The Editors

KRISTIN O. LAUER is Associate Professor of English at Fordham University. Her publications include *Edith Wharton: The Contemporary Reviews* (with James Tuttleton and Margaret P. Murray) and *Edith Wharton: An Annotated Secondary Bibliography* (with Margaret P. Murray). Her psychological study, *Gallery of the Damned: The Inner World of Edith Wharton's Women*, is forthcoming. She has published psychological essays on George Eliot, Henry James, and Edith Wharton.

CYNTHIA GRIFFIN WOLFF is Class of 1922 Professor of Humanities at the Massachusetts Institute of Technology. She is the author of *A Feast of Words: The Triumph of Edith Wharton, Emily Dickinson,* and *Samuel Richardson and The Eighteenth-Century Puritan Character.* She has edited many literary works, including *Short Fiction of Major American Women Writers: Jewett, Chopin, Wharton, and Cather; Four Works by American Women Writers;* and Edith Wharton's *Summer, The House of Mirth, The Custom of the Country,* and *The Touchstone.* Her essays and articles have appeared in many journals in the United States and Canada.

ETHAN FROME

AUTHORITATIVE TEXT
BACKGROUNDS AND CONTEXTS
CRITICISM

A NORTON CRITICAL EDITION

Edith Wharton
ETHAN FROME

AUTHORITATIVE TEXT
BACKGROUNDS AND CONTEXTS
CRITICISM

Edited by

Kristin O. Lauer
FORDHAM UNIVERSITY

and

Cynthia Griffin Wolff
MASSACHUSETTS INSTITUTE OF TECHNOLOGY

W. W. NORTON & COMPANY · *New York* · *London*

The text of this book is composed in Electra
with the display set in Bernhard Modern
Composition and Manufacturing by Maple-Vail

Library of Congress Cataloging-in-Publication Data

Wharton, Edith, 1862–1937.
Ethan Frome : authoritative text, backgrounds and contexts,
criticism / Edith Wharton ; edited by Kristin O. Lauer, Cynthia
Griffin Wolff.
p.   cm.—(A Norton critical edition)
Includes bibliographical references and index.
1. New England—Social life and customs—Fiction.   2. Wharton,
Edith, 1862–1937.   Ethan Frome.   3. Married people—New England—
Fiction.   4. Rural poor—New England—Fiction.   5. Farm life—New
England—Fiction.   I. Lauer, Kristin O.   II. Wolff,
Cynthia Griffin.   III. Title.
PS3545.H16E7   1994
813'.52—dc20   94-17385

ISBN 0-393-96635-6

W. W. Norton & Company, Inc., 500 Fifth Avenue, New York, N.Y. 10110
W. W. Norton & Company Ltd., 10 Coptic Street, London WC1A 1PU
5 6 7 8 9 0

Contents

Criticism 111

Preface

The history of *Ethan Frome*, Edith Wharton's most famous tale, is as paradoxical as its chill beauty. The tragic story of an impoverished New England small farmer was hardly what her public expected in 1911 of the wealthy, well-born Mrs. Wharton, known for her novels and stories exposing the follies of the inner circles of fashionable society in *fin de siècle* New York.

Ethan Frome was decidedly outside the subject matter of the literature of manners. From the earliest reviews, critics, bewildered but universally moved by its power, went back to the Greeks to place it. They termed the story classical, shocking, beautiful, unforgettable, brilliant. Nonetheless, many questioned Edith Wharton's right to tell it.

Before *Ethan Frome*, Edith Wharton had been celebrated for her acerbic wit, her culture and vast knowledge of Italian and French history, art, architecture, and literature. At forty-nine, she had become an international hostess enjoying French salon society, a traveler of indefatigable energy, in love with the new joys of chauffeured motoring. A leisure-class descendent of heroes of the Revolution, she divided her year between her country estate in Lenox, Massachusetts, and her apartment in the exclusive Faubourg Saint-Germain of Paris. No one expected the celebrated satirist to give voice to the sufferings of a cripple trapped in the isolated Berkshire hamlet she emphatically labeled Starkfield.

Critical reservations, born of the public image of an elitist, intellectual Mrs. Wharton, gradually focused on two aspects of the work: structure—particularly the framing narrative—and setting. The first was termed clumsy and artificial; the second, condescending.

Still, the powerful little novel prospered. Of all the long shelf of her work—her twenty-two novels and novellas, her eighty-seven short stories, her nine volumes of nonfiction, and her two volumes of poetry—only *Ethan Frome* (except for the Pulitzer Prize-winning 1920 *Age of Innocence*) has remained consistently in print and widely read. A mainstay of American secondary education, it has been studied by more Americans than anything else she wrote. *Ethan Frome* staked out an unassailable position within the traditional American canon long before the 1975 R. W. B. Lewis biography of Wharton and the feminist revival unearthed many of her buried masterpieces—that is, long before the veritable Wharton revolution in both critical and popular consciousness began.

To Edith Wharton herself, this was an important book, for with it she felt for the first time "the artisan's full control of his implements." Perhaps for that reason (and perhaps also because she was acutely aware of the charges that she was merely a "literary" observer who had gone slumming in the Berkshire neighborhoods of her estate), in 1922 she wrote the first introduction she had ever penned for one of her works. In it she defended both her narrative structure and her intimacy with her fictional world. She argued that her vision of the economically and emotionally starved life of the small New England farmer was more realistic than that of the New England local color regional writers whom she was to accuse in her autobiography of wearing "rose-coloured spectacles."

In the tradition of *Ethan Frome* criticism, this edition offers a survey of varied responses to the narrative structure and sheds new light on the question of the book's psychological, historical, and cultural authenticity. Edith Wharton's public could never know the most poignant paradox of the novel: how close her private world was to the emotional reality of Ethan Frome himself. Trapped in a loveless marriage to a mentally unbalanced man, suffering since childhood from painful shyness and feelings of isolation, scarred at the end of a passionate, bruising love affair with an unfaithful American journalist, Edith Wharton, approaching fifty, rejected the illusions of romanticism, felt keenly the crushing demands of the household invalid, and fought a valiant inner battle to remain active, involved, and strong like her framing engineer, who abandons the seductive numbness of resignation and despair.

Such valuable biographical data, the wealth of material recently gathered on the position of poor farm women like Zeena Frome, the documentation of the nineteenth-century stunting of the potentialities of young women like Mattie Silver—all these riches of modern scholarship illuminate the text and make *Ethan Frome* a completely new subject of study.

Renowned for the beauty and lucidity of its style, *Ethan Frome* was actually begun in French as an assignment for her Parisian tutor, probably in early 1907. Yet in the long list of paradoxes, perhaps the greatest is that this, Edith Wharton's most famous, if controversial, fiction, has been eclipsed in the modern Wharton revival by feminist attention to *The House of Mirth* with its doomed Lily Bart whose career is a pointed lesson in fatal acculturation. Those familiar with the ironic history of *Ethan Frome*, however, will find in feminist theory new approaches only reaffirming *Ethan Frome*'s vitality and now indisputable authenticity.

ACKNOWLEDGMENTS

Lev Raphael located the elusive Van Deusen material, illuminated difficult French expressions and served as a knowledgeable consultant and enthusiastic best friend in all aspects of the editorial process. American historian Larry Menna supplied valuable data on the economic conditions in New England. Mark Sigerson was an ingenious research detective. Scott Marshall of the Edith Wharton Restoration was singularly important to the success of this volume with his encyclopedic knowledge of Wharton and Lenox and his sound suggestions. The editors are, as always, indebted to the gracious staff at the Beinecke Library at Yale. Carol Bemis was the gifted, attentive editor of which authors dream. Wharton scholar Margaret P. Murray lent her considerable expertise and devoted partnership to this project. Heartfelt thanks to Professor James Tuttleton and Lowell Acola for special research services, to superb copy editor Josepha Gutelius, and to Norton's ever-helpful Ann R. Tappert. Particularly warm gratitude to Darrell Lauer for a multitude of those unsung, generous daily gifts of time and encouragement which lighten the scholar's load immeasurably.

A NOTE ON THE TEXT

This edition of *Ethan Frome* is reprinted from the original 1911 edition published by Charles Scribner's Sons. No editorial changes have been made.

Introduction to the 1922 Edition

I had known something of New England village life long before I made my home in the same county as my imaginary Starkfield; though, during the years spent there, certain of its aspects became much more familiar to me.[1]

Even before that final initiation, however, I had had an uneasy sense that the New England of fiction[2] bore little—except a vague botanical and dialectical—resemblance to the harsh and beautiful land as I had seen it. Even the abundant enumeration of sweet-fern, asters and mountain-laurel, and the conscientious reproduction of the vernacular, left me with the feeling that the outcropping granite had in both cases been overlooked. I give the impression merely as a personal one; it accounts for "Ethan Frome," and may, to some readers, in a measure justify it.

So much for the origin of the story; there is nothing else of interest to say of it, except as concerns its construction.

The problem before me, as I saw in the first flash, was this: I had to deal with a subject of which the dramatic climax, or rather the anti-climax, occurs a generation later than the first acts of the tragedy. This enforced lapse of time would seem to anyone persuaded—as I have always been—that every subject (in the novelist's sense of the term) implicitly *contains its own form and dimensions*, to mark Ethan Frome as the subject for a novel. But I never thought this for a moment, for I had felt, at the same time, that the theme of my tale was not one on which many variations could be played. It must be treated as starkly and summarily as life had always presented itself to my protagonists; any attempt to elaborate and complicate their sentiments would necessarily have falsified the whole. They were, in truth, these figures, my *granite outcroppings*; but half-emerged from the soil, and scarcely more articulate.

---

1. Refers to her summer residence at The Mount, her country estate in Lenox, Massachusetts, in the foothills of the Berkshire Mountains, 1902–1911.
2. Refers to the fiction of the local color regional writers, specifically Sarah Orne Jewett (1849–1909), famous for her studies of rural life in Maine, and Mary E. Wilkins Freeman (1852–1930), chronicler of rural life in Massachusetts.

This incompatibility between subject and plan would perhaps have seemed to suggest that my "situation" was after all one to be rejected. Every novelist has been visited by the insinuating wraiths of false "good situations," siren-subjects[3] luring his cockle-shell to the rocks; their voice is oftenest heard, and their mirage-sea beheld, as he traverses the waterless desert which awaits him half-way through whatever work is actually in hand. I knew well enough what song those sirens sang, and had often tied myself to my dull job until they were out of hearing— perhaps carrying a lost masterpiece in their rainbow veils. But I had no such fear of them in the case of Ethan Frome. It was the first subject I had ever approached with full confidence in its value, for my own purpose, and a relative faith in my power to render at least a part of what I saw in it.

Every novelist, again, who "intends upon"[4] his art, has lit upon such subjects, and been fascinated by the difficulty of presenting them in the fullest relief, yet without an added ornament, or a trick of drapery or lighting. This was my task, if I were to tell the story of Ethan Frome; and my scheme of construction[5]—which met with the immediate and unqualified disapproval of the few friends to whom I tentatively outlined it—I still think justified in the given case. It appears to me, indeed, that, while an air of artificiality is lent to a tale of complex and sophisticated people which the novelist causes to be guessed at and interpreted by any mere looker-on, there need be no such drawback if the looker-on is sophisticated, and the people he interprets are simple. If he is capable of seeing all around them, no violence is done to probability in allowing him to exercise this faculty; it is natural enough that he should act as the sympathizing intermediary between his rudimentary characters and the more complicated minds to whom he is trying to present them. But this is all self-evident, and needs explaining only to those who have never thought of fiction as an art of composition.

The real merit of my construction seems to me to lie in a minor detail. I had to find means to bring my tragedy, in a way at once natural and picture-making, to the knowledge of its narrator. I might have sat him down before a village gossip who would have poured out the whole affair to him in a breath, but in doing this I should have been false to two essential elements of my picture: first, the deep-rooted reticence and inarticulateness of the people I was trying to draw, and secondly the effect of "roundness" (in the plastic sense) produced by letting their case be seen through eyes as different as those of Harmon Gow and Mrs.

3. Sirens were mythical monsters, in some legends half-woman, half-bird, whose bewitching singing lured seamen to their deaths as ships dashed on the rocks. "Siren-subjects" are characters or plots that tempt a writer away from a current project.
4. Thinks with purpose about.
5. The scheme of construction, controversial throughout the history of the novel, refers to Wharton's use of the frame and the engineer-narrator.

Ned Hale. Each of my chroniclers contributes to the narrative *just so much as he or she is capable of understanding* of what, to them, is a complicated and mysterious case; and only the narrator of the tale has scope enough to see it all, to resolve it back into simplicity, and to put it in its rightful place among his larger categories.

I make no claim for originality in following a method of which "La Grande Bretêche" and "The Ring and the Book"[6] had set me the magnificent example; my one merit is, perhaps, to have guessed that the proceeding there employed was also applicable to my small tale.

I have written this brief analysis—the first I have ever published of any of my books—because, as an author's introduction to his work, I can imagine nothing of any value to his readers except a statement as to why he decided to attempt the work in question, and why he selected one form rather than another for its embodiment. These primary aims, the only ones that can be explicitly stated, must, by the artist, be almost instinctively felt and acted upon before there can pass into his creation that imponderable something more which causes life to circulate in it, and preserves it for a little from decay.

EDITH WHARTON.

6. "La Grande Bretêche" by the French author Honoré de Balzac (1799–1850), a short story of an illicit love affair which employs a double narrator; "The Ring and the Book" (1868–1869) by English poet Robert Browning (1812–1889), a poem in twelve books based on an Italian murder case of 1698, presented in dramatic monologues spoken by twelve characters.

The Text of
ETHAN FROME

Ethan Frome

I had the story, bit by bit, from various people, and, as generally
happens in such cases, each time it was a different story.

If you know Starkfield, Massachusetts,[1] you know the post-office. If
you know the post-office you must have seen Ethan[2] Frome drive up to
it, drop the reins on his hollow-backed bay and drag himself across the
brick pavement to the white colonnade; and you must have asked who
he was.

It was there that, several years ago, I saw him for the first time; and
the sight pulled me up sharp. Even then he was the most striking figure
in Starkfield, though he was but the ruin of a man. It was not so much
his great height that marked him, for the "natives" were easily singled
out by their lank longitude from the stockier foreign breed: it was the
careless powerful look he had, in spite of a lameness checking each step
like the jerk of a chain. There was something bleak and unapproachable
in his face, and he was so stiffened and grizzled that I took him for an
old man and was surprised to hear that he was not more than fifty-two.
I had this from Harmon Gow, who had driven the stage from Bettsbridge
to Starkfield in pre-trolley days and knew the chronicle of all the families
on his line.[3]

"He's looked that way ever since he had his smash-up; and that's
twenty-four years ago come next February," Harmon threw out between
reminiscent pauses.

The "smash-up" it was—I gathered from the same informant—
which, besides drawing the red gash across Ethan Frome's forehead, had
so shortened and warped his right side that it cost him a visible effort to
take the few steps from his buggy to the post-office window. He used to
drive in from his farm every day at about noon, and as that was my own
hour for fetching my mail I often passed him in the porch or stood
beside him while we waited on the motions of the distributing hand
behind the grating. I noticed that, though he came so punctually, he

---

1. Identified by Wharton as a typical village in the foothills of the Berkshire Mountains of western
   Massachusetts, supposedly in the vicinity of Lenox where she summered on her country estate
   from 1902–1911.
2. Name Ethan suggests Nathaniel Hawthorne's (1804–1864) short story, "Ethan Brand" (1851),
   in which Ethan Brand finds the Unpardonable Sin in his own heart—intellect divorced from
   love. Echoes of the New England Hawthorne recur throughout in setting, imagery, and
   names.
3. Trolley lines were laid in Lenox 1901–1902.

seldom received anything but a copy of the *Bettsbridge Eagle*, which he put without a glance into his sagging pocket. At intervals, however, the post-master would hand him an envelope addressed to Mrs. Zenobia— or Mrs. Zeena—Frome, and usually bearing conspicuously in the upper left-hand corner the address of some manufacturer of patent medicine and the name of his specific.[4] These documents my neighbour would also pocket without a glance, as if too much used to them to wonder at their number and variety, and would then turn away with a silent nod to the post-master.

Every one in Starkfield knew him and gave him a greeting tempered to his own grave mien; but his taciturnity was respected and it was only on rare occasions that one of the older men of the place detained him for a word. When this happened he would listen quietly, his blue eyes on the speaker's face, and answer in so low a tone that his words never reached me; then he would climb stiffly into his buggy, gather up the reins in his left hand and drive slowly away in the direction of his farm.

"It was a pretty bad smash-up?" I questioned Harmon, looking after Frome's retreating figure, and thinking how gallantly his lean brown head, with its shock of light hair, must have sat on his strong shoulders before they were bent out of shape.

"Wust kind," my informant assented. "More'n enough to kill most men. But the Fromes are tough. Ethan'll likely touch a hundred."

"Good God!" I exclaimed. At the moment Ethan Frome, after climbing to his seat, had leaned over to assure himself of the security of a wooden box—also with a druggist's label on it—which he had placed in the back of the buggy, and I saw his face as it probably looked when he thought himself alone. "*That* man touch a hundred? He looks as if he was dead and in hell now!"

Harmon drew a slab of tobacco from his pocket, cut off a wedge and pressed it into the leather pouch of his cheek. "Guess he's been in Starkfield too many winters. Most of the smart ones get away."

"Why didn't *he?*"

"Somebody had to stay and care for the folks. There warn't ever anybody but Ethan. Fust his father—then his mother—then his wife."

"And then the smash-up?"

Harmon chuckled sardonically. "That's so. He *had* to stay then."

"I see. And since then they've had to care for him?"

Harmon thoughtfully passed his tobacco to the other cheek. "Oh, as to that: I guess it's always Ethan done the caring."

Though Harmon Gow developed the tale as far as his mental and moral reach permitted there were perceptible gaps between his facts, and

---

4. Zenobia suggests Nathaniel Hawthorne's (1804–1864) dark, queenly Zenobia in *The Blithedale Romance* (1852), named after Zenobia, Queen of Palmyra, who openly defied the Roman emperor in A.D. 270. Thus any powerful, ambitious woman. A specific is a medicine indicated for a particular sickness. In the nineteenth century these mail-order medicines often contained alcohol.

I had the sense that the deeper meaning of the story was in the gaps. But one phrase stuck in my memory and served as the nucleus about which I grouped my subsequent inferences: "Guess he's been in Starkfield too many winters."

Before my own time there was up I had learned to know what that meant. Yet I had come in the degenerate day of trolley, bicycle and rural delivery, when communication was easy between the scattered mountain villages, and the bigger towns in the valleys, such as Betts-bridge and Shadd's Falls, had libraries, theatres and Y. M. C. A.[5] halls to which the youth of the hills could descend for recreation. But when winter shut down on Starkfield, and the village lay under a sheet of snow perpetually renewed from the pale skies, I began to see what life there— or rather its negation—must have been in Ethan Frome's young manhood.

I had been sent up by my employers on a job connected with the big power-house[6] at Corbury Junction, and a long-drawn carpenters' strike had so delayed the work that I found myself anchored at Starkfield—the nearest habitable spot—for the best part of the winter. I chafed at first, and then, under the hypnotising effect of routine, gradually began to find a grim satisfaction in the life. During the early part of my stay I had been struck by the contrast between the vitality of the climate and the deadness of the community. Day by day, after the December snows were over, a blazing blue sky poured down torrents of light and air on the white landscape, which gave them back in an intenser glitter. One would have supposed that such an atmosphere must quicken the emo-tions as well as the blood; but it seemed to produce no change except that of retarding still more the sluggish pulse of Starkfield. When I had been there a little longer, and had seen this phase of crystal clearness followed by long stretches of sunless cold; when the storms of February had pitched their white tents about the devoted village and the wild cavalry of March winds had charged down to their support; I began to understand why Starkfield emerged from its six months' siege like a starved garrison capitulating without quarter. Twenty years earlier the means of resistance must have been far fewer, and the enemy in com-mand of almost all the lines of access between the beleaguered villages; and, considering these things, I felt the sinister force of Harmon's phrase: "Most of the smart ones get away." But if that were the case, how could any combination of obstacles have hindered the flight of a man like Ethan Frome?

During my stay at Starkfield I lodged with a middle-aged widow collo-

5. Young Men's Christian Association. Britain-founded, international organization promoting Christian ideals and health, first in U.S. in Boston, 1851. Provided inexpensive lodging and recreation for young men.
6. A station generating electricity. Edith Wharton's home, The Mount, was electrically lit, rare in 1902. In 1886, one of the first main streets in America electrically lit was in Great Bar-rington, close to Lenox.

quially known as Mrs. Ned Hale. Mrs. Hale's father had been the village lawyer of the previous generation, and "lawyer Varnum's house," where my landlady still lived with her mother, was the most considerable mansion in the village. It stood at one end of the main street, its classic portico and small-paned windows looking down a flagged path between Norway spruces to the slim white steeple of the Congregational church. It was clear that the Varnum fortunes were at the ebb, but the two women did what they could to preserve a decent dignity; and Mrs. Hale, in particular, had a certain wan refinement not out of keeping with her pale old-fashioned house.

In the "best parlour," with its black horse-hair and mahogany weakly illuminated by a gurgling Carcel lamp,[7] I listened every evening to another and more delicately shaded version of the Starkfield chronicle. It was not that Mrs. Ned Hale felt, or affected, any social superiority to the people about her; it was only that the accident of a finer sensibility and a little more education had put just enough distance between herself and her neighbours to enable her to judge them with detachment. She was not unwilling to exercise this faculty, and I had great hopes of getting from her the missing facts of Ethan Frome's story, or rather such a key to his character as should co-ordinate the facts I knew. Her mind was a store-house of innocuous anecdote and any question about her acquaintances brought forth a volume of detail; but on the subject of Ethan Frome I found her unexpectedly reticent. There was no hint of disapproval in her reserve; I merely felt in her an insurmountable reluctance to speak of him or his affairs, a low "Yes, I knew them both . . . it was awful . . ." seeming to be the utmost concession that her distress could make to my curiosity.

So marked was the change in her manner, such depths of sad initiation did it imply, that, with some doubts as to my delicacy, I put the case anew to my village oracle, Harmon Gow; but got for my pains only an uncomprehending grunt.

"Ruth Varnum was always as nervous as a rat; and, come to think of it, she was the first one to see 'em after they was picked up. It happened right below lawyer Varnum's, down at the bend of the Corbury road, just round about the time that Ruth got engaged to Ned Hale.[8] The young folks was all friends, and I guess she just can't bear to talk about it. She's had troubles enough of her own."

All the dwellers in Starkfield, as in more notable communities, had had troubles enough of their own to make them comparatively indifferent to those of their neighbours; and though all conceded that Ethan

7. Carcel lamp pumps oil steadily up its wick, therefore gurgles, invented by Frenchman B. G. Carcel (1750–1812). Horse-hair fabric, of horse hair, mostly manes and tails, covered furniture; mahogany, fine-grained reddish hardwood, indicates quality furniture.
8. Wharton based the sledding accident on the March 11, 1904, tragedy on Courthouse Hill in the center of Lenox; one girl died and four companions were injured. See p. 86.

Frome's had been beyond the common measure, no one gave me an explanation of the look in his face which, as I persisted in thinking, neither poverty nor physical suffering could have put there. Nevertheless, I might have contented myself with the story pieced together from these hints had it not been for the provocation of Mrs. Hale's silence, and—a little later—for the accident of personal contact with the man.

On my arrival at Starkfield, Denis Eady, the rich Irish grocer, who was the proprietor of Starkfield's nearest approach to a livery stable, had entered into an agreement to send me over daily to Corbury Flats, where I had to pick up my train for the Junction. But about the middle of the winter Eady's horses fell ill of a local epidemic. The illness spread to the other Starkfield stables and for a day or two I was put to it to find a means of transport. Then Harmon Gow suggested that Ethan Frome's bay was still on his legs and that his owner might be glad to drive me over.

I stared at the suggestion. "Ethan Frome? But I've never even spoken to him. Why on earth should he put himself out for me?"

Harmon's answer surprised me still more. "I don't know as he would; but I know he wouldn't be sorry to earn a dollar."[9]

I had been told that Frome was poor, and that the saw-mill and the arid acres of his farm yielded scarcely enough to keep his household through the winter; but I had not supposed him to be in such want as Harmon's words implied, and I expressed my wonder.

"Well, matters ain't gone any too well with him," Harmon said. "When a man's been setting round like a hulk for twenty years or more, seeing things that want doing, it eats inter him, and he loses his grit. That Frome farm was always 'bout as bare's a milkpan when the cat's been round; and you know what one of them old water-mills[1] is wuth nowadays. When Ethan could sweat over 'em both from sun-up to dark he kinder choked a living out of 'em; but his folks ate up most everything, even then, and I don't see how he makes out now. Fust his father got a kick, out haying, and went soft in the brain, and gave away money like Bible texts afore he died. Then his mother got queer and dragged along for years as weak as a baby; and his wife Zeena, she's always been the greatest hand at doctoring in the county. Sickness and trouble: that's what Ethan's had his plate full up with, ever since the very first helping."

The next morning, when I looked out, I saw the hollow-backed bay between the Varnum spruces, and Ethan Frome, throwing back his worn bearskin, made room for me in the sleigh at his side. After that, for a week, he drove me over every morning to Corbury Flats, and on my return in the afternoon met me again and carried me back through

9. Sample 1900 wages and prices: railroad conductor, $989 a year; laborer, $535. Breakfast was 25 cents, lunch, 50. Apartments could be had for $3.50 a week; a newspaper was 2 cents; postage, 2 cents an ounce. Train fares: fifty miles, 85 cents, one hundred, $1.50.
1. Old-fashioned source of power for sawing logs, obsolete with the new powerhouses.

the icy night to Starkfield. The distance each way was barely three miles, but the old bay's pace was slow, and even with firm snow under the runners we were nearly an hour on the way. Ethan Frome drove in silence, the reins loosely held in his left hand, his brown seamed profile, under the helmet-like peak of the cap, relieved against the banks of snow like the bronze image of a hero. He never turned his face to mine, or answered, except in monosyllables, the questions I put, or such slight pleasantries as I ventured. He seemed a part of the mute melancholy landscape, an incarnation of its frozen woe, with all that was warm and sentient in him fast bound below the surface; but there was nothing unfriendly in his silence. I simply felt that he lived in a depth of moral isolation too remote for casual access, and I had the sense that his loneliness was not merely the result of his personal plight, tragic as I guessed that to be, but had in it, as Harmon Gow had hinted, the profound accumulated cold of many Starkfield winters.

Only once or twice was the distance between us bridged for a moment; and the glimpses thus gained confirmed my desire to know more. Once I happened to speak of an engineering job I had been on the previous year in Florida, and of the contrast between the winter landscape about us and that in which I had found myself the year before; and to my surprise Frome said suddenly: "Yes: I was down there once, and for a good while afterward I could call up the sight of it in winter. But now it's all snowed under."

He said no more, and I had to guess the rest from the inflection of his voice and his sharp relapse into silence.

Another day, on getting into my train at the Flats, I missed a volume of popular science—I think it was on some recent discoveries in biochemistry—which I had carried with me to read on the way. I thought no more about it till I got into the sleigh again that evening, and saw the book in Frome's hand.

"I found it after you were gone," he said.

I put the volume into my pocket and we dropped back into our usual silence; but as we began to crawl up the long hill from Corbury Flats to the Starkfield ridge I became aware in the dusk that he had turned his face to mine.

"There are things in that book that I didn't know the first word about," he said.

I wondered less at his words than at the queer note of resentment in his voice. He was evidently surprised and slightly aggrieved at his own ignorance.

"Does that sort of thing interest you?" I asked.

"It used to."

"There are one or two rather new things in the book: there have been some big strides lately in that particular line of research." I waited a moment for an answer that did not come; then I said: "If you'd like to look the book through I'd be glad to leave it with you."

He hesitated, and I had the impression that he felt himself about to yield to a stealing tide of inertia; then, "Thank you—I'll take it," he answered shortly.

I hoped that this incident might set up some more direct communication between us. Frome was so simple and straightforward that I was sure his curiosity about the book was based on a genuine interest in its subject. Such tastes and acquirements in a man of his condition made the contrast more poignant between his outer situation and his inner needs, and I hoped that the chance of giving expression to the latter might at least unseal his lips. But something in his past history, or in his present way of living, had apparently driven him too deeply into himself for any casual impulse to draw him back to his kind. At our next meeting he made no allusion to the book, and our intercourse seemed fated to remain as negative and one-sided as if there had been no break in his reserve.

Frome had been driving me over to the Flats for about a week when one morning I looked out of my window into a thick snow-fall. The height of the white waves massed against the garden-fence and along the wall of the church showed that the storm must have been going on all night, and that the drifts were likely to be heavy in the open. I thought it probable that my train would be delayed; but I had to be at the power-house for an hour or two that afternoon, and I decided, if Frome turned up, to push through to the Flats and wait there till my train came in. I don't know why I put it in the conditional, however, for I never doubted that Frome would appear. He was not the kind of man to be turned from his business by any commotion of the elements; and at the appointed hour his sleigh glided up through the snow like a stage-apparition behind thickening veils of gauze.

I was getting to know him too well to express either wonder or gratitude at his keeping his appointment; but I exclaimed in surprise as I saw him turn his horse in a direction opposite to that of the Corbury road.

"The railroad's blocked by a freight-train that got stuck in a drift below the Flats," he explained, as we jogged off into the stinging whiteness.

"But look here—where are you taking me, then?"

"Straight to the Junction, by the shortest way," he answered, pointing up School House Hill with his whip.

"To the Junction—in this storm? Why, it's a good ten miles!"

"The bay'll do it if you give him time. You said you had some business there this afternoon. I'll see you get there."

He said it so quietly that I could only answer: "You're doing me the biggest kind of a favour."

"That's all right," he rejoined.

Abreast of the schoolhouse the road forked, and we dipped down a lane to the left, between hemlock[2] boughs bent inward to their trunks by the weight of the snow. I had often walked that way on Sundays, and knew that the solitary roof showing through bare branches near the bottom of the hill was that of Frome's saw-mill. It looked exanimate[3] enough, with its idle wheel looming above the black stream dashed with yellow-white spume, and its cluster of sheds sagging under their white load. Frome did not even turn his head as we drove by, and still in silence we began to mount the next slope. About a mile farther, on a road I had never travelled, we came to an orchard of starved apple-trees writhing over a hillside among outcroppings of slate that nuzzled up through the snow like animals pushing out their noses to breathe. Beyond the orchard lay a field or two, their boundaries lost under drifts; and above the fields, huddled against the white immensities of land and sky, one of those lonely New England farm-houses that make the landscape lonelier.

"That's my place," said Frome, with a sideway jerk of his lame elbow; and in the distress and oppression of the scene I did not know what to answer. The snow had ceased, and a flash of watery sunlight exposed the house on the slope above us in all its plaintive ugliness. The black wraith of a deciduous creeper flapped from the porch, and the thin wooden walls, under their worn coat of paint, seemed to shiver in the wind that had risen with the ceasing of the snow.

"The house was bigger in my father's time: I had to take down the 'L,' a while back," Frome continued, checking with a twitch of the left rein the bay's evident intention of turning in through the broken-down gate.

I saw then that the unusually forlorn and stunted look of the house was partly due to the loss of what is known in New England as the "L": that long deep-roofed adjunct usually built at right angles to the main house, and connecting it, by way of storerooms and tool-house, with the wood-shed and cow-barn. Whether because of its symbolic sense, the image it presents of a life linked with the soil, and enclosing in itself the chief sources of warmth and nourishment, or whether merely because of the consolatory thought that it enables the dwellers in that harsh climate to get to their morning's work without facing the weather, it is certain that the "L" rather than the house itself seems to be the centre, the actual hearth-stone, of the New England farm. Perhaps this connection of ideas, which had often occurred to me in my rambles about Starkfield, caused me to hear a wistful note in Frome's words, and to see in the diminished dwelling the image of his own shrunken body.

"We're kinder side-tracked here now," he added, "but there was considerable passing before the railroad was carried through to the Flats."

2. A poisonous herb used medicinally as a strong sedative, or a poisonous drink made from the herb.
3. Lifeless, dead.

He roused the lagging bay with another twitch; then, as if the mere sight of the house had let me too deeply into his confidence for any farther pretence of reserve, he went on slowly: "I've always set down the worst of mother's trouble to that. When she got the rheumatism so bad she couldn't move around she used to sit up there and watch the road by the hour; and one year, when they was six months mending the Bettsbridge pike after the floods, and Harmon Gow had to bring his stage round this way, she picked up so that she used to get down to the gate most days to see him. But after the trains begun running nobody ever come by here to speak of, and mother never could get it through her head what had happened, and it preyed on her right along till she died."

As we turned into the Corbury road the snow began to fall again, cutting off our last glimpse of the house; and Frome's silence fell with it, letting down between us the old veil of reticence. This time the wind did not cease with the return of the snow. Instead, it sprang up to a gale which now and then, from a tattered sky, flung pale sweeps of sunlight over a landscape chaotically tossed. But the bay was as good as Frome's word, and we pushed on to the Junction through the wild white scene.

In the afternoon the storm held off, and the clearness in the west seemed to my inexperienced eye the pledge of a fair evening. I finished my business as quickly as possible, and we set out for Starkfield with a good chance of getting there for supper. But at sunset the clouds gathered again, bringing an earlier night, and the snow began to fall straight and steadily from a sky without wind, in a soft universal diffusion more confusing than the gusts and eddies of the morning. It seemed to be a part of the thickening darkness, to be the winter night itself descending on us layer by layer.

The small ray of Frome's lantern was soon lost in this smothering medium, in which even his sense of direction, and the bay's homing instinct, finally ceased to serve us. Two or three times some ghostly landmark sprang up to warn us that we were astray, and then was sucked back into the mist; and when we finally regained our road the old horse began to show signs of exhaustion. I felt myself to blame for having accepted Frome's offer, and after a short discussion I persuaded him to let me get out of the sleigh and walk along through the snow at the bay's side. In this way we struggled on for another mile or two, and at last reached a point where Frome, peering into what seemed to me formless night, said: "That's my gate down yonder."

The last stretch had been the hardest part of the way. The bitter cold and the heavy going had nearly knocked the wind out of me, and I could feel the horse's side ticking like a clock under my hand.

"Look here, Frome," I began, "there's no earthly use in your going any farther—" but he interrupted me: "Nor you neither. There's been about enough of this for anybody."

I understood that he was offering me a night's shelter at the farm, and without answering I turned into the gate at his side, and followed him to the barn, where I helped him to unharness and bed down the tired horse. When this was done he unhooked the lantern from the sleigh, stepped out again into the night, and called to me over his shoulder: "This way."

Far off above us a square of light trembled through the screen of snow. Staggering along in Frome's wake I floundered toward it, and in the darkness almost fell into one of the deep drifts against the front of the house. Frome scrambled up the slippery steps of the porch, digging a way through the snow with his heavily booted foot. Then he lifted his lantern, found the latch, and led the way into the house. I went after him into a low unlit passage, at the back of which a ladder-like staircase rose into obscurity. On our right a line of light marked the door of the room which had sent its ray across the night; and behind the door I heard a woman's voice droning querulously.

Frome stamped on the worn oil-cloth to shake the snow from his boots, and set down his lantern on a kitchen chair which was the only piece of furniture in the hall. Then he opened the door.

"Come in," he said; and as he spoke the droning voice grew still . . .

It was that night that I found the clue to Ethan Frome, and began to put together this vision of his story.[4]..
....
....

I

The village lay under two feet of snow, with drifts at the windy corners. In a sky of iron the points of the Dipper hung like icicles and Orion flashed his cold fires.[1] The moon had set, but the night was so transparent that the white housefronts between the elms looked gray against the snow, clumps of bushes made black stains on it, and the basement windows of the church sent shafts of yellow light far across the endless undulations.

Young Ethan Frome walked at a quick pace along the deserted street, past the bank and Michael Eady's new brick store and Lawyer Varnum's house with the two black Norway spruces at the gate. Opposite the Var-

---

4. Use of word "vision" has led some critics to see the story as fundamentally the narrator's rather than Ethan's. Concerned about the placing of the extended ellipsis, Wharton exchanged letters with Scribner's over its form and type. The gist of her request was that an important break be immediately apparent to the eye, signifying the flashback of twenty-four years.

1. Wharton means either the "Little" or "Big Dipper" (both constellations shaped like ladles) near the celestial north pole. Orion, handsome, mythical giant hero killed (probably for jealousy) by the fierce and vengeful Artemis, goddess of the hunt, whom he served. Orion follows the Pleiades, or seven sisters; in mythology, the seven daughters of Atlas. Orion pursued them unsuccessfully until Zeus, king of the gods, made them stars, where Orion still pursues them—persistent and frustrated eternally.

num gate, where the road fell away toward the Corbury valley, the church reared its slim white steeple and narrow peristyle.[2] As the young man walked toward it the upper windows drew a black arcade along the side wall of the building, but from the lower openings, on the side where the ground sloped steeply down to the Corbury road, the light shot its long bars, illuminating many fresh furrows in the track leading to the basement door, and showing, under an adjoining shed, a line of sleighs with heavily blanketed horses.

The night was perfectly still, and the air so dry and pure that it gave little sensation of cold. The effect produced on Frome was rather of a complete absence of atmosphere, as though nothing less tenuous than ether intervened between the white earth under his feet and the metallic dome overhead. "It's like being in an exhausted receiver,"[3] he thought. Four or five years earlier he had taken a year's course at a technological college at Worcester, and dabbled in the laboratory with a friendly professor of physics; and the images supplied by that experience still cropped up, at unexpected moments, through the totally different associations of thought in which he had since been living. His father's death, and the misfortunes following it, had put a premature end to Ethan's studies; but though they had not gone far enough to be of much practical use they had fed his fancy and made him aware of huge cloudy meanings behind the daily face of things.

As he strode along through the snow the sense of such meanings glowed in his brain and mingled with the bodily flush produced by his sharp tramp. At the end of the village he paused before the darkened front of the church. He stood there a moment, breathing quickly, and looking up and down the street, in which not another figure moved. The pitch of the Corbury road, below lawyer Varnum's spruces, was the favourite coasting-ground of Starkfield, and on clear evenings the church corner rang till late with the shouts of the coasters; but to-night not a sled darkened the whiteness of the long declivity. The hush of midnight lay on the village, and all its waking life was gathered behind the church windows, from which strains of dance-music flowed with the broad bands of yellow light.

The young man, skirting the side of the building, went down the slope toward the basement door. To keep out of range of the revealing rays from within he made a circuit through the untrodden snow and gradually approached the farther angle of the basement wall. Thence, still hugging the shadow, he edged his way cautiously forward to the nearest window, holding back his straight spare body and craning his neck till he got a glimpse of the room.

Seen thus, from the pure and frosty darkness in which he stood, it seemed to be seething in a mist of heat. The metal reflectors of the gas-

2. The short decorative columns at base of a New England church steeple.
3. From physics, referring to the bell jar or glass used to create a vacuum.

jets sent crude waves of light against the whitewashed walls, and the iron flanks of the stove at the end of the hall looked as though they were heaving with volcanic fires. The floor was thronged with girls and young men. Down the side wall facing the window stood a row of kitchen chairs from which the older women had just risen. By this time the music had stopped, and the musicians—a fiddler, and the young lady who played the harmonium[4] on Sundays—were hastily refreshing themselves at one corner of the supper-table which aligned its devastated pie-dishes and ice-cream saucers on the platform at the end of the hall. The guests were preparing to leave, and the tide had already set toward the passage where coats and wraps were hung, when a young man with a sprightly foot and a shock of black hair shot into the middle of the floor and clapped his hands. The signal took instant effect. The musicians hurried to their instruments, the dancers—some already half-muf-fled for departure—fell into line down each side of the room, the older spectators slipped back to their chairs, and the lively young man, after diving about here and there in the throng, drew forth a girl who had already wound a cherry-coloured "fascinator"[5] about her head, and, leading her up to the end of the floor, whirled her down its length to the bounding tune of a Virginia reel.

Frome's heart was beating fast. He had been straining for a glimpse of the dark head under the cherry-coloured scarf and it vexed him that another eye should have been quicker than his. The leader of the reel, who looked as if he had Irish blood in his veins, danced well, and his partner caught his fire. As she passed down the line, her light figure swinging from hand to hand in circles of increasing swiftness, the scarf flew off her head and stood out behind her shoulders, and Frome, at each turn, caught sight of her laughing panting lips, the cloud of dark hair about her forehead, and the dark eyes which seemed the only fixed points in a maze of flying lines.

The dancers were going faster and faster, and the musicians, to keep up with them, belaboured their instruments like jockeys lashing their mounts on the home-stretch; yet it seemed to the young man at the window that the reel would never end. Now and then he turned his eyes from the girl's face to that of her partner, which, in the exhilaration of the dance, had taken on a look of almost impudent ownership. Denis Eady was the son of Michael Eady, the ambitious Irish grocer, whose suppleness and effrontery had given Starkfield its first notion of "smart" business methods, and whose new brick store testified to the success of the attempt. His son seemed likely to follow in his steps, and was mean-while applying the same arts to the conquest of the Starkfield maiden-hood. Hitherto Ethan Frome had been content to think him a mean fellow; but now he positively invited a horse-whipping. It was strange

4. A type of reed organ.
5. Woman's head covering.

that the girl did not seem aware of it: that she could lift her rapt face to her dancer's, and drop her hands into his, without appearing to feel the offence of his look and touch.

Frome was in the habit of walking into Starkfield to fetch home his wife's cousin, Mattie Silver, on the rare evenings when some chance of amusement drew her to the village. It was his wife who had suggested, when the girl came to live with them, that such opportunities should be put in her way. Mattie Silver came from Stamford, and when she entered the Fromes' household to act as her cousin Zeena's aid it was thought best, as she came without pay, not to let her feel too sharp a contrast between the life she had left and the isolation of a Starkfield farm. But for this—as Frome sardonically reflected—it would hardly have occurred to Zeena to take any thought for the girl's amusement.

When his wife first proposed that they should give Mattie an occasional evening out he had inwardly demurred at having to do the extra two miles to the village and back after his hard day on the farm; but not long afterward he had reached the point of wishing that Starkfield might give all its nights to revelry.

Mattie Silver had lived under his roof for a year, and from early morning till they met at supper he had frequent chances of seeing her; but no moments in her company were comparable to those when, her arm in his, and her light step flying to keep time with his long stride, they walked back through the night to the farm. He had taken to the girl from the first day, when he had driven over to the Flats to meet her, and she had smiled and waved to him from the train, crying out "You must be Ethan!" as she jumped down with her bundles, while he reflected, looking over her slight person: "She don't look much on housework, but she ain't a fretter, anyhow." But it was not only that the coming to his house of a bit of hopeful young life was like the lighting of a fire on a cold hearth. The girl was more than the bright serviceable creature he had thought her. She had an eye to see and an ear to hear: he could show her things and tell her things, and taste the bliss of feeling that all he imparted left long reverberations and echoes he could wake at will.

It was during their night walks back to the farm that he felt most intensely the sweetness of this communion. He had always been more sensitive than the people about him to the appeal of natural beauty. His unfinished studies had given form to this sensibility and even in his unhappiest moments field and sky spoke to him with a deep and powerful persuasion. But hitherto the emotion had remained in him as a silent ache, veiling with sadness the beauty that evoked it. He did not even know whether any one else in the world felt as he did, or whether he was the sole victim of this mournful privilege. Then he learned that one other spirit had trembled with the same touch of wonder: that at his side, living under his roof and eating his bread, was a creature to whom he could say: "That's Orion down yonder; the big fellow to the right is

Aldebaran, and the bunch of little ones—like bees swarming—they're the Pleiades . . . "[6] or whom he could hold entranced before a ledge of granite thrusting up through the fern while he unrolled the huge panorama of the ice age, and the long dim stretches of succeeding time. The fact that admiration for his learning mingled with Mattie's wonder at what he taught was not the least part of his pleasure. And there were other sensations, less definable but more exquisite, which drew them together with a shock of silent joy: the cold red of sunset behind winter hills, the flight of cloud-flocks over slopes of golden stubble, or the intensely blue shadows of hemlocks on sunlit snow. When she said to him once: "It looks just as if it was painted!" it seemed to Ethan that the art of definition could go no farther, and that words had at last been found to utter his secret soul. . . .

As he stood in the darkness outside the church these memories came back with the poignancy of vanished things. Watching Mattie whirl down the floor from hand to hand he wondered how he could ever have thought that his dull talk interested her. To him, who was never gay but in her presence, her gaiety seemed plain proof of indifference. The face she lifted to her dancers was the same which, when she saw him, always looked like a window that has caught the sunset. He even noticed two or three gestures which, in his fatuity, he had thought she kept for him: a way of throwing her head back when she was amused, as if to taste her laugh before she let it out, and a trick of sinking her lids slowly when anything charmed or moved her.

The sight made him unhappy, and his unhappiness roused his latent fears. His wife had never shown any jealousy of Mattie, but of late she had grumbled increasingly over the house-work and found oblique ways of attracting attention to the girl's inefficiency. Zeena had always been what Starkfield called "sickly," and Frome had to admit that, if she were as ailing as she believed, she needed the help of a stronger arm than the one which lay so lightly in his during the night walks to the farm. Mattie had no natural turn for housekeeping, and her training had done nothing to remedy the defect. She was quick to learn, but forgetful and dreamy, and not disposed to take the matter seriously. Ethan had an idea that if she were to marry a man she was fond of the dormant instinct would wake, and her pies and biscuits become the pride of the county; but domesticity in the abstract did not interest her. At first she was so awkward that he could not help laughing at her; but she laughed with him and that made them better friends. He did his best to supplement her unskilled efforts, getting up earlier than usual to light the kitchen fire, carrying in the wood overnight, and neglecting the mill for the farm that he might help her about the house during the day. He even crept

6. See p. 12 for Orion and the Pleiades. Aldebaran, a red star, one of the twenty brightest, lies in the constellation Taurus. In Arabic, "follower of the Pleiades."

down on Saturday nights to scrub the kitchen floor after the women had gone to bed; and Zeena, one day, had surprised him at the churn[7] and had turned away silently, with one of her queer looks.

Of late there had been other signs of her disfavour, as intangible but more disquieting. One cold winter morning, as he dressed in the dark, his candle flickering in the draught of the ill-fitting window, he had heard her speak from the bed behind him.

"The doctor don't want I should be left without anybody to do for me," she said in her flat whine.

He had supposed her to be asleep, and the sound of her voice had startled him, though she was given to abrupt explosions of speech after long intervals of secretive silence.

He turned and looked at her where she lay indistinctly outlined under the dark calico quilt, her high-boned face taking a grayish tinge from the whiteness of the pillow.

"Nobody to do for you?" he repeated.

"If you say you can't afford a hired girl when Mattie goes."

Frome turned away again, and taking up his razor stooped to catch the reflection of his stretched cheek in the blotched looking-glass above the wash-stand.

"Why on earth should Mattie go?"

"Well, when she gets married, I mean," his wife's drawl came from behind him.

"Oh, she'd never leave us as long as you needed her," he returned, scraping hard at his chin.

"I wouldn't ever have it said that I stood in the way of a poor girl like Mattie marrying a smart fellow like Denis Eady," Zeena answered in a tone of plaintive self-effacement.

Ethan, glaring at his face in the glass, threw his head back to draw the razor from ear to chin. His hand was steady, but the attitude was an excuse for not making an immediate reply.

"And the doctor don't want I should be left without anybody," Zeena continued. "He wanted I should speak to you about a girl he's heard about, that might come—"

Ethan laid down the razor and straightened himself with a laugh.

"Denis Eady! If that's all I guess there's no such hurry to look round for a girl."

"Well, I'd like to talk to you about it," said Zeena obstinately.

He was getting into his clothes in fumbling haste. "All right. But I haven't got the time now; I'm late as it is," he returned, holding his old silver turnip-watch to the candle.

Zeena, apparently accepting this as final, lay watching him in silence

7. Agitates milk or cream to make butter.

while he pulled his suspenders over his shoulders and jerked his arms
into his coat; but as he went toward the door she said, suddenly and
incisively: "I guess you're always late, now you shave every morning."

That thrust had frightened him more than any vague insinuations
about Denis Eady. It was a fact that since Mattie Silver's coming he had
taken to shaving every day; but his wife always seemed to be asleep when
he left her side in the winter darkness, and he had stupidly assumed that
she would not notice any change in his appearance. Once or twice in
the past he had been faintly disquieted by Zenobia's way of letting things
happen without seeming to remark them, and then, weeks afterward, in
a casual phrase, revealing that she had all along taken her notes and
drawn her inferences. Of late, however, there had been no room in his
thoughts for such vague apprehensions. Zeena herself, from an oppressive reality, had faded into an insubstantial shade. All his life was lived
in the sight and sound of Mattie Silver, and he could no longer conceive
of its being otherwise. But now, as he stood outside the church, and saw
Mattie spinning down the floor with Denis Eady, a throng of disregarded
hints and menaces wove their cloud about his brain . . .

II

As the dancers poured out of the hall Frome, drawing back behind
the projecting stormdoor, watched the segregation of the grotesquely
muffled groups, in which a moving lantern ray now and then lit up a
face flushed with food and dancing. The villagers, being afoot, were the
first to climb the slope to the main street, while the country neighbours
packed themselves more slowly into the sleighs under the shed.

"Ain't you riding, Mattie?" a woman's voice called back from the
throng about the shed, and Ethan's heart gave a jump. From where he
stood he could not see the persons coming out of the hall till they had
advanced a few steps beyond the wooden sides of the storm-door; but
through its cracks he heard a clear voice answer: "Mercy no! Not on
such a night."

She was there, then, close to him, only a thin board between. In
another moment she would step forth into the night, and his eyes,
accustomed to the obscurity, would discern her as clearly as though she
stood in daylight. A wave of shyness pulled him back into the dark angle
of the wall, and he stood there in silence instead of making his presence
known to her. It had been one of the wonders of their intercourse that
from the first, she, the quicker, finer, more expressive, instead of crushing him by the contrast, had given him something of her own ease and
freedom; but now he felt as heavy and loutish as in his student days,
when he had tried to "jolly" the Worcester girls at a picnic.

He hung back, and she came out alone and paused within a few yards of him. She was almost the last to leave the hall, and she stood looking uncertainly about her as if wondering why he did not show himself. Then a man's figure approached, coming so close to her that under their formless wrappings they seemed merged in one dim outline.

"Gentleman friend gone back on you? Say, Matt, that's tough! No, I wouldn't be mean enough to tell the other girls. I ain't as low-down as that." (How Frome hated his cheap banter!) "But look at here, ain't it lucky I got the old man's cutter[1] down there waiting for us?"

Frome heard the girl's voice, gaily incredulous: "What on earth's your father's cutter doin' down there?"

"Why, waiting for me to take a ride. I got the roan colt too. I kinder knew I'd want to take a ride to-night," Eady, in his triumph, tried to put a sentimental note into his bragging voice.

The girl seemed to waver, and Frome saw her twirl the end of her scarf irresolutely about her fingers. Not for the world would he have made a sign to her, though it seemed to him that his life hung on her next gesture.

"Hold on a minute while I unhitch the colt," Denis called to her, springing toward the shed.

She stood perfectly still, looking after him, in an attitude of tranquil expectancy torturing to the hidden watcher. Frome noticed that she no longer turned her head from side to side, as though peering through the night for another figure. She let Denis Eady lead out the horse, climb into the cutter and fling back the bearskin to make room for her at his side; then, with a swift motion of flight, she turned about and darted up the slope toward the front of the church.

"Good-bye! Hope you'll have a lovely ride!" she called back to him over her shoulder.

Denis laughed, and gave the horse a cut that brought him quickly abreast of her retreating figure.

"Come along! Get in quick! It's as slippery as thunder on this turn," he cried, leaning over to reach out a hand to her.

She laughed back at him: "Good-night! I'm not getting in."

By this time they had passed beyond Frome's earshot and he could only follow the shadowy pantomime of their silhouettes as they continued to move along the crest of the slope above him. He saw Eady, after a moment, jump from the cutter and go toward the girl with the reins over one arm. The other he tried to slip through hers; but she eluded him nimbly, and Frome's heart, which had swung out over a black void, trembled back to safety. A moment later he heard the jingle of departing sleigh bells and discerned a figure advancing alone toward the empty expanse of snow before the church.

---

1. Small one-horse sleigh.

In the black shade of the Varnum spruces he caught up with her and she turned with a quick "Oh!"

"Think I'd forgotten you, Matt?" he asked with sheepish glee.

She answered seriously: "I thought maybe you couldn't come back for me."

"Couldn't? What on earth could stop me?"

"I knew Zeena wasn't feeling any too good to-day."

"Oh, she's in bed long ago." He paused, a question struggling in him. "Then you meant to walk home all alone?"

"Oh, I ain't afraid!" she laughed.

They stood together in the gloom of the spruces, an empty world glimmering about them wide and grey under the stars. He brought his question out.

"If you thought I hadn't come, why didn't you ride back with Denis Eady?"

"Why, where *were* you? How did you know? I never saw you!"

Her wonder and his laughter ran together like spring rills[2] in a thaw. Ethan had the sense of having done something arch and ingenious. To prolong the effect he groped for a dazzling phrase, and brought out, in a growl of rapture: "Come along."

He slipped an arm through hers, as Eady had done, and fancied it was faintly pressed against her side; but neither of them moved. It was so dark under the spruces that he could barely see the shape of her head beside his shoulder. He longed to stoop his cheek and rub it against her scarf. He would have liked to stand there with her all night in the blackness. She moved forward a step or two and then paused again above the dip of the Corbury road. Its icy slope, scored by innumerable runners, looked like a mirror scratched by travellers at an inn.

"There was a whole lot of them coasting before the moon set," she said.

"Would you like to come in and coast with them some night?" he asked.

"Oh, *would* you, Ethan? It would be lovely!"

"We'll come to-morrow if there's a moon."

She lingered, pressing closer to his side. "Ned Hale and Ruth Varnum came just as *near* running into the big elm at the bottom. We were all sure they were killed." Her shiver ran down his arm. "Wouldn't it have been too awful? They're so happy!"

"Oh, Ned ain't much at steering. I guess I can take you down all right!" he said disdainfully.

He was aware that he was "talking big," like Denis Eady; but his reaction of joy had unsteadied him, and the inflection with which she had

2. Very small brooks.

said of the engaged couple "They're so happy!" made the words sound as if she had been thinking of herself and him.

"The elm *is* dangerous, though. It ought to be cut down," she insisted.

"Would you be afraid of it, with me?"

"I told you I ain't the kind to be afraid," she tossed back, almost indifferently; and suddenly she began to walk on with a rapid step.

These alterations of mood were the despair and joy of Ethan Frome. The motions of her mind were as incalculable as the flit of a bird in the branches. The fact that he had no right to show his feelings, and thus provoke the expression of hers, made him attach a fantastic importance to every change in her look and tone. Now he thought she understood him, and feared; now he was sure she did not, and despaired. To-night the pressure of accumulated misgivings sent the scale drooping toward despair, and her indifference was the more chilling after the flush of joy into which she had plunged him by dismissing Denis Eady. He mounted School House Hill at her side and walked on in silence till they reached the lane leading to the saw-mill; then the need of some definite assurance grew too strong for him.

"You'd have found me right off if you hadn't gone back to have that last reel with Denis," he brought out awkwardly. He could not pronounce the name without a stiffening of the muscles of his throat.

"Why, Ethan, how could I tell you were there?"

"I suppose what folks say is true," he jerked out at her, instead of answering.

She stopped short, and he felt, in the darkness, that her face was lifted quickly to his. "Why, what do folks say?"

"It's natural enough you should be leaving us," he floundered on, following his thought.

"Is that what they say?" she mocked back at him; then, with a sudden drop of her sweet treble: "You mean that Zeena—ain't suited with me any more?" she faltered.

Their arms had slipped apart and they stood motionless, each seeking to distinguish the other's face.

"I know I ain't anything like as smart as I ought to be," she went on, while he vainly struggled for expression. "There's lots of things a hired girl could do that come awkward to me still—and I haven't got much strength in my arms. But if she'd only tell me I'd try. You know she hardly ever says anything, and sometimes I can see she ain't suited, and yet I don't know why." She turned on him with a sudden flash of indignation. "You'd ought to tell me, Ethan Frome—you'd ought to! Unless *you* want me to go too—"

Unless he wanted her to go too! The cry was balm to his raw wound. The iron heavens seemed to melt and rain down sweetness. Again he struggled for the all-expressive word, and again, his arm in hers, found only a deep "Come along."

They walked on in silence through the blackness of the hemlock-shaded lane, where Ethan's saw-mill gloomed through the night, and out again into the comparative clearness of the fields. On the farther side of the hemlock belt the open country rolled away before them gray and lonely under the stars. Sometimes their way led them under the shade of an overhanging bank or through the thin obscurity of a clump of leafless trees. Here and there a farmhouse stood far back among the fields, mute and cold as a grave-stone. The night was so still that they heard the frozen snow crackle under their feet. The crash of a loaded branch falling far off in the woods reverberated like a musket-shot, and once a fox barked, and Mattie shrank closer to Ethan, and quickened her steps.

At length they sighted the group of larches at Ethan's gate, and as they drew near it the sense that the walk was over brought back his words.

"Then you don't want to leave us, Matt?"

He had to stoop his head to catch her stifled whisper: "Where'd I go, if I did?"

The answer sent a pang through him but the tone suffused him with joy. He forgot what else he had meant to say and pressed her against him so closely that he seemed to feel her warmth in his veins.

"You ain't crying are you, Matt?"

"No, of course I'm not," she quavered.

They turned in at the gate and passed under the shaded knoll where, enclosed in a low fence, the Frome grave-stones slanted at crazy angles through the snow. Ethan looked at them curiously. For years that quiet company had mocked his restlessness, his desire for change and free-dom. "We never got away—how should you?" seemed to be written on every headstone; and whenever he went in or out of his gate he thought with a shiver: "I shall just go on living here till I join them." But now all desire for change had vanished, and the sight of the little enclosure gave him a warm sense of continuance and stability.

"I guess we'll never let you go, Matt," he whispered, as though even the dead, lovers once, must conspire with him to keep her; and brushing by the graves, he thought: "We'll always go on living here together, and some day she'll lie there beside me."

He let the vision possess him as they climbed the hill to the house. He was never so happy with her as when he abandoned himself to these dreams. Half-way up the slope Mattie stumbled against some unseen obstruction and clutched his sleeve to steady herself. The wave of warmth that went through him was like the prolongation of his vision. For the first time he stole his arm about her, and she did not resist. They walked on as if they were floating on a summer stream.

Zeena always went to bed as soon as she had had her supper, and the shutterless windows of the house were dark. A dead cucumber-vine dangled from the porch like the crape streamer tied to the door for a death, and the thought flashed through Ethan's brain: "If it was there for Zeena—" Then he had a distinct sight of his wife lying in their bedroom asleep, her mouth slightly open, her false teeth in a tumbler by the bed . . .

They walked around to the back of the house, between the rigid gooseberry bushes. It was Zeena's habit, when they came back late from the village, to leave the key of the kitchen door under the mat. Ethan stood before the door, his head heavy with dreams, his arm still about Mattie. "Matt—" he began, not knowing what he meant to say.

She slipped out of his hold without speaking, and he stooped down and felt for the key.

"It's not there!" he said, straightening himself with a start.

They strained their eyes at each other through the icy darkness. Such a thing had never happened before.

"Maybe she's forgotten it," Mattie said in a tremulous whisper; but both of them knew that it was not like Zeena to forget.

"It might have fallen off into the snow," Mattie continued, after a pause during which they had stood intently listening.

"It must have been pushed off, then," he rejoined in the same tone. Another wild thought tore through him. What if tramps had been there—what if . . .

Again he listened, fancying he heard a distant sound in the house; then he felt in his pocket for a match, and kneeling down, passed its light slowly over the rough edges of snow about the doorstep.

He was still kneeling when his eyes, on a level with the lower panel of the door, caught a faint ray beneath it. Who could be stirring in that silent house? He heard a step on the stairs, and again for an instant the thought of tramps tore through him. Then the door opened and he saw his wife.

Against the dark background of the kitchen she stood up tall and angular, one hand drawing a quilted counterpane to her flat breast, while the other held a lamp. The light, on a level with her chin, drew out of the darkness her puckered throat and the projecting wrist of the hand that clutched the quilt, and deepened fantastically the hollows and prominences of her high-boned face under its ring of crimping-pins.[3] To Ethan, still in the rosy haze of his hour with Mattie, the sight came with the intense precision of the last dream before waking. He felt as if he had never before known what his wife looked like.

She drew aside without speaking, and Mattie and Ethan passed into the kitchen, which had the deadly chill of a vault after the dry cold of the night.

3. To curl the hair.

"Guess you forgot about us, Zeena," Ethan joked, stamping the snow from his boots.

"No. I just felt so mean I couldn't sleep."

Mattie came forward, unwinding her wraps, the colour of the cherry scarf in her fresh lips and cheeks. "I'm so sorry, Zeena! Isn't there anything I can do?"

"No; there's nothing." Zeena turned away from her. "You might 'a' shook off that snow outside," she said to her husband.

She walked out of the kitchen ahead of them and pausing in the hall raised the lamp at arm's-length, as if to light them up the stairs.

Ethan paused also, affecting to fumble for the peg on which he hung his coat and cap. The doors of the two bedrooms faced each other across the narrow upper landing, and to-night it was peculiarly repugnant to him that Mattie should see him follow Zeena.

"I guess I won't come up yet awhile," he said, turning as if to go back to the kitchen.

Zeena stopped short and looked at him. "For the land's sake—what you going to do down here?"

"I've got the mill accounts to go over."

She continued to stare at him, the flame of the unshaded lamp bringing out with microscopic cruelty the fretful lines of her face.

"At this time o' night? You'll ketch your death. The fire's out long ago."

Without answering he moved away toward the kitchen. As he did so his glance crossed Mattie's and he fancied that a fugitive warning gleamed through her lashes. The next moment they sank to her flushed cheeks and she began to mount the stairs ahead of Zeena.

"That's so. It *is* powerful cold down here," Ethan assented; and with lowered head he went up in his wife's wake, and followed her across the threshold of their room.

III

There was some hauling to be done at the lower end of the wood-lot, and Ethan was out early the next day.

The winter morning was as clear as crystal. The sunrise burned red in a pure sky, the shadows on the rim of the wood-lot were darkly blue, and beyond the white and scintillating fields patches of far-off forest hung like smoke.

It was in the early morning stillness, when his muscles were swinging to their familiar task and his lungs expanding with long draughts of mountain air, that Ethan did his clearest thinking. He and Zeena had not exchanged a word after the door of their room had closed on them.

She had measured out some drops from a medicine-bottle on a chair by the bed and, after swallowing them, and wrapping her head in a piece of yellow flannel, had lain down with her face turned away. Ethan undressed hurriedly and blew out the light so that he should not see her when he took his place at her side. As he lay there he could hear Mattie moving about in her room, and her candle, sending its small ray across the landing, drew a scarcely perceptible line of light under his door. He kept his eyes fixed on the light till it vanished. Then the room grew perfectly black, and not a sound was audible but Zeena's asthmatic breathing. Ethan felt confusedly that there were many things he ought to think about, but through his tingling veins and tired brain only one sensation throbbed: the warmth of Mattie's shoulder against his. Why had he not kissed her when he held her there? A few hours earlier he would not have asked himself the question. Even a few minutes earlier, when they had stood alone outside the house, he would not have dared to think of kissing her. But since he had seen her lips in the lamplight he felt that they were his.

Now, in the bright morning air, her face was still before him. It was part of the sun's red and of the pure glitter on the snow. How the girl had changed since she had come to Starkfield! He remembered what a colourless slip of a thing she had looked the day he had met her at the station. And all the first winter, how she had shivered with cold when the northerly gales shook the thin clapboards and the snow beat like hail against the loose-hung windows!

He had been afraid that she would hate the hard life, the cold and loneliness; but not a sign of discontent escaped her. Zeena took the view that Mattie was bound to make the best of Starkfield since she hadn't any other place to go to; but this did not strike Ethan as conclusive. Zeena, at any rate, did not apply the principle in her own case.

He felt all the more sorry for the girl because misfortune had, in a sense, indentured her to them. Mattie Silver was the daughter of a cousin of Zenobia Frome's, who had inflamed his clan with mingled sentiments of envy and admiration by descending from the hills to Connecticut, where he had married a Stamford girl and succeeded to her father's thriving "drug" business. Unhappily Orin Silver, a man of far-reaching aims, had died too soon to prove that the end justifies the means. His accounts revealed merely what the means had been; and these were such that it was fortunate for his wife and daughter that his books were examined only after his impressive funeral. His wife died of the disclosure, and Mattie, at twenty, was left alone to make her way on the fifty dollars obtained from the sale of her piano. For this purpose her equipment, though varied, was inadequate. She could trim a hat, make molasses candy, recite "Curfew shall not ring to-night," and play "The

Lost Chord" and a pot-pourri from "Carmen."[1] When she tried to extend the field of her activities in the direction of stenography and book-keeping her health broke down, and six months on her feet behind the counter of a department store did not tend to restore it. Her nearest relations had been induced to place their savings in her father's hands, and though, after his death, they ungrudgingly acquitted themselves of the Christian duty of returning good for evil by giving his daughter all the advice at their disposal, they could hardly be expected to supplement it by material aid. But when Zenobia's doctor recommended her looking about for some one to help her with the house-work the clan instantly saw the chance of exacting a compensation from Mattie. Zenobia, though doubtful of the girl's efficiency, was tempted by the freedom to find fault without much risk of losing her; and so Mattie came to Starkfield.

Zenobia's fault-finding was of the silent kind, but not the less penetrating for that. During the first months Ethan alternately burned with the desire to see Mattie defy her and trembled with fear of the result. Then the situation grew less strained. The pure air, and the long summer hours in the open, gave back life and elasticity to Mattie, and Zeena, with more leisure to devote to her complex ailments, grew less watchful of the girl's omissions; so that Ethan, struggling on under the burden of his barren farm and failing saw-mill, could at least imagine that peace reigned in his house.

There was really, even now, no tangible evidence to the contrary; but since the previous night a vague dread had hung on his sky-line. It was formed of Zeena's obstinate silence, of Mattie's sudden look of warning, of the memory of just such fleeting imperceptible signs as those which told him, on certain stainless mornings, that before night there would be rain.

His dread was so strong that, man-like, he sought to postpone certainty. The hauling was not over till mid-day, and as the lumber was to be delivered to Andrew Hale, the Starkfield builder, it was really easier for Ethan to send Jotham Powell, the hired man, back to the farm on foot, and drive the load down to the village himself. He had scrambled up on the logs, and was sitting astride of them, close over his shaggy grays, when, coming between him and their steaming necks, he had a vision of the warning look that Mattie had given him the night before.

"If there's going to be any trouble I want to be there," was his vague

1. "Curfew shall not ring to-night": line from Rosa Hartwick Thorpe's (1850–1939) famous sentimental poem of a girl who saves her lover's life; "The Lost Chord": popular religious song of mystical experience from poem by Adelaide Anne Procter (1825–1864) composed by Englishman Sir Arthur Sullivan (1842–1900); selections from *Carmen*, French opera by Georges Bizet (1838–1875) based on Prosper Mérimée's (1803–1870) French novella of Spanish gypsy passions. Thus, Mattie has no practical skills and only a superficial training in "proper" feminine culture.

reflection, as he threw to Jotham the unexpected order to unhitch the team and lead them back to the barn.

It was a slow trudge home through the heavy fields, and when the two men entered the kitchen Mattie was lifting the coffee from the stove and Zeena was already at the table. Her husband stopped short at sight of her. Instead of her usual calico wrapper and knitted shawl she wore her best dress of brown merino, and above her thin strands of hair, which still preserved the tight undulations of the crimping-pins, rose a hard perpendicular bonnet, as to which Ethan's clearest notion was that he had to pay five dollars for it at the Bettsbridge Emporium. On the floor beside her stood his old valise and a bandbox[2] wrapped in newspapers.

"Why, where are you going, Zeena?" he exclaimed.

"I've got my shooting pains so bad that I'm going over to Bettsbridge to spend the night with Aunt Martha Pierce and see that new doctor," she answered in a matter-of-fact tone, as if she had said she was going into the store-room to take a look at the preserves, or up to the attic to go over the blankets.

In spite of her sedentary habits such abrupt decisions were not without precedent in Zeena's history. Twice or thrice before she had suddenly packed Ethan's valise and started off to Bettsbridge, or even Springfield, to seek the advice of some new doctor, and her husband had grown to dread these expeditions because of their cost. Zeena always came back laden with expensive remedies, and her last visit to Springfield had been commemorated by her paying twenty dollars for an electric battery of which she had never been able to learn the use. But for the moment his sense of relief was so great as to preclude all other feelings. He had now no doubt that Zeena had spoken the truth in saying, the night before, that she had sat up because she felt "too mean" to sleep: her abrupt resolve to seek medical advice showed that, as usual, she was wholly absorbed in her health.

As if expecting a protest, she continued plaintively; "If you're too busy with the hauling I presume you can let Jotham Powell drive me over with the sorrel in time to ketch the train at the Flats."

Her husband hardly heard what she was saying. During the winter months there was no stage between Starkfield and Bettsbridge, and the trains which stopped at Corbury Flats were slow and infrequent. A rapid calculation showed Ethan that Zeena could not be back at the farm before the following evening. . . .

"If I'd supposed you'd 'a' made any objection to Jotham Powell's driving me over—" she began again, as though his silence had implied refusal. On the brink of departure she was always seized with a flux of words. "All I know is," she continued, "I can't go on the way I am much

2. Usually, cylindrical box of paperboard or thin wood for holding light clothing.

longer. The pains are clear away down to my ankles now, or I'd 'a'
walked in to Starkfield on my own feet, sooner'n put you out, and asked
Michael Eady to let me ride over on his wagon to the Flats, when he
sends to meet the train that brings his groceries. I'd 'a' had two hours to
wait in the station, but I'd sooner 'a' done it, even with this cold, than
to have you say—"

"Of course Jotham'll drive you over," Ethan roused himself to answer.
He became suddenly conscious that he was looking at Mattie while
Zeena talked to him, and with an effort he turned his eyes to his wife.
She sat opposite the window, and the pale light reflected from the banks
of snow made her face look more than usually drawn and bloodless,
sharpened the three parallel creases between ear and cheek, and drew
querulous lines from her thin nose to the corners of her mouth. Though
she was but seven years her husband's senior, and he was only twenty-
eight, she was already an old woman.

Ethan tried to say something befitting the occasion, but there was
only one thought in his mind: the fact that, for the first time since Mattie
had come to live with them, Zeena was to be away for a night. He
wondered if the girl were thinking of it too. . . .

He knew that Zeena must be wondering why he did not offer to drive
her to the Flats and let Jotham Powell take the lumber to Starkfield, and
at first he could not think of a pretext for not doing so; then he said: "I'd
take you over myself, only I've got to collect the cash for the lumber."

As soon as the words were spoken he regretted them, not only because
they were untrue—there being no prospect of his receiving cash payment from Hale—but also because he knew from experience the imprudence of letting Zeena think he was in funds on the eve of one of her
therapeutic excursions. At the moment, however, his one desire was to
avoid the long drive with her behind the ancient sorrel who never went
out of a walk.

Zeena made no reply: she did not seem to hear what he had said. She
had already pushed her plate aside, and was measuring out a draught
from a large bottle at her elbow.

"It ain't done me a speck of good, but I guess I might as well use it
up," she remarked; adding, as she pushed the empty bottle toward Mattie: "If you can get the taste out it'll do for pickles."

IV

As soon as his wife had driven off Ethan took his coat and cap from
the peg. Mattie was washing up the dishes, humming one of the dance
tunes of the night before. He said "So long, Matt," and she answered
gaily "So long, Ethan"; and that was all.

It was warm and bright in the kitchen. The sun slanted through the south window on the girl's moving figure, on the cat dozing in a chair, and on the geraniums brought in from the door-way, where Ethan had planted them in the summer to "make a garden" for Mattie. He would have liked to linger on, watching her tidy up and then settle down to her sewing; but he wanted still more to get the hauling done and be back at the farm before night.

All the way down to the village he continued to think of his return to Mattie. The kitchen was a poor place, not "spruce" and shining as his mother had kept it in his boyhood; but it was surprising what a homelike look the mere fact of Zeena's absence gave it. And he pictured what it would be like that evening, when he and Mattie were there after supper. For the first time they would be alone together indoors, and they would sit there, one on each side of the stove, like a married couple, he in his stocking feet and smoking his pipe, she laughing and talking in that funny way she had, which was always as new to him as if he had never heard her before.

The sweetness of the picture, and the relief of knowing that his fears of "trouble" with Zeena were unfounded, sent up his spirits with a rush, and he, who was usually so silent, whistled and sang aloud as he drove through the snowy fields. There was in him a slumbering spark of sociability which the long Starkfield winters had not yet extinguished. By nature grave and inarticulate, he admired recklessness and gaiety in others and was warmed to the marrow by friendly human intercourse. At Worcester, though he had the name of keeping to himself and not being much of a hand at a good time, he had secretly gloried in being clapped on the back and hailed as "Old Ethe" or "Old Stiff"; and the cessation of such familiarities had increased the chill of his return to Starkfield.

There the silence had deepened about him year by year. Left alone, after his father's accident, to carry the burden of farm and mill, he had had no time for convivial loiterings in the village; and when his mother fell ill the loneliness of the house grew more oppressive than that of the fields. His mother had been a talker in her day, but after her "trouble" the sound of her voice was seldom heard, though she had not lost the power of speech. Sometimes, in the long winter evenings, when in desperation her son asked her why she didn't "say something," she would lift a finger and answer: "Because I'm listening"; and on stormy nights, when the loud wind was about the house, she would complain, if he spoke to her: "They're talking so out there that I can't hear you."

It was only when she drew toward her last illness, and his cousin Zenobia Pierce came over from the next valley to help him nurse her, that human speech was heard again in the house. After the mortal silence of his long imprisonment Zeena's volubility was music in his ears. He felt that he might have "gone like his mother" if the sound of a new voice had not come to steady him. Zeena seemed to understand his case at a glance. She laughed at him for not knowing the simplest sick-bed duties and told him to "go right along out" and leave her to see to things. The mere fact of obeying her orders, of feeling free to go about his business again and talk with other men, restored his shaken balance and magnified his sense of what he owed her. Her efficiency shamed and dazzled him. She seemed to possess by instinct all the household wisdom that his long apprenticeship had not instilled in him. When the end came it was she who had to tell him to hitch up and go for the undertaker, and she thought it "funny" that he had not settled before-hand who was to have his mother's clothes and the sewing-machine. After the funeral, when he saw her preparing to go away, he was seized with an unreasoning dread of being left alone on the farm; and before he knew what he was doing he had asked her to stay there with him. He had often thought since that it would not have happened if his mother had died in spring instead of winter . . .

When they married it was agreed that, as soon as he could straighten out the difficulties resulting from Mrs. Frome's long illness, they would sell the farm and saw-mill and try their luck in a large town. Ethan's love of nature did not take the form of a taste for agriculture. He had always wanted to be an engineer, and to live in towns, where there were lectures and big libraries and "fellows doing things." A slight engineering job in Florida, put in his way during his period of study at Worcester, increased his faith in his ability as well as his eagerness to see the world; and he felt sure that, with a "smart" wife like Zeena, it would not be long before he had made himself a place in it.

Zeena's native village was slightly larger and nearer to the railway than Starkfield, and she had let her husband see from the first that life on an isolated farm was not what she had expected when she married. But purchasers were slow in coming, and while he waited for them Ethan learned the impossibility of transplanting her. She chose to look down on Starkfield, but she could not have lived in a place which looked down on her. Even Bettsbridge or Shadd's Falls would not have been sufficiently aware of her, and in the greater cities which attracted Ethan she would have suffered a complete loss of identity. And within a year of their marriage she developed the "sickliness" which had since made her notable even in a community rich in pathological instances. When she came to take care of his mother she had seemed to Ethan like the very genius of health, but he soon saw that her skill as a nurse had been acquired by the absorbed observation of her own symptoms.

Then she too fell silent. Perhaps it was the inevitable effect of life on the farm, or perhaps, as she sometimes said, it was because Ethan "never listened." The charge was not wholly unfounded. When she spoke it was only to complain, and to complain of things not in his power to remedy; and to check a tendency to impatient retort he had first formed the habit of not answering her, and finally of thinking of other things while she talked. Of late, however, since he had had reasons for observing her more closely, her silence had begun to trouble him. He recalled his mother's growing taciturnity, and wondered if Zeena were also turning "queer." Women did, he knew. Zeena, who had at her fingers' ends the pathological chart of the whole region, had cited many cases of the kind while she was nursing his mother; and he himself knew of certain lonely farm-houses in the neighbourhood where stricken creatures pined, and of others where sudden tragedy had come of their presence. At times, looking at Zeena's shut face, he felt the chill of such forebodings. At other times her silence seemed deliberately assumed to conceal far-reaching intentions, mysterious conclusions drawn from suspicions and resentments impossible to guess. That supposition was even more disturbing than the other; and it was the one which had come to him the night before, when he had seen her standing in the kitchen door.

Now her departure for Bettsbridge had once more eased his mind, and all his thoughts were on the prospect of his evening with Mattie. Only one thing weighed on him, and that was his having told Zeena that he was to receive cash for the lumber. He foresaw so clearly the consequences of this imprudence that with considerable reluctance he decided to ask Andrew Hale for a small advance on his load.

When Ethan drove into Hale's yard the builder was just getting out of his sleigh.

"Hello, Ethe!" he said. "This comes handy."

Andrew Hale was a ruddy man with a big gray moustache and a stubbly double-chin unconstrained by a collar; but his scrupulously clean shirt was always fastened by a small diamond stud. This display of opulence was misleading, for though he did a fairly good business it was known that his easy-going habits and the demands of his large family frequently kept him what Starkfield called "behind." He was an old friend of Ethan's family, and his house one of the few to which Zeena occasionally went, drawn there by the fact that Mrs. Hale, in her youth, had done more "doctoring" than any other woman in Starkfield, and was still a recognised authority on symptoms and treatment.

Hale went up to the grays and patted their sweating flanks.

"Well, sir," he said, "you keep them two as if they was pets."

Ethan set about unloading the logs and when he had finished his job he pushed open the glazed door of the shed which the builder used as his office. Hale sat with his feet up on the stove, his back propped against a battered desk strewn with papers: the place, like the man, was warm, genial and untidy.

"Sit right down and thaw out," he greeted Ethan.

The latter did not know how to begin, but at length he managed to bring out his request for an advance of fifty dollars. The blood rushed to his thin skin under the sting of Hale's astonishment. It was the builder's custom to pay at the end of three months, and there was no precedent between the two men for a cash settlement.

Ethan felt that if he had pleaded an urgent need Hale might have made shift to pay him; but pride, and an instinctive prudence, kept him from resorting to this argument. After his father's death it had taken time to get his head above water, and he did not want Andrew Hale, or any one else in Starkfield, to think he was going under again. Besides, he hated lying; if he wanted the money he wanted it, and it was nobody's business to ask why. He therefore made his demand with the awkwardness of a proud man who will not admit to himself that he is stooping; and he was not much surprised at Hale's refusal.

The builder refused genially, as he did everything else: he treated the matter as something in the nature of a practical joke, and wanted to know if Ethan meditated buying a grand piano or adding a "cupolo"[1] to his house; offering, in the latter case, to give his services free of cost.

Ethan's arts were soon exhausted, and after an embarrassed pause he wished Hale good day and opened the door of the office. As he passed out the builder suddenly called after him: "See here—you ain't in a tight place, are you?"

"Not a bit," Ethan's pride retorted before his reason had time to intervene.

"Well, that's good! Because I *am*, a shade. Fact is, I was going to ask you to give me a little extra time on that payment. Business is pretty slack, to begin with, and then I'm fixing up a little house for Ned and Ruth when they're married. I'm glad to do it for 'em, but it costs." His look appealed to Ethan for sympathy. "The young people like things nice. You know how it is yourself: it's not so long ago since you fixed up your own place for Zeena."

Ethan left the grays in Hale's stable and went about some other business in the village. As he walked away the builder's last phrase lingered in his ears, and he reflected grimly that his seven years with Zeena seemed to Starkfield "not so long."

The afternoon was drawing to an end, and here and there a lighted pane spangled the cold gray dusk and made the snow look whiter. The bitter weather had driven every one indoors and Ethan had the long rural street to himself. Suddenly he heard the brisk play of sleigh-bells and a cutter passed him, drawn by a free-going horse. Ethan recognised Michael Eady's roan colt, and young Denis Eady, in a handsome new fur cap, leaned forward and waved a greeting. "Hello, Ethe!" he shouted and spun on.

The cutter was going in the direction of the Frome farm, and Ethan's

---

1. Cupola. Small, vaulted structure, usually hemispherical, rising above the roof of a building; here meaning adding an extravagant decoration to the farmhouse.

heart contracted as he listened to the dwindling bells. What more likely than that Denis Eady had heard of Zeena's departure for Bettsbridge, and was profiting by the opportunity to spend an hour with Mattie? Ethan was ashamed of the storm of jealousy in his breast. It seemed unworthy of the girl that his thoughts of her should be so violent.

He walked on to the church corner and entered the shade of the Varnum spruces, where he had stood with her the night before. As he passed into their gloom he saw an indistinct outline just ahead of him. At his approach it melted for an instant into two separate shapes and then conjoined again, and he heard a kiss, and a half-laughing "Oh!" provoked by the discovery of his presence. Again the outline hastily disunited and the Varnum gate slammed on one half while the other hurried on ahead of him. Ethan smiled at the discomfiture he had caused. What did it matter to Ned Hale and Ruth Varnum if they were caught kissing each other? Everybody in Starkfield knew they were engaged. It pleased Ethan to have surprised a pair of lovers on the spot where he and Mattie had stood with such a thirst for each other in their hearts; but he felt a pang at the thought that these two need not hide their happiness.

He fetched the grays from Hale's stable and started on his long climb back to the farm. The cold was less sharp than earlier in the day and a thick fleecy sky threatened snow for the morrow. Here and there a star pricked through, showing behind it a deep well of blue. In an hour or two the moon would push up over the ridge behind the farm, burn a gold-edged rent in the clouds, and then be swallowed by them. A mournful peace hung on the fields, as though they felt the relaxing grasp of the cold and stretched themselves in their long winter sleep.

Ethan's ears were alert for the jingle of sleighbells, but not a sound broke the silence of the lonely road. As he drew near the farm he saw, through the thin screen of larches at the gate, a light twinkling in the house above him. "She's up in her room," he said to himself, "fixing herself up for supper"; and he remembered Zeena's sarcastic stare when Mattie, on the evening of her arrival, had come down to supper with smoothed hair and a ribbon at her neck.

He passed by the graves on the knoll and turned his head to glance at one of the older headstones, which had interested him deeply as a boy because it bore his name.

SACRED TO THE MEMORY OF

ETHAN FROME AND ENDURANCE HIS WIFE,

WHO DWELLED TOGETHER IN PEACE

FOR FIFTY YEARS.

He used to think that fifty years sounded like a long time to live together; but now it seemed to him that they might pass in a flash. Then, with a sudden dart of irony, he wondered if, when their turn came, the same epitaph would be written over him and Zeena.

He opened the barn-door and craned his head into the obscurity, half-fearing to discover Denis Eady's roan colt in the stall beside the sorrel. But the old horse was there alone, mumbling his crib with toothless jaws, and Ethan whistled cheerfully while he bedded down the grays and shook an extra measure of oats into their managers. His was not a tuneful throat, but harsh melodies burst from it as he locked the barn and sprang up the hill to the house. He reached the kitchen-porch and turned the door-handle; but the door did not yield to his touch.

Startled at finding it locked he rattled the handle violently; then he reflected that Mattie was alone and that it was natural she should barricade herself at nightfall. He stood in the darkness expecting to hear her step. It did not come, and after vainly straining his ears he called out in a voice that shook with joy: "Hello, Matt!"

Silence answered; but in a minute or two he caught a sound on the stairs and saw a line of light about the door-frame, as he had seen it the night before. So strange was the precision with which the incidents of the previous evening were repeating themselves that he half expected, when he heard the key turn, to see his wife before him on the threshold; but the door opened, and Mattie faced him.

She stood just as Zeena had stood, a lifted lamp in her hand, against the black background of the kitchen. She held the light at the same level, and it drew out with the same distinctness her slim young throat and the brown wrist no bigger than a child's. Then, striking upward, it threw a lustrous fleck on her lips, edged her eyes with velvet shade, and laid a milky whiteness above the black curve of her brows.

She wore her usual dress of darkish stuff, and there was no bow at her neck; but through her hair she had run a streak of crimson ribbon. This tribute to the unusual transformed and glorified her. She seemed to Ethan taller, fuller, more womanly in shape and motion. She stood aside, smiling silently, while he entered, and then moved away from him with something soft and flowing in her gait. She set the lamp on the table, and he saw that it was carefully laid for supper, with fresh dough-nuts, stewed blueberries and his favourite pickles in a dish of gay red glass. A bright fire glowed in the stove and the cat lay stretched before it, watching the table with a drowsy eye.

Ethan was suffocated with the sense of well-being. He went out into the passage to hang up his coat and pull off his wet boots. When he came back Mattie had set the teapot on the table and the cat was rubbing itself persuasively against her ankles.

"Why, Puss! I nearly tripped over you," she cried, the laughter sparkling through her lashes.

Again Ethan felt a sudden twinge of jealousy. Could it be his coming that gave her such a kindled face?

"Well, Matt, any visitors?" he threw off, stooping down carelessly to examine the fastening of the stove.

She nodded and laughed "Yes, one," and he felt a blackness settling on his brows.

"Who was that?" he questioned, raising himself up to slant a glance at her beneath his scowl.

Her eyes danced with malice. "Why, Jotham Powell. He came in after he got back, and asked for a drop of coffee before he went down home."

The blackness lifted and light flooded Ethan's brain. "That all? Well, I hope you made out to let him have it." And after a pause he felt it right to add: "I suppose he got Zeena over to the Flats all right?"

"Oh, yes; in plenty of time."

The name threw a chill between them, and they stood a moment looking sideways at each other before Mattie said with a shy laugh: "I guess it's about time for supper."

They drew their seats up to the table, and the cat, unbidden, jumped between them into Zeena's empty chair. "Oh, Puss!" said Mattie, and they laughed again.

Ethan, a moment earlier, had felt himself on the brink of eloquence; but the mention of Zeena had paralysed him. Mattie seemed to feel the contagion of his embarrassment, and sat with downcast lids, sipping her tea, while he feigned an insatiable appetite for dough-nuts and sweet pickles. At last, after casting about for an effective opening, he took a long gulp of tea, cleared his throat, and said: "Looks as if there'd be more snow."

She feigned great interest. "Is that so? Do you suppose it'll interfere with Zeena's getting back?" She flushed red as the question escaped her, and hastily set down the cup she was lifting.

Ethan reached over for another helping of pickles. "You never can tell, this time of year, it drifts so bad on the Flats." The name had benumbed him again, and once more he felt as if Zeena were in the room between them.

"Oh, Puss, you're too greedy!" Mattie cried.

The cat, unnoticed, had crept up on muffled paws from Zeena's seat to the table, and was stealthily elongating its body in the direction of the milk-jug, which stood between Ethan and Mattie. The two leaned forward at the same moment and their hands met on the handle of the jug. Mattie's hand was underneath, and Ethan kept his clasped on it a moment longer than was necessary. The cat, profiting by this unusual demonstration, tried to effect an unnoticed retreat, and in doing so backed into the pickle-dish, which fell to the floor with a crash.

Mattie, in an instant, had sprung from her chair and was down on her knees by the fragments.

"Oh, Ethan, Ethan—it's all to pieces! What will Zeena say?"

But this time his courage was up. "Well, she'll have to say it to the cat, any way!" he rejoined with a laugh, kneeling down at Mattie's side to scrape up the swimming pickles.

She lifted stricken eyes to him. "Yes, but, you see, she never meant it should be used, not even when there was company; and I had to get up on the step-ladder to reach it down from the top shelf of the china-closet, where she keeps it with all her best things, and of course she'll want to know why I did it——"

The case was so serious that it called forth all of Ethan's latent resolution.

"She needn't know anything about it if you keep quiet. I'll get another just like it to-morrow. Where did it come from? I'll go to Shadd's Falls for it if I have to!"

"Oh, you'll never get another even there! It was a wedding present—don't you remember? It came all the way from Philadelphia, from Zeena's aunt that married the minister. That's why she wouldn't ever use it. Oh, Ethan, Ethan, what in the world shall I do?"

She began to cry, and he felt as if every one of her tears were pouring over him like burning lead. "Don't, Matt, don't—oh, *don't!*" he implored her.

She struggled to her feet, and he rose and followed her helplessly while she spread out the pieces of glass on the kitchen dresser. It seemed to him as if the shattered fragments of their evening lay there.

"Here, give them to me," he said in a voice of sudden authority.

She drew aside, instinctively obeying his tone. "Oh, Ethan, what are you going to do?"

Without replying he gathered the pieces of glass into his broad palm and walked out of the kitchen to the passage. There he lit a candle-end, opened the china-closet, and, reaching his long arm up to the highest shelf, laid the pieces together with such accuracy of touch that a close inspection convinced him of the impossibility of detecting from below that the dish was broken. If he glued it together the next morning months might elapse before his wife noticed what had happened, and meanwhile he might after all be able to match the dish at Shadd's Falls or Bettsbridge. Having satisfied himself that there was no risk of immediate discovery he went back to the kitchen with a lighter step, and found Mattie disconsolately removing the last scraps of pickle from the floor.

"It's all right, Matt. Come back and finish supper," he commanded her.

Completely reassured, she shone on him through tear-hung lashes, and his soul swelled with pride as he saw how his tone subdued her. She did not even ask what he had done. Except when he was steering a big log down the mountain to his mill he had never known such a thrilling sense of mastery.

V

They finished supper, and while Mattie cleared the table Ethan went to look at the cows and then took a last turn about the house. The earth lay dark under a muffled sky and the air was so still that now and then he heard a lump of snow come thumping down from a tree far off on the edge of the wood-lot.

When he returned to the kitchen Mattie had pushed up his chair to the stove and seated herself near the lamp with a bit of sewing. The scene was just as he had dreamed of it that morning. He sat down, drew his pipe from his pocket and stretched his feet to the glow. His hard day's work in the keen air made him feel at once lazy and light of mood, and he had a confused sense of being in another world, where all was warmth and harmony and time could bring no change. The only drawback to his complete well-being was the fact that he could not see Mattie from where he sat; but he was too indolent to move and after a moment he said: "Come over here and sit by the stove."

Zeena's empty rocking-chair stood facing him. Mattie rose obediently, and seated herself in it. As her young brown head detached itself against the patch-work cushion that habitually framed his wife's gaunt countenance, Ethan had a momentary shock. It was almost as if the other face, the face of the superseded woman, had obliterated that of the intruder. After a moment Mattie seemed to be affected by the same sense of constraint. She changed her position, leaning forward to bend her head above her work, so that he saw only the foreshortened tip of her nose and the streak of red in her hair; then she slipped to her feet, saying "I can't see to sew," and went back to her chair by the lamp.

Ethan made a pretext of getting up to replenish the stove, and when he returned to his seat he pushed it sideways that he might get a view of her profile and of the lamplight falling on her hands. The cat, who had been a puzzled observer of these unusual movements, jumped up into Zeena's chair, rolled itself into a ball, and lay watching them with narrowed eyes.

Deep quiet sank on the room. The clock ticked above the dresser, a piece of charred wood fell now and then in the stove, and the faint sharp scent of the geraniums mingled with the odour of Ethan's smoke, which began to throw a blue haze about the lamp and to hang its greyish cobwebs in the shadowy corners of the room.

All constraint had vanished between the two, and they began to talk easily and simply. They spoke of every-day things, of the prospect of snow, of the next church sociable, of the loves and quarrels of Starkfield. The commonplace nature of what they said produced in Ethan an illusion of long-established intimacy which no outburst of emotion could have given, and he set his imagination adrift on the fiction that they had always spent their evenings thus and would always go on doing so . . .

"This is the night we were to have gone coasting, Matt," he said at length, with the rich sense, as he spoke, that they could go on any other night they chose, since they had all time before them.

She smiled back at him. "I guess you forgot!"

"No, I didn't forget; but it's as dark as Egypt outdoors. We might go to-morrow if there's a moon."

She laughed with pleasure, her head tilted back, the lamplight sparkling on her lips and teeth. "That would be lovely, Ethan!"

He kept his eyes fixed on her, marvelling at the way her face changed with each turn of their talk, like a wheat-field under a summer breeze. It was intoxicating to find such magic in his clumsy words, and he longed to try new ways of using it.

"Would you be scared to go down the Corbury road with me on a night like this?" he asked.

Her cheeks burned redder. "I ain't any more scared than you are!"

"Well, I'd be scared, then; I wouldn't do it. That's an ugly corner down by the big elm. If a fellow didn't keep his eyes open he'd go plumb into it." He luxuriated in the sense of protection and authority which his words conveyed. To prolong and intensify the feeling he added: "I guess we're well enough here."

She let her lids sink slowly, in the way he loved. "Yes, we're well enough here," she sighed.

Her tone was so sweet that he took the pipe from his mouth and drew his chair up to the table. Leaning forward, he touched the farther end of the strip of brown stuff that she was hemming. "Say, Matt," he began with a smile, "what do you think I saw under the Varnum spruces, coming along home just now? I saw a friend of yours getting kissed."

The words had been on his tongue all the evening, but now that he had spoken them they struck him as inexpressibly vulgar and out of place.

Mattie blushed to the roots of her hair and pulled her needle rapidly twice or thrice through her work, insensibly drawing the end of it away from him. "I suppose it was Ruth and Ned," she said in a low voice, as though he had suddenly touched on something grave.

Ethan had imagined that his allusion might open the way to the accepted pleasantries, and these perhaps in turn to a harmless caress, if only a mere touch on her hand. But now he felt as if her blush had set a flaming guard about her. He supposed it was his natural awkwardness that made him feel so. He knew that most young men made nothing at all of giving a pretty girl a kiss, and he remembered that the night before, when he had put his arm about Mattie, she had not resisted. But that had been out-of-doors, under the open irresponsible night. Now, in the warm lamplit room, with all its ancient implications of conformity and order, she seemed infinitely farther away from him and more unapproachable.

To ease his constraint he said: "I suppose they'll be setting a date before long."

"Yes. I shouldn't wonder if they got married some time along in the summer." She pronounced the word *married* as if her voice caressed it. It seemed a rustling covert leading to enchanted glades. A pang shot through Ethan, and he said, twisting away from her in his chair: "It'll be your turn next, I wouldn't wonder."

She laughed a little uncertainly. "Why do you keep on saying that?"

He echoed her laugh. "I guess I do it to get used to the idea."

He drew up to the table again and she sewed on in silence, with dropped lashes, while he sat in fascinated contemplation of the way in which her hands went up and down above the strip of stuff, just as he had seen a pair of birds make short perpendicular flights over a nest they were building. At length, without turning her head or lifting her lids, she said in a low tone: "It's not because you think Zeena's got anything against me, is it?"

His former dread started up full-armed at the suggestion. "Why, what do you mean?" he stammered.

She raised distressed eyes to his, her work dropping on the table between them. "I don't know. I thought last night she seemed to have."

"I'd like to know what," he growled.

"Nobody can tell with Zeena." It was the first time they had ever spoken so openly of her attitude toward Mattie, and the repetition of the name seemed to carry it to the farther corners of the room and send it back to them in long repercussions of sound. Mattie waited, as if to give the echo time to drop, and then went on: "She hasn't said anything to *you?*"

He shook his head. "No, not a word."

She tossed the hair back from her forehead with a laugh. "I guess I'm just nervous, then. I'm not going to think about it any more."

"Oh, no—don't let's think about it, Matt!"

The sudden heat of his tone made her colour mount again, not with a rush, but gradually, delicately, like the reflection of a thought stealing slowly across her heart. She sat silent, her hands clasped on her work, and it seemed to him that a warm current flowed toward him along the strip of stuff that still lay unrolled between them. Cautiously he slid his hand palm-downward along the table till his finger-tips touched the end of the stuff. A faint vibration of her lashes seemed to show that she was aware of his gesture, and that it had sent a counter-current back to her; and she let her hands lie motionless on the other end of the strip.

As they sat thus he heard a sound behind him and turned his head. The cat had jumped from Zeena's chair to dart at a mouse in the wainscot, and as a result of the sudden movement the empty chair had set up a spectral rocking.

"She'll be rocking in it herself this time to-morrow," Ethan thought. "I've been in a dream, and this is the only evening we'll ever have together." The return to reality was as painful as the return to consciousness after taking an anæsthetic. His body and brain ached with indescribable weariness, and he could think of nothing to say or to do that should arrest the mad flight of the moments.

His alteration of mood seemed to have communicated itself to Mattie. She looked up at him languidly, as though her lids were weighted with sleep and it cost her an effort to raise them. Her glance fell on his hand, which now completely covered the end of her work and grasped it as if it were a part of herself. He saw a scarcely perceptible tremor cross her face, and without knowing what he did he stooped his head and kissed the bit of stuff in his hold. As his lips rested on it he felt it glide slowly from beneath them, and saw that Mattie had risen and was silently rolling up her work. She fastened it with a pin, and then, finding her thimble and scissors, put them with the roll of stuff into the box covered with fancy paper which he had once brought to her from Bettsbridge.

He stood up also, looking vaguely about the room. The clock above the dresser struck eleven.

"Is the fire all right?" she asked in a low voice.

He opened the door of the stove and poked aimlessly at the embers. When he raised himself again he saw that she was dragging toward the stove the old soap-box lined with carpet in which the cat made its bed. Then she recrossed the floor and lifted two of the geranium pots in her arms, moving them away from the cold window. He followed her and brought the other geraniums, the hyacinth bulbs in a cracked custard bowl and the German ivy trained over an old croquet hoop.

When these nightly duties were performed there was nothing left to do but to bring in the tin candlestick from the passage, light the candle and blow out the lamp. Ethan put the candlestick in Mattie's hand and she went out of the kitchen ahead of him, the light that she carried before her making her dark hair look like a drift of mist on the moon.

"Good night, Matt," he said as she put her foot on the first step of the stairs.

She turned and looked at him a moment. "Good night, Ethan," she answered, and went up.

When the door of her room had closed on her he remembered that he had not even touched her hand.

VI

The next morning at breakfast Jotham Powell was between them, and Ethan tried to hide his joy under an air of exaggerated indifference, lounging back in his chair to throw scraps to the cat, growling at the weather, and not so much as offering to help Mattie when she rose to clear away the dishes.

He did not know why he was so irrationally happy, for nothing was changed in his life or hers. He had not even touched the tip of her fingers or looked her full in the eyes. But their evening together had given him a vision of what life at her side might be, and he was glad now that he had done nothing to trouble the sweetness of the picture. He had a fancy that she knew what had restrained him . . .

There was a last load of lumber to be hauled to the village, and Jotham Powell—who did not work regularly for Ethan in winter—had "come round" to help with the job. But a wet snow, melting to sleet, had fallen in the night and turned the roads to glass. There was more wet in the air and it seemed likely to both men that the weather would "milden" toward afternoon and make the going safer. Ethan therefore proposed to his assistant that they should load the sledge at the wood-lot, as they had done on the previous morning, and put off the "teaming" to Starkfield till later in the day. This plan had the advantage of enabling him to send Jotham to the Flats after dinner to meet Zenobia, while he himself took the lumber down to the village.

He told Jotham to go out and harness up the grays, and for a moment he and Mattie had the kitchen to themselves. She had plunged the breakfast dishes into a tin dish-pan and was bending above it with her slim arms bared to the elbow, the steam from the hot water beading her forehead and tightening her rough hair into little brown rings like the tendrils on the traveller's joy.[1]

Ethan stood looking at her, his heart in his throat. He wanted to say: "We shall never be alone again like this." Instead, he reached down his tobacco-pouch from a shelf of the dresser, put it into his pocket and said: "I guess I can make out to be home for dinner."

She answered "All right, Ethan," and he heard her singing over the dishes as he went.

As soon as the sledge was loaded he meant to send Jotham back to the farm and hurry on foot into the village to buy the glue for the pickle-dish. With ordinary luck he should have had time to carry out this plan; but everything went wrong from the start. On the way over to the wood-lot one of the grays slipped on a glare of ice and cut his knee; and when they got him up again Jotham had to go back to the barn for a strip of

---

1. Popular name of a hardy, climbing, flowering vine, common in low grounds.

rag to bind the cut. Then, when the loading finally began, a sleety rain was coming down once more, and the tree trunks were so slippery that it took twice as long as usual to lift them and get them in place on the sledge. It was what Jotham called a sour morning for work, and the horses, shivering and stamping under their wet blankets, seemed to like it as little as the men. It was long past the dinner-hour when the job was done, and Ethan had to give up going to the village because he wanted to lead the injured horse home and wash the cut himself.

He thought that by starting out again with the lumber as soon as he had finished his dinner he might get back to the farm with the glue before Jotham and the old sorrel had had time to fetch Zenobia from the Flats; but he knew the chance was a slight one. It turned on the state of the roads and on the possible lateness of the Bettsbridge train. He remembered afterward, with a grim flash of self-derision, what importance he had attached to the weighing of these probabilities . . .

As soon as dinner was over he set out again for the wood-lot, not daring to linger till Jotham Powell left. The hired man was still drying his wet feet at the stove, and Ethan could only give Mattie a quick look as he said beneath his breath: "I'll be back early."

He fancied that she nodded her comprehension; and with that scant solace he had to trudge off through the rain.

He had driven his load half-way to the village when Jotham Powell overtook him, urging the reluctant sorrel toward the Flats. "I'll have to hurry up to do it," Ethan mused, as the sleigh dropped down ahead of him over the dip of the school-house hill. He worked like ten at the unloading, and when it was over hastened on to Michael Eady's for the glue. Eady and his assistant were both "down street," and young Denis, who seldom deigned to take their place, was lounging by the stove with a knot of the golden youth of Starkfield. They hailed Ethan with ironic compliment and offers of conviviality; but no one knew where to find the glue. Ethan, consumed with the longing for a last moment alone with Mattie, hung about impatiently while Denis made an ineffectual search in the obscurer corners of the store.

"Looks as if we were all sold out. But if you'll wait around till the old man comes along maybe he can put his hand on it."

"I'm obliged to you, but I'll try if I can get it down at Mrs. Homan's," Ethan answered, burning to be gone.

Denis's commercial instinct compelled him to aver on oath that what Eady's store could not produce would never be found at the widow Homan's; but Ethan, heedless of this boast, had already climbed to the sledge and was driving on to the rival establishment. Here, after considerable search, and sympathetic questions as to what he wanted it for, and whether ordinary flour paste wouldn't do as well if she couldn't find it, the widow Homan finally hunted down her solitary bottle of glue to its hiding-place in a medley of cough-lozenges and corset-laces.

"I hope Zeena ain't broken anything she sets store by," she called after him as he turned the grays toward home.

The fitful bursts of sleet had changed into a steady rain and the horses had heavy work even without a load behind them. Once or twice, hearing sleigh-bells, Ethan turned his head, fancying that Zeena and Jotham might overtake him; but the old sorrel was not in sight, and he set his face against the rain and urged on his ponderous pair.

The barn was empty when the horses turned into it and, after giving them the most perfunctory ministrations they had ever received from him, he strode up to the house and pushed open the kitchen door.

Mattie was there alone, as he had pictured her. She was bending over a pan on the stove; but at the sound of his step she turned with a start and sprang to him.

"See, here, Matt, I've got some stuff to mend the dish with! Let me get at it quick," he cried, waving the bottle in one hand while he put her lightly aside; but she did not seem to hear him.

"Oh, Ethan—Zeena's come," she said in a whisper, clutching his sleeve.

They stood and stared at each other, pale as culprits.

"But the sorrel's not in the barn!" Ethan stammered.

"Jotham Powell brought some goods over from the Flats for his wife, and he drove right on home with them," she explained.

He gazed blankly about the kitchen, which looked cold and squalid in the rainy winter twilight.

"How is she?" he asked, dropping his voice to Mattie's whisper.

She looked away from him uncertainly. "I don't know. She went right up to her room."

"She didn't say anything?"

"No."

Ethan let out his doubts in a low whistle and thrust the bottle back into his pocket. "Don't fret; I'll come down and mend it in the night," he said. He pulled on his wet coat again and went back to the barn to feed the grays.

While he was there Jotham Powell drove up with the sleigh, and when the horses had been attended to Ethan said to him: "You might as well come back up for a bite." He was not sorry to assure himself of Jotham's neutralising presence at the supper table, for Zeena was always "nervous" after a journey. But the hired man, though seldom loth to accept a meal not included in his wages, opened his stiff jaws to answer slowly: "I'm obliged to you, but I guess I'll go along back."

Ethan looked at him in surprise. "Better come up and dry off. Looks as if there'd be something hot for supper."

Jotham's facial muscles were unmoved by this appeal and, his vocabulary being limited, he merely repeated: "I guess I'll go along back."

To Ethan there was something vaguely ominous in this stolid rejection of free food and warmth, and he wondered what had happened on the drive to nerve Jotham to such stoicism. Perhaps Zeena had failed to see the new doctor or had not liked his counsels: Ethan knew that in such cases the first person she met was likely to be held responsible for her grievance.

When he re-entered the kitchen the lamp lit up the same scene of shining comfort as on the previous evening. The table had been as carefully laid, a clear fire glowed in the stove, the cat dozed in its warmth, and Mattie came forward carrying a plate of dough-nuts.

She and Ethan looked at each other in silence; then she said, as she had said the night before: "I guess it's about time for supper."

VII

Ethan went out into the passage to hang up his wet garments. He listened for Zeena's step and, not hearing it, called her name up the stairs. She did not answer, and after a moment's hesitation he went up and opened her door. The room was almost dark, but in the obscurity he saw her sitting by the window, bolt upright, and knew by the rigidity of the outline projected against the pane that she had not taken off her travelling dress.

"Well, Zeena," he ventured from the threshold.

She did not move, and he continued: "Supper's about ready. Ain't you coming?"

She replied: "I don't feel as if I could touch a morsel."

It was the consecrated formula, and he expected it to be followed, as usual, by her rising and going down to supper. But she remained seated, and he could think of nothing more felicitous than: "I presume you're tired after the long ride."

Turning her head at this, she answered solemnly: "I'm a great deal sicker than you think."

Her words fell on his ear with a strange shock of wonder. He had often heard her pronounce them before—what if at last they were true?

He advanced a step or two into the dim room. "I hope that's not so, Zeena," he said.

She continued to gaze at him through the twilight with a mien of wan authority, as of one consciously singled out for a great fate. "I've got complications," she said.

Ethan knew the word for one of exceptional import. Almost everybody in the neighbourhood had "troubles," frankly localized and specified; but only the chosen had "complications." To have them was in itself a distinction, though it was also, in most cases, a death-warrant.

People struggled on for years with "troubles," but they almost always succumbed to "complications."

Ethan's heart was jerking to and fro between two extremities of feeling, but for the moment compassion prevailed. His wife looked so hard and lonely, sitting there in the darkness with such thoughts.

"Is that what the new doctor told you?" he asked, instinctively lowering his voice.

"Yes. He says any regular doctor would want me to have an operation."

Ethan was aware that, in regard to the important question of surgical intervention, the female opinion of the neighbourhood was divided, some glorying in the prestige conferred by operations while others shunned them as indelicate. Ethan, from motives of economy, had always been glad that Zeena was of the latter faction.

In the agitation caused by the gravity of her announcement he sought a consolatory short cut. "What do you know about this doctor anyway? Nobody ever told you that before."

He saw his blunder before she could take it up: she wanted sympathy, not consolation.

"I didn't need to have anybody tell me I was losing ground every day. Everybody but you could see it. And everybody in Bettsbridge knows about Dr. Buck. He has his office in Worcester, and comes over once a fortnight to Shadd's Falls and Bettsbridge for consultations. Eliza Spears was wasting away with kidney trouble before she went to him, and now she's up and around, and singing in the choir."

"Well, I'm glad of that. You must do just what he tells you," Ethan answered sympathetically.

She was still looking at him. "I mean to," she said. He was struck by a new note in her voice. It was neither whining nor reproachful, but drily resolute.

"What does he want you should do?" he asked, with a mounting vision of fresh expenses.

"He wants I should have a hired girl. He says I oughtn't to have to do a single thing around the house."

"A hired girl?" Ethan stood transfixed.

"Yes. And Aunt Martha found me one right off. Everybody said I was lucky to get a girl to come away out here, and I agreed to give her a dollar extry to make sure. She'll be over to-morrow afternoon."

Wrath and dismay contended in Ethan. He had foreseen an immediate demand for money, but not a permanent drain on his scant resources. He no longer believed what Zeena had told him of the supposed seriousness of her state: he saw in her expedition to Bettsbridge only a plot hatched between herself and her Pierce relations to foist on him the cost of a servant; and for the moment wrath predominated.

"If you meant to engage a girl you ought to have told me before you started," he said.

"How could I tell you before I started? How did I know what Dr. Buck would say?"

"Oh, Dr. Buck—" Ethan's incredulity escaped in a short laugh. "Did Dr. Buck tell you how I was to pay her wages?"

Her voice rose furiously with his. "No, he didn't. For I'd 'a' been ashamed to tell *him* that you grudged me the money to get back my health, when I lost it nursing your own mother!"

"*You* lost your health nursing mother?"

"Yes; and my folks all told me at the time you couldn't do no less than marry me after——"

"Zeena!"

Through the obscurity which hid their faces their thoughts seemed to dart at each other like serpents shooting venom. Ethan was seized with horror of the scene and shame at his own share in it. It was as senseless and savage as a physical fight between two enemies in the darkness.

He turned to the shelf above the chimney, groped for matches and lit the one candle in the room. At first its weak flame made no impression on the shadows; then Zeena's face stood grimly out against the uncurtained pane, which had turned from gray to black.

It was the first scene of open anger between the couple in their sad seven years together, and Ethan felt as if he had lost an irretrievable advantage in descending to the level of recrimination. But the practical problem was there and had to be dealt with.

"You know I haven't got the money to pay for a girl, Zeena. You'll have to send her back: I can't do it."

"The doctor says it'll be my death if I go on slaving the way I've had to. He doesn't understand how I've stood it as long as I have."

"Slaving!—" He checked himself again, "You sha'n't lift a hand, if he says so. I'll do everything round the house myself——"

She broke in: "You're neglecting the farm enough already," and this being true, he found no answer, and left her time to add ironically: "Better send me over to the almshouse[1] and done with it . . . I guess there's been Fromes there afore now."

The taunt burned into him, but he let it pass. "I haven't got the money. That settles it."

There was a moment's pause in the struggle, as though the combatants were testing their weapons. Then Zeena said in a level voice: "I thought you were to get fifty dollars from Andrew Hale for that lumber."

"Andrew Hale never pays under three months." He had hardly spoken when he remembered the excuse he had made for not accompanying

---

1. House where paupers are supported, a poorhouse.

his wife to the station the day before; and the blood rose to his frowning brows.

"Why, you told me yesterday you'd fixed it up with him to pay cash down. You said that was why you couldn't drive me over to the Flats."

Ethan had no suppleness in deceiving. He had never before been convicted of a lie, and all the resources of evasion failed him. "I guess that was a misunderstanding," he stammered.

"You ain't got the money?"

"No."

"And you ain't going to get it?"

"No."

"Well, I couldn't know that when I engaged the girl, could I?"

"No." He paused to control his voice. "But you know it now. I'm sorry, but it can't be helped. You're a poor man's wife, Zeena; but I'll do the best I can for you."

For a while she sat motionless, as if reflecting, her arms stretched along the arms of her chair, her eyes fixed on vacancy. "Oh, I guess we'll make out," she said mildly.

The change in her tone reassured him. "Of course we will! There's a whole lot more I can do for you, and Mattie——"

Zeena, while he spoke, seemed to be following out some elaborate mental calculation. She emerged from it to say: "There'll be Mattie's board less, anyhow——"

Ethan, supposing the discussion to be over, had turned to go down to supper. He stopped short, not grasping what he heard. "Mattie's board less—?" he began.

Zeena laughed. It was an odd unfamiliar sound—he did not remember ever having heard her laugh before. "You didn't suppose I was going to keep two girls, did you? No wonder you were scared at the expense!"

He still had but a confused sense of what she was saying. From the beginning of the discussion he had instinctively avoided the mention of Mattie's name, fearing he hardly knew what: criticism, complaints, or vague allusions to the imminent probability of her marrying. But the thought of a definite rupture had never come to him, and even now could not lodge itself in his mind.

"I don't know what you mean," he said. "Mattie Silver's not a hired girl. She's your relation."

"She's a pauper that's hung onto us all after her father'd done his best to ruin us. I've kep' her here a whole year: it's somebody else's turn now."

As the shrill words shot out Ethan heard a tap on the door, which he had drawn shut when he turned back from the threshold.

"Ethan—Zeena!" Mattie's voice sounded gaily from the landing, "do you know what time it is? Supper's been ready half an hour."

Inside the room there was a moment's silence; then Zeena called out from her seat: "I'm not coming down to supper."

"Oh, I'm sorry! Aren't you well? Sha'n't I bring you up a bite of something?"

Ethan roused himself with an effort and opened the door. "Go along down, Matt. Zeena's just a little tired. I'm coming."

He heard her "All right!" and her quick step on the stairs; then he shut the door and turned back into the room. His wife's attitude was unchanged, her face inexorable, and he was seized with the despairing sense of his helplessness.

"You ain't going to do it, Zeena?"

"Do what?" she emitted between flattened lips.

"Send Mattie away—like this?"

"I never bargained to take her for life!"

He continued with rising vehemence: "You can't put her out of the house like a thief—a poor girl without friends or money. She's done her best for you and she's got no place to go to. You may forget she's your kin but everybody else'll remember it. If you do a thing like that what do you suppose folks'll say of you?"

Zeena waited a moment, as if giving him time to feel the full force of the contrast between his own excitement and her composure. Then she replied in the same smooth voice: "I know well enough what they say of my having kep' her here as long as I have."

Ethan's hand dropped from the door-knob, which he had held clenched since he had drawn the door shut on Mattie. His wife's retort was like a knife-cut across the sinews and he felt suddenly weak and powerless. He had meant to humble himself, to argue that Mattie's keep didn't cost much, after all, that he could make out to buy a stove and fix up a place in the attic for the hired girl—but Zeena's words revealed the peril of such pleadings.

"You mean to tell her she's got to go—at once?" he faltered out, in terror of letting his wife complete her sentence.

As if trying to make him see reason she replied impartially; "The girl will be over from Bettsbridge to-morrow, and I presume she's got to have somewheres to sleep."

Ethan looked at her with loathing. She was no longer the listless creature who had lived at his side in a state of sullen self-absorption, but a mysterious alien presence, an evil energy secreted from the long years of silent brooding. It was the sense of his helplessness that sharpened his antipathy. There had never been anything in her that one could appeal to; but as long as he could ignore and command he had remained indifferent. Now she had mastered him and he abhorred her. Mattie was her relation, not his: there were no means by which he could compel her to keep the girl under her roof. All the long misery of his baffled past, of his youth of failure, hardship and vain effort, rose up in his soul in bitterness and seemed to take shape before him in the woman who at every turn had barred his way. She had taken everything else from him; and now she meant to take the one thing that made up for all the others. For a moment such a flame of hate rose in him that it ran down his arm and clenched his fist against her. He took a wild step forward and then stopped.

"You're—you're not coming down?" he said in a bewildered voice.

"No. I guess I'll lay down on the bed a little while," she answered mildly; and he turned and walked out of the room.

In the kitchen Mattie was sitting by the stove, the cat curled up on her knees. She sprang to her feet as Ethan entered and carried the covered dish of meat-pie to the table.

"I hope Zeena isn't sick?" she asked.

"No."

She shone at him across the table. "Well, sit right down then. You must be starving." She uncovered the pie and pushed it over to him. So they were to have one more evening together, her happy eyes seemed to say!

He helped himself mechanically and began to eat; then disgust took him by the throat and he laid down his fork.

Mattie's tender gaze was on him and she marked the gesture.

"Why, Ethan, what's the matter? Don't it taste right?"

"Yes—it's first-rate. Only I—" He pushed his plate away, rose from his chair, and walked around the table to her side. She started up with frightened eyes.

"Ethan, there's something wrong! I *knew* there was!"

She seemed to melt against him in her terror, and he caught her in his arms, held her fast there, felt her lashes beat his cheek like netted butterflies.

"What is it—what is it?" she stammered; but he had found her lips at last and was drinking unconsciousness of everything but the joy they gave him.

She lingered a moment, caught in the same strong current; then she slipped from him and drew back a step or two, pale and troubled. Her look smote him with compunction, and he cried out, as if he saw her drowning in a dream: "You can't go, Matt! I'll never let you!"

"Go—go?" she stammered. "Must I go?"

The words went on sounding between them as though a torch of warning flew from hand to hand through a black landscape.

Ethan was overcome with shame at his lack of self-control in flinging the news at her so brutally. His head reeled and he had to support himself against the table. All the while he felt as if he were still kissing her, and yet dying of thirst for her lips.

"Ethan what has happened? Is Zeena mad with me?"

Her cry steadied him, though it deepened his wrath and pity. "No, no," he assured her, "it's not that. But this new doctor has scared her about herself. You know she believes all they say the first time she sees them. And this one's told her she won't get well unless she lays up and don't do a thing about the house—not for months—"

He paused, his eyes wandering from her miserably. She stood silent a moment, drooping before him like a broken branch. She was so small and weak-looking that it wrung his heart; but suddenly she lifted her head and looked straight at him. "And she wants somebody handier in my place? Is that it?"

"That's what she says to-night."

"If she says it to-night she'll say it to-morrow."

Both bowed to the inexorable truth: they knew that Zeena never changed her mind, and that in her case a resolve once taken was equivalent to an act performed.

There was a long silence between them; then Mattie said in a low voice: "Don't be too sorry, Ethan."

"Oh, God—oh, God," he groaned. The glow of passion he had felt for her had melted to an aching tenderness. He saw her quick lids beating back the tears, and longed to take her in his arms and soothe her.

"You're letting your supper get cold," she admonished him with a pale gleam of gaiety.

"Oh, Matt—Matt—where'll you go to?"

Her lids sank and a tremor crossed her face. He saw that for the first time the thought of the future came to her distinctly. "I might get something to do over at Stamford," she faltered, as if knowing that he knew she had no hope.

He dropped back into his seat and hid his face in his hands. Despair seized him at the thought of her setting out alone to renew the weary quest for work. In the only place where she was known she was surrounded by indifference or animosity; and what chance had she, inexperienced and untrained, among the million bread-seekers of the cities? There came back to him miserable tales he had heard at Worcester,[2] and the faces of girls whose lives had begun as hopefully as Mattie's. . . . It was not possible to think of such things without a revolt of his whole being. He sprang up suddenly.

"You can't go, Matt! I won't let you! She's always had her way, but I mean to have mine now—"

Mattie lifted her hand with a quick gesture, and he heard his wife's step behind him.

2. In 1880, in the city of Boston, twenty-thousand women were employed in other than domestic service; sixty-nine percent of them lived at home. Average annual income was $269.07; average annual expenses were $261.30. Working in Worcester, Mattie could be expected to make even less. Hours were long and grueling, shop girls required to stand all day. Mattie, if she did manage to find employment, with no family home environment, would be at a particular disadvantage.

Zeena came into the room with her dragging down-at-the-heel step, and quietly took her accustomed seat between them.

"I felt a little mite better, and Dr. Buck says I ought to eat all I can to keep my stren'th up, even if I ain't got any appetite," she said in her flat whine, reaching across Mattie for the teapot. Her "good" dress had been replaced by the black calico and brown knitted shawl which formed her daily wear, and with them she had put on her usual face and manner. She poured out her tea, added a great deal of milk to it, helped herself largely to pie and pickles, and made the familiar gesture of adjusting her false teeth before she began to eat. The cat rubbed itself ingratiatingly against her, and she said "Good Pussy," stooped to stroke it and gave it a scrap of meat from her plate.

Ethan sat speechless, not pretending to eat, but Mattie nibbled valiantly at her food and asked Zeena one or two questions about her visit to Bettsbridge. Zeena answered in her every-day tone and, warming to the theme, regaled them with several vivid descriptions of intestinal disturbances among her friends and relatives. She looked straight at Mattie as she spoke, a faint smile deepening the vertical lines between her nose and chin.

When supper was over she rose from her seat and pressed her hand to the flat surface over the region of the heart. "That pie of yours always sets a mite heavy, Matt," she said, not ill-naturedly. She seldom abbreviated the girl's name, and when she did so it was always a sign of affability.

"I've a good mind to go and hunt up those stomach powders I got last year over in Springfield," she continued. "I ain't tried them for quite a while, and maybe they'll help the heartburn."

Mattie lifted her eyes. "Can't I get them for you, Zeena?" she ventured.

"No. They're in a place you don't know about," Zeena answered darkly, with one of her secret looks.

She went out of the kitchen and Mattie, rising, began to clear the dishes from the table. As she passed Ethan's chair their eyes met and clung together desolately. The warm still kitchen looked as peaceful as the night before. The cat had sprung to Zeena's rocking-chair, and the heat of the fire was beginning to draw out the faint sharp scent of the geraniums. Ethan dragged himself wearily to his feet.

"I'll go out and take a look round," he said, going toward the passage to get his lantern.

As he reached the door he met Zeena coming back into the room, her lips twitching with anger, a flush of excitement on her sallow face. The shawl had slipped from her shoulders and was dragging at her down-trodden heels, and in her hands she carried the fragments of the red glass pickle-dish.

"I'd like to know who done this," she said, looking sternly from Ethan to Mattie.

There was no answer, and she continued in a trembling voice: "I went to get those powders I'd put away in father's old spectacle-case, top of the china-closet, where I keep the things I set store by, so's folks sha'n't meddle with them—" Her voice broke, and two small tears hung on her lashless lids and ran slowly down her cheeks. "It takes the step-ladder to get at the top shelf, and I put Aunt Philura Maple's pickle-dish up there o' purpose when we was married, and it's never been down since 'cept for the spring cleaning, and then I always lifted it with my own hands, so's 't it shouldn't get broke." She laid the fragments reverently on the table. "I want to know who done this," she quavered.

At the challenge Ethan turned back into the room and faced her. "I can tell you, then. The cat done it."

"The *cat?*"

"That's what I said."

She looked at him hard, and then turned her eyes to Mattie, who was carrying the dish-pan to the table.

"I'd like to know how the cat got into my china-closet," she said.

"Chasin' mice, I guess," Ethan rejoined. "There was a mouse round the kitchen all last evening."

Zeena continued to look from one to the other; then she emitted her small strange laugh. "I knew the cat was a smart cat," she said in a high voice, "but I didn't know he was smart enough to pick up the pieces of my pickle-dish and lay 'em edge to edge on the very shelf he knocked 'em off of."

Mattie suddenly drew her arms out of the steaming water. "It wasn't Ethan's fault, Zeena! The cat *did* break the dish; but I got it down from the china-closet, and I'm the one to blame for its getting broken."

Zeena stood beside the ruin of her treasure, stiffening into a stony image of resentment. "*You* got down my pickle-dish—what for?"

A bright flush flew to Mattie's cheeks. "I wanted to make the supper-table pretty," she said.

"You wanted to make the supper-table pretty; and you waited till my back was turned, and took the thing I set most store by of anything I've got, and wouldn't never use it, not even when the minister come to dinner, or Aunt Martha Pierce come over from Bettsbridge—" Zeena paused with a gasp, as if terrified by her own evocation of the sacrilege. "You're a bad girl, Mattie Silver, and I always known it. It's the way your father begun, and I was warned of it when I took you, and I tried to keep my things where you couldn't get at 'em—and now you've took from me the one I cared for most of all—" She broke off in a short spasm of sobs that passed and left her more than ever like a shape of stone.

"If I'd 'a' listened to folks, you'd 'a' gone before now, and this wouldn't

'a' happened," she said; and gathering up the bits of broken glass she
went out of the room as if she carried a dead body . . .

VIII

When Ethan was called back to the farm by his father's illness his
mother gave him, for his own use, a small room behind the untenanted
"best parlour." Here he had nailed up shelves for his books, built himself
a box-sofa out of boards and a mattress, laid out his papers on a kitchen-
table, hung on the rough plaster wall an engraving of Abraham Lincoln
and a calendar with "Thoughts from the Poets," and tried, with these
meagre properties to produce some likeness to the study of a "minister"
who had been kind to him and lent him books when he was at Worcester. He still took refuge there in summer, but when Mattie came to live
at the farm he had had to give her his stove, and consequently the room
was uninhabitable for several months of the year.

To this retreat he descended as soon as the house was quiet, and
Zeena's steady breathing from the bed had assured him that there was to
be no sequel to the scene in the kitchen. After Zeena's departure he and
Mattie had stood speechless, neither seeking to approach the other.
Then the girl had returned to her task of clearing up the kitchen for the
night and he had taken his lantern and gone on his usual round outside
the house. The kitchen was empty when he came back to it; but his
tobacco-pouch and pipe had been laid on the table, and under them
was a scrap of paper torn from the back of a seedsman's catalogue, on
which three words were written: "Don't trouble, Ethan."

Going into his cold dark "study" he placed the lantern on the table
and, stooping to its light, read the message again and again. It was the
first time that Mattie had ever written to him, and the possession of the
paper gave him a strange new sense of her nearness; yet it deepened his
anguish by reminding him that henceforth they would have no other
way of communicating with each other. For the life of her smile, the
warmth of her voice, only cold paper and dead words!

Confused motions of rebellion stormed in him. He was too young,
too strong, too full of the sap of living, to submit so easily to the destruction of his hopes. Must he wear out all his years at the side of a bitter
querulous woman? Other possibilities had been in him, possibilities sacrificed, one by one, to Zeena's narrow-mindedness and ignorance. And
what good had come of it? She was a hundred times bitterer and more
discontented than when he had married her. the one pleasure left her
was to inflict pain on him. All the healthy instincts of self-defence rose
up in him against such waste . . .

He bundled himself into his old coon-skin coat and lay down on the box-sofa to think. Under his cheek he felt a hard object with strange protuberances. It was a cushion which Zeena had made for him when they were engaged—the only piece of needlework he had ever seen her do. He flung it across the floor and propped his head against the wall . . .

He knew a case of a man over the mountain—a young fellow of about his own age—who had escaped from just such a life of misery by going West with the girl he cared for. His wife had divorced him, and he had married the girl and prospered. Ethan had seen the couple the summer before at Shadd's Falls, where they had come to visit relatives. They had a little girl with fair curls, who wore a gold locket and was dressed like a princess. The deserted wife had not done badly either. Her husband had given her the farm and she had managed to sell it, and with that and the alimony she had started a lunch-room at Bettsbridge and bloomed into activity and importance. Ethan was fired by the thought. Why should he not leave with Mattie the next day, instead of letting her go alone? He would hide his valise under the seat of the sleigh, and Zeena would suspect nothing till she went upstairs for her afternoon nap and found a letter on the bed . . .

His impulses were still near the surface, and he sprang up, re-lit the lantern, and sat down at the table. He rummaged in the drawer for a sheet of paper, found one, and began to write.

"Zeena, I've done all I could for you, and I don't see as it's been any use. I don't blame you, nor I don't blame myself. Maybe both of us will do better separate. I'm going to try my luck West, and you can sell the farm and mill, and keep the money—"

His pen paused on the word, which brought home to him the relentless conditions of his lot. If he gave the farm and mill to Zeena what would be left him to start his own life with? Once in the West he was sure of picking up work—he would not have feared to try his chance alone. But with Mattie depending on him the case was different. And what of Zeena's fate? Farm and mill were mortgaged to the limit of their value, and even if she found a purchaser—in itself an unlikely chance—it was doubtful if she could clear a thousand dollars on the sale. Meanwhile, how could she keep the farm going? It was only by incessant labour and personal supervision that Ethan drew a meagre living from his land, and his wife, even if she were in better health than she imagined, could never carry such a burden alone.

Well, she could go back to her people, then, and see what they would do for her. It was the fate she was forcing on Mattie—why not let her try it herself? By the time she had discovered his whereabouts, and brought suit for divorce, he would probably—wherever he was—be earning enough to pay her a sufficient alimony. And the alternative was to let Mattie go forth alone, with far less hope of ultimate provision . . .

He had scattered the contents of the table-drawer in his search for a sheet of paper, and as he took up his pen his eye fell on an old copy of the *Bettsbridge Eagle*. The advertising sheet was folded uppermost, and he read the seductive words: "Trips to the West: Reduced Rates."

He drew the lantern nearer and eagerly scanned the fares; then the paper fell from his hand and he pushed aside his unfinished letter. A moment ago he had wondered what he and Mattie were to live on when they reached the West; now he saw that he had not even the money to take her there. Borrowing was out of the question: six months before he had given his only security to raise funds for necessary repairs to the mill, and he knew that without security no one at Starkfield would lend him ten dollars.[1] The inexorable facts closed in on him like prison-warders hand-cuffing a convict. There was no way out—none. He was a prisoner for life, and now his one ray of light was to be extinguished.

He crept back heavily to the sofa, stretching himself out with limbs so leaden that he felt as if they would never move again. Tears rose in his throat and slowly burned their way to his lids.

As he lay there, the window-pane that faced him, growing gradually lighter, inlaid upon the darkness a square of moon-suffused sky. A crooked tree-branch crossed it, a branch of the apple-tree under which, on summer evenings, he had sometimes found Mattie sitting when he came up from the mill. Slowly the rim of the rainy vapours caught fire and burnt away, and a pure moon swung into the blue. Ethan, rising on his elbow, watched the landscape whiten and shape itself under the sculpture of the moon. This was the night on which he was to have taken Mattie coasting, and there hung the lamp to light them! He looked out at the slopes bathed in lustre, the silver-edged darkness of the woods, the spectral purple of the hills against the sky, and it seemed as though all the beauty of the night had been poured out to mock his wretchedness . . .

He fell asleep, and when he woke the chill of the winter dawn was in the room. He felt cold and stiff and hungry, and ashamed of being hungry. He rubbed his eyes and went to the window. A red sun stood over the gray rim of the fields, behind trees that looked black and brittle. He said to himself: "This is Matt's last day," and tried to think what the place would be without her.

As he stood there he heard a step behind him and she entered.

"Oh, Ethan—were you here all night?"

She looked so small and pinched, in her poor dress, with the red scarf wound about her, and the cold light turning her paleness sallow, that Ethan stood before her without speaking.

"You must be frozen," she went on, fixing lustreless eyes on him.

He drew a step nearer. "How did you know I was here?"

---

1. Train fares averaged $1.50 for one hundred miles, $5.00 for five hundred.

"Because I heard you go down stairs again after I went to bed, and I listened all night, and you didn't come up."

All his tenderness rushed to his lips. He looked at her and said: "I'll come right along and make up the kitchen fire."

They went back to the kitchen, and he fetched the coal and kindlings and cleared out the stove for her, while she brought in the milk and the cold remains of the meat-pie. When warmth began to radiate from the stove, and the first ray of sunlight lay on the kitchen floor, Ethan's dark thoughts melted in the mellower air. The sight of Mattie going about her work as he had seen her on so many mornings made it seem impossible that she should ever cease to be a part of the scene. He said to himself that he had doubtless exaggerated the significance of Zeena's threats, and that she too, with the return of daylight, would come to a saner mood.

He went up to Mattie as she bent above the stove, and laid his hand on her arm. "I don't want you should trouble either," he said, looking down into her eyes with a smile.

She flushed up warmly and whispered back: "No, Ethan, I ain't going to trouble."

"I guess things'll straighten out," he added.

There was no answer but a quick throb of her lids, and he went on: "She ain't said anything this morning?"

"No. I haven't seen her yet."

"Don't you take any notice when you do."

With this injunction he left her and went out to the cow-barn. He saw Jotham Powell walking up the hill through the morning mist, and the familiar sight added to his growing conviction of security.

As the two men were clearing out the stalls Jotham rested on his pitchfork to say: "Dan'l Byrne's goin' over to the Flats to-day noon, an' he c'd take Mattie's trunk along, and make it easier ridin' when I take her over in the sleigh."

Ethan looked at him blankly, and he continued: "Mis' Frome said the new girl'd be at the Flats at five, and I was to take Mattie then, so's 't she could ketch the six o'clock train for Stamford."

Ethan felt the blood drumming in his temples. He had to wait a moment before he could find voice to say: "Oh, it ain't so sure about Mattie's going——"

"That so?" said Jotham indifferently; and they went on with their work.

When they returned to the kitchen the two women were already at breakfast. Zeena had an air of unusual alertness and activity. She drank two cups of coffee and fed the cat with the scraps left in the pie-dish; then she rose from her seat and, walking over to the window, snipped two or three yellow leaves from the geraniums. "Aunt Martha's ain't got a faded leaf on 'em; but they pine away when they ain't cared for," she

said reflectively. Then she turned to Jotham and asked: "What time'd
you say Dan'l Byrne'd be along?"

The hired man threw a hesitating glance at Ethan. "Round about
noon," he said.

Zeena turned to Mattie. "That trunk of yours is too heavy for the
sleigh, and Dan'l Byrne'll be round to take it over to the Flats," she said.

"I'm much obliged to you, Zeena," said Mattie.

"I'd like to go over things with you first," Zeena continued in an
unperturbed voice. "I know there's a huckabuck towel[2] missing; and I
can't make out what you done with that match-safe 't used to stand
behind the stuffed owl in the parlour."

She went out, followed by Mattie, and when the men were alone
Jotham said to his employer: "I guess I better let Dan'l come round,
then."

Ethan finished his usual morning tasks about the house and barn;
then he said to Jotham: "I'm going down to Starkfield. Tell them not to
wait dinner."

The passion of rebellion had broken out in him again. That which
had seemed incredible in the sober light of day had really come to pass,
and he was to assist as a helpless spectator at Mattie's banishment. His
manhood was humbled by the part he was compelled to play and by the
thought of what Mattie must think of him. Confused impulses struggled
in him as he strode along to the village. He had made up his mind to
do something, but he did not know what it would be.

The early mist had vanished and the fields lay like a silver shield
under the sun. It was one of the days when the glitter of winter shines
through a pale haze of spring. Every yard of the road was alive with
Mattie's presence, and there was hardly a branch against the sky or a
tangle of brambles on the bank in which some bright shred of memory
was not caught. Once, in the stillness, the call of a bird in a mountain
ash was so like her laughter that his heart tightened and then grew large;
and all these things made him see that something must be done at once.

Suddenly it occurred to him that Andrew Hale, who was a kind-
hearted man, might be induced to reconsider his refusal and advance a
small sum on the lumber if he were told that Zeena's ill-health made it
necessary to hire a servant. Hale, after all, knew enough of Ethan's
situation to make it possible for the latter to renew his appeal without
too much loss of pride; and, moreover, how much did pride count in
the ebullition of passions in his breast?

The more he considered his plan the more hopeful it seemed. If he
could get Mrs. Hale's ear he felt certain of success, and with fifty dollars
in his pocket nothing could keep him from Mattie . . .

---

2. Towel made from an absorbent durable fabric of cotton, linen, or both.

His first object was to reach Starkfield before Hale had started for his work; he knew the carpenter had a job down the Corbury road and was likely to leave his house early. Ethan's long strides grew more rapid with the accelerated beat of his thoughts, and as he reached the foot of School House Hill he caught sight of Hale's sleigh in the distance. He hurried forward to meet it, but as it drew nearer he saw that it was driven by the carpenter's youngest boy and that the figure at his side, looking like a large upright cocoon in spectacles, was that of Mrs. Hale. Ethan signed to them to stop, and Mrs. Hale leaned forward, her pink wrinkles twinkling with benevolence.

"Mr. Hale? Why, yes, you'll find him down home now. He ain't going to his work this forenoon. He woke up with a touch o' lumbago, and I just made him put on one of old Dr. Kidder's plasters[3] and set right up into the fire."

Beaming maternally on Ethan, she bent over to add: "I on'y just heard from Mr. Hale 'bout Zeena's going over to Bettsbridge to see that new doctor. I'm real sorry she's feeling so bad again! I hope he thinks he can do something for her? I don't know anybody round here's had more sickness than Zeena. I always tell Mr. Hale I don't know what she'd 'a' done if she hadn't 'a' had you to look after her; and I used to say the same thing 'bout your mother. You've had an awful mean time, Ethan Frome."

She gave him a last nod of sympathy while her son chirped to the horse; and Ethan, as she drove off, stood in the middle of the road and stared after the retreating sleigh.

It was a long time since any one had spoken to him as kindly as Mrs. Hale. Most people were either indifferent to his troubles, or disposed to think it natural that a young fellow of his age should have carried without repining the burden of three crippled lives. But Mrs. Hale had said "You've had an awful mean time, Ethan Frome," and he felt less alone with his misery. If the Hales were sorry for him they would surely respond to his appeal . . .

He started down the road toward their house, but at the end of a few yards he pulled up sharply, the blood in his face. For the first time, in the light of the words he had just heard, he saw what he was about to do. He was planning to take advantage of the Hales' sympathy to obtain money from them on false pretences. That was a plain statement of the cloudy purpose which had driven him in headlong to Starkfield.

With the sudden perception of the point to which his madness had carried him, the madness fell and he saw his life before him as it was. He was a poor man, the husband of a sickly woman, whom his desertion would leave alone and destitute; and even if he had had the heart to

---

3. Lumbago is a painful muscular rheumatism involving the lumbar region; a plaster, a medicated dressing consisting of a film as of cloth or plaster spread with a medicated substance.

desert her he could have done so only by deceiving two kindly people who had pitied him.

He turned and walked slowly back to the farm.

IX

At the kitchen door Daniel Byrne sat in his sleigh behind a big-boned gray who pawed the snow and swung his long head restlessly from side to side.

Ethan went into the kitchen and found his wife by the stove. Her head was wrapped in her shawl, and she was reading a book called "Kidney Troubles And Their Cure" on which he had had to pay extra postage only a few days before.

Zeena did not move or look up when he entered, and after a moment he asked: "Where's Mattie?"

Without lifting her eyes from the page she replied: "I presume she's getting down her trunk."

The blood rushed to his face. "Getting down her trunk—alone?"

"Jotham Powell's down in the wood-lot, and Dan'l Byrne says he darsn't leave that horse," she returned.

Her husband, without stopping to hear the end of the phrase, had left the kitchen and sprung up the stairs. The door of Mattie's room was shut, and he wavered a moment on the landing. "Matt," he said in a low voice; but there was no answer, and he put his hand on the door-knob.

He had never been in her room except once, in the early summer, when he had gone there to plaster up a leak in the eaves, but he remembered exactly how everything had looked: the red and white quilt on her narrow bed, the pretty pin-cushion on the chest of drawers, and over it the enlarged photograph of her mother, in an oxydized frame, with a bunch of dyed grasses at the back. Now these and all other tokens of her presence had vanished, and the room looked as bare and comfortless as when Zeena had shown her into it on the day of her arrival. In the middle of the floor stood her trunk, and on the trunk she sat in her Sunday dress, her back turned to the door and her face in her hands. She had not heard Ethan's call because she was sobbing; and she did not hear his step till he stood close behind her and laid his hands on her shoulders.

"Matt—oh, don't—oh, *Matt!*"

She started up, lifting her wet face to his. "Ethan—I thought I wasn't ever going to see you again!"

He took her in his arms, pressing her close, and with a trembling hand smoothed away the hair from her forehead.

"Not see me again? What do you mean?"

She sobbed out: "Jotham said you told him we wasn't to wait dinner for you, and I thought—"

"You thought I meant to cut it?" he finished for her grimly.

She clung to him without answering, and he laid his lips on her hair, which was soft yet springy, like certain mosses on warm slopes, and had the faint woody fragrance of fresh sawdust in the sun.

Through the door they heard Zeena's voice calling out from below: "Dan'l Byrne says you better hurry up if you want him to take that trunk."

They drew apart with stricken faces. Words of resistance rushed to Ethan's lips and died there. Mattie found her handkerchief and dried her eyes; then, bending down, she took hold of a handle of the trunk.

Ethan put her aside. "You let go, Matt," he ordered her.

She answered: "It takes two to coax it round the corner"; and submitting to this argument he grasped the other handle, and together they manœuvred the heavy trunk out to the landing.

"Now let go," he repeated; then he shouldered the trunk and carried it down the stairs and across the passage to the kitchen. Zeena, who had gone back to her seat by the stove, did not lift her head from her book as he passed. Mattie followed him out of the door and helped him to lift the trunk into the back of the sleigh. When it was in place they stood side by side on the door-step, watching Daniel Byrne plunge off behind his fidgety horse.

It seemed to Ethan that his heart was bound with cords which an unseen hand was tightening with every tick of the clock. Twice he opened his lips to speak to Mattie and found no breath. At length, as she turned to re-enter the house, he laid a detaining hand on her.

"I'm going to drive you over, Matt," he whispered.

She murmured back: "I think Zeena wants I should go with Jotham."

"I'm going to drive you over," he repeated; and she went into the kitchen without answering.

At dinner Ethan could not eat. If he lifted his eyes they rested on Zeena's pinched face, and the corners of her straight lips seemed to quiver away into a smile. She ate well, declaring that the mild weather made her feel better, and pressed a second helping of beans on Jotham Powell, whose wants she generally ignored.

Mattie, when the meal was over, went about her usual task of clearing the table and washing up the dishes. Zeena, after feeding the cat, had returned to her rocking-chair by the stove, and Jotham Powell, who always lingered last, reluctantly pushed back his chair and moved toward the door.

On the threshold he turned back to say to Ethan: "What time'll I come round for Mattie?"

Ethan was standing near the window, mechanically filling his pipe while he watched Mattie move to and fro. He answered: "You needn't come round; I'm going to drive her over myself."

He saw the rise of the colour in Mattie's averted cheek, and the quick lifting of Zeena's head.

"I want you should stay here this afternoon, Ethan," his wife said. "Jotham can drive Mattie over."

Mattie flung an imploring glance at him, but he repeated curtly: "I'm going to drive her over myself."

Zeena continued in the same even tone: "I wanted you should stay and fix up that stove in Mattie's room afore the girl gets here. It ain't been drawing right for nigh on a month now."

Ethan's voice rose indignantly. "If it was good enough for Mattie I guess it's good enough for a hired girl."

"That girl that's coming told me she was used to a house where they had a furnace," Zeena persisted with the same monotonous mildness.

"She'd better ha' stayed there then," he flung back at her; and turning to Mattie he added in a hard voice: "You be ready by three, Matt; I've got business at Corbury."

Jotham Powell had started for the barn, and Ethan strode down after him aflame with anger. The pulses in his temples throbbed and a fog was in his eyes. He went about his task without knowing what force directed him, or whose hands and feet were fulfilling its orders. It was not till he led out the sorrel and backed him between the shafts of the sleigh that he once more became conscious of what he was doing. As he passed the bridle over the horse's head, and wound the traces around the shafts, he remembered the day when he had made the same preparations in order to drive over and meet his wife's cousin at the Flats. It was little more than a year ago, on just such a soft afternoon, with a "feel" of spring in the air. The sorrel, turning the same big ringed eye on him, nuzzled the palm of his hand in the same way; and one by one all the days between rose up and stood before him . . .

He flung the bearskin into the sleigh, climbed to the seat, and drove up to the house. When he entered the kitchen it was empty, but Mattie's bag and shawl lay ready by the door. He went to the foot of the stairs and listened. No sound reached him from above, but presently he thought he heard some one moving about in his deserted study, and pushing open the door he saw Mattie, in her hat and jacket, standing with her back to him near the table.

She started at his approach and turning quickly, said: "Is it time?"

"What are you doing here, Matt?" he asked her.

She looked at him timidly. "I was just taking a look round—that's all," she answered, with a wavering smile.

They went back into the kitchen without speaking, and Ethan picked up her bag and shawl.

"Where's Zeena?" he asked.

"She went upstairs right after dinner. She said she had those shooting pains again, and didn't want to be disturbed."

"Didn't she say good-bye to you?"

"No. That was all she said."

Ethan, looking slowly about the kitchen, said to himself with a shudder that in a few hours he would be returning to it alone. Then the sense of unreality overcame him once more, and he could not bring himself to believe that Mattie stood there for the last time before him.

"Come on," he said almost gaily, opening the door and putting her bag into the sleigh. He sprang to his seat and bent over to tuck the rug about her as she slipped into the place at his side. "Now then, go 'long," he said, with a shake of the reins that sent the sorrel placidly jogging down the hill.

"We got lots of time for a good ride, Matt!" he cried, seeking her hand beneath the fur and pressing it in his. His face tingled and he felt dizzy, as if he had stopped in at the Starkfield saloon on a zero day [1] for a drink.

At the gate, instead of making for Starkfield, he turned the sorrel to the right, up the Bettsbridge road. Mattie sat silent, giving no sign of surprise; but after a moment she said: "Are you going round by Shadow Pond?"

He laughed and answered: "I knew you'd know!"

She drew closer under the bearskin, so that, looking sideways around his coat-sleeve, he could just catch the tip of her nose and a blown brown wave of hair. They drove slowly up the road between fields glistening under the pale sun, and then bent to the right down a lane edged with spruce and larch. Ahead of them, a long way off, a range of hills stained by mottlings of black forest flowed away in round white curves against the sky. The lane passed into a pine-wood with boles reddening in the afternoon sun and delicate blue shadows on the snow. As they entered it the breeze fell and a warm stillness seemed to drop from the branches with the dropping needles. Here the snow was so pure that the tiny tracks of wood-animals had left on it intricate lace-like patterns, and the bluish cones caught in its surface stood out like ornaments of bronze.

Ethan drove on in silence till they reached a part of the wood where the pines were more widely spaced; then he drew up and helped Mattie to get out of the sleigh. They passed between the aromatic trunks, the snow breaking crisply under their feet, till they came to a small sheet of water with steep wooded sides. Across its frozen surface, from the farther bank, a single hill rising against the western sun threw the long conical shadow which gave the lake its name. It was a shy secret spot, full of the same dumb melancholy that Ethan felt in his heart.

---

1. Zero-degree day (Fahrenheit; or −18 Celsius.).

He looked up and down the little pebbly beach till his eye lit on a fallen tree-trunk half submerged in snow.

"There's where we sat at the picnic," he reminded her.

The entertainment of which he spoke was one of the few that they had taken part in together: a "church picnic" which, on a long afternoon of the preceding summer, had filled the retired place with merry-making. Mattie had begged him to go with her but he had refused. Then, toward sunset, coming down from the mountain where he had been felling timber, he had been caught by some strayed revellers and drawn into the group by the lake, where Mattie, encircled by facetious youths, and bright as a blackberry under her spreading hat, was brewing coffee over a gipsy fire. He remembered the shyness he had felt at approaching her in his uncouth clothes, and then the lighting up of her face, and the way she had broken through the group to come to him with a cup in her hand. They had sat for a few minutes on the fallen log by the pond, and she had missed her gold locket, and set the young men searching for it; and it was Ethan who had spied it in the moss . . . That was all; but all their intercourse had been made up of just such inarticulate flashes, when they seemed to come suddenly upon happiness as if they had surprised a butterfly in the winter woods . . .

"It was right there I found your locket," he said, pushing his foot into a dense tuft of blueberry bushes.

"I never saw anybody with such sharp eyes!" she answered.

She sat down on the tree-trunk in the sun and he sat down beside her.

"You were as pretty as a picture in that pink hat," he said.

She laughed with pleasure. "Oh, I guess it was the hat!" she rejoined.

They had never before avowed their inclination so openly, and Ethan, for a moment, had the illusion that he was a free man, wooing the girl he meant to marry. He looked at her hair and longed to touch it again, and to tell her that it smelt of the woods; but he had never learned to say such things.

Suddenly she rose to her feet and said: "We mustn't stay here any longer."

He continued to gaze at her vaguely, only half-roused from his dream. "There's plenty of time," he answered.

They stood looking at each other as if the eyes of each were straining to absorb and hold fast the other's image. There were things he had to say to her before they parted, but he could not say them in that place of summer memories, and he turned and followed her in silence to the sleigh. As they drove away the sun sank behind the hill and the pine-boles turned from red to gray.

By a devious track between the fields they wound back to the Starkfield road. Under the open sky the light was still clear, with a reflection of cold red on the eastern hills. The clumps of trees in the snow seemed to draw together in ruffled lumps, like birds with their heads under their wings; and the sky, as it paled, rose higher, leaving the earth more alone.

As they turned into the Starkfield road Ethan said: "Matt, what do you mean to do?"

She did not answer at once, but at length she said: "I'll try to get a place in a store."

"You know you can't do it. The bad air and the standing all day nearly killed you before."

"I'm a lot stronger than I was before I came to Starkfield."

"And now you're going to throw away all the good it's done you!"

There seemed to be no answer to this, and again they drove on for a while without speaking. With every yard of the way some spot where they had stood, and laughed together or been silent, clutched at Ethan and dragged him back.

"Isn't there any of your father's folks could help you?"

"There isn't any of 'em I'd ask."

He lowered his voice to say: "You know there's nothing I wouldn't do for you if I could."

"I know there isn't."

"But I can't——"

She was silent, but he felt a slight tremor in the shoulder against his.

"Oh, Matt," he broke out, "if I could ha' gone with you now I'd ha' done it——"

She turned to him, pulling a scrap of paper from her breast. "Ethan— I found this," she stammered. Even in the failing light he saw it was the letter to his wife that he had begun the night before and forgotten to destroy. Through his astonishment there ran a fierce thrill of joy. "Matt—" he cried; "if I could ha' done it, would you?"

"Oh, Ethan, Ethan—what's the use?" With a sudden movement she tore the letter in shreds and sent them fluttering off into the snow.

"Tell me, Matt! Tell me!" he adjured her.

She was silent for a moment; then she said, in such a low tone that he had to stoop his head to hear her: "I used to think of it sometimes, summer nights, when the moon was so bright I couldn't sleep."

His heart reeled with the sweetness of it. "As long ago as that?"

She answered, as if the date had long been fixed for her: "The first time was at Shadow Pond."

"Was that why you gave me my coffee before the others?"

"I don't know. Did I? I was dreadfully put out when you wouldn't go to the picnic with me; and then, when I saw you coming down the road, I thought maybe you'd gone home that way o' purpose; and that made me glad."

They were silent again. They had reached the point where the road dipped to the hollow by Ethan's mill and as they descended the darkness descended with them, dropping down like a black veil from the heavy hemlock boughs.

"I'm tied hand and foot, Matt. There isn't a thing I can do," he began again.

"You must write to me sometimes, Ethan."

"Oh, what good'll writing do? I want to put my hand out and touch you. I want to do for you and care for you. I want to be there when you're sick and when you're lonesome."

"You mustn't think but what I'll do all right."

"You won't need me, you mean? I suppose you'll marry!"

"Oh, Ethan!" she cried.

"I don't know how it is you make me feel, Matt. I'd a'most rather have you dead than that!"

"Oh, I wish I was, I wish I was!" she sobbed.

The sound of her weeping shook him out of his dark anger, and he felt ashamed.

"Don't let's talk that way," he whispered.

"Why shouldn't we, when it's true? I've been wishing it every minute of the day."

"Matt! You be quiet! Don't you say it."

"There's never anybody been good to me but you."

"Don't say that either, when I can't lift a hand for you!"

"Yes; but it's true just the same."

They had reached the top of School House Hill and Starkfield lay below them in the twilight. A cutter, mounting the road from the village, passed them by in a joyous flutter of bells, and they straightened themselves and looked ahead with rigid faces. Along the main street lights had begun to shine from the house-fronts and stray figures were turning in here and there at the gates. Ethan, with a touch of his whip, roused the sorrel to a languid trot.

As they drew near the end of the village the cries of children reached them, and they saw a knot of boys, with sleds behind them, scattering across the open space before the church.

"I guess this'll be their last coast for a day or two," Ethan said, looking up at the mild sky.

Mattie was silent, and he added: "We were to have gone down last night."

Still she did not speak and, prompted by an obscure desire to help himself and her through their miserable last hour, he went on discursively: "Ain't it funny we haven't been down together but just that once last winter?"

She answered: "It wasn't often I got down to the village."

"That's so," he said.

They had reached the crest of the Corbury road, and between the indistinct white glimmer of the church and the black curtain of the Varnum spruces the slope stretched away below them without a sled on its length. Some erratic impulse prompted Ethan to say: "How'd you like me to take you down now?"

She forced a laugh. "Why, there isn't time!"

"There's all the time we want. Come along!" His one desire now was to postpone the moment of turning the sorrel toward the Flats.

"But the girl," she faltered. "The girl'll be waiting at the station."

"Well, let her wait. You'd have to if she didn't. Come!"

The note of authority in his voice seemed to subdue her, and when he had jumped from the sleigh he let him help her out, saying only, with a vague feint of reluctance: "But there isn't a sled round any wheres."

"Yes, there is! Right over there under the spruces."

He threw the bearskin over the sorrel, who stood passively by the roadside, hanging a meditative head. Then he caught Mattie's hand and drew her after him toward the sled.

She seated herself obediently and he took his place behind her, so close that her hair brushed his face. "All right, Matt?" he called out, as if the width of the road had been between them.

She turned her head to say: "It's dreadfully dark. Are you sure you can see?"

He laughed contemptuously: "I could go down this coast with my eyes tied!" and she laughed with him, as if she liked his audacity. Nevertheless he sat still a moment, straining his eyes down the long hill, for it was the most confusing hour of the evening, the hour when the last clearness from the upper sky is merged with the rising night in a blur that disguises landmarks and falsifies distances.

"Now!" he cried.

The sled started with a bound, and they flew on through the dusk, gathering smoothness and speed as they went, with the hollow night opening out below them and the air singing by like an organ. Mattie sat perfectly still, but as they reached the bend at the foot of the hill, where the big elm thrust out a deadly elbow, he fancied that she shrank a little closer.

"Don't be scared, Matt!" he cried exultantly, as they spun safely past it and flew down the second slope; and when they reached the level ground beyond, and the speed of the sled began to slacken, he heard her give a little laugh of glee.

They sprang off and started to walk back up the hill. Ethan dragged the sled with one hand and passed the other through Mattie's arm.

"Were you scared I'd run you into the elm?" he asked with a boyish laugh.

"I told you I was never scared with you," she answered.

The strange exaltation of his mood had brought on one of his rare fits of boastfulness. "It *is* a tricky place, though. The least swerve, and we'd never ha' come up again. But I can measure distances to a hair's-breadth—always could."

She murmured: "I always say you've got the surest eye . . ."

Deep silence had fallen with the starless dusk, and they leaned on each other without speaking; but at every step of their climb Ethan said to himself: "It's the last time we'll ever walk together."

They mounted slowly to the top of the hill. When they were abreast of the church he stooped his head to her to ask: "Are you tired?" and she answered, breathing quickly: "It was splendid!"

With a pressure of his arm he guided her toward the Norway spruces. "I guess this sled must be Ned Hale's. Anyhow I'll leave it where I found it." He drew the sled up to the Varnum gate and rested it against the fence. As he raised himself he suddenly felt Mattie close to him among the shadows.

"Is this where Ned and Ruth kissed each other?" she whispered breathlessly, and flung her arms about him. Her lips, groping for his, swept over his face, and he held her fast in a rapture of surprise.

"Good-bye—good-bye," she stammered, and kissed him again.

"Oh, Matt I can't let you go!" broke from him in the same old cry.

She freed herself from his hold and he heard her sobbing. "Oh, I can't go either!" she wailed.

"Matt! What'll we do? What'll we do?"

They clung to each other's hands like children, and her body shook with desperate sobs.

Through the stillness they heard the church clock striking five.

"Oh, Ethan, it's time!" she cried.

He drew her back to him. "Time for what? You don't suppose I'm going to leave you now?"

"If I missed my train where'd I go?"

"Where are you going if you catch it?"

She stood silent, her hands lying cold and relaxed in his.

"What's the good of either of us going anywheres without the other one now?" he said.

She remained motionless, as if she had not heard him. Then she snatched her hands from his, threw her arms about his neck, and pressed a sudden drenched cheek against his face. "Ethan! Ethan! I want you to take me down again!"

"Down where?"

"The coast. Right off," she panted. "So 't we'll never come up any more."

"Matt! What on earth do you mean?"

She put her lips close against his ear to say: "Right into the big elm.

You said you could. So 't we'd never have to leave each other any more."

"Why, what are you talking of? You're crazy!"

"I'm not crazy; but I will be if I leave you."

"Oh, Matt, Matt—" he groaned.

She tightened her fierce hold about his neck. Her face lay close to his face.

"Ethan, where'll I go if I leave you? I don't know how to get along alone. You said so yourself just now. Nobody but you was ever good to me. And there'll be that strange girl in the house . . . and she'll sleep in my bed, where I used to lay nights and listen to hear you come up the stairs . . ."

The words were like fragments torn from his heart. With them came the hated vision of the house he was going back to—of the stairs he would have to go up every night, of the woman who would wait for him there. And the sweetness of Mattie's avowal, the wild wonder of knowing at last that all that had happened to him had happened to her too, made the other vision more abhorrent, the other life more intolerable to return to . . .

Her pleadings still came to him between short sobs, but he no longer heard what she was saying. Her hat had slipped back and he was stroking her hair. He wanted to get the feeling of it into his hand, so that it would sleep there like a seed in winter. Once he found her mouth again, and they seemed to be by the pond together in the burning August sun. But his cheek touched hers, and it was cold and full of weeping, and he saw the road to the Flats under the night and heard the whistle of the train up the line.

The spruces swathed them in blackness and silence. They might have been in their coffins underground. He said to himself: "Perhaps it'll feel like this . . ." and then again: "After this I sha'n't feel anything . . ."

Suddenly he heard the old sorrel whinny across the road, and thought: "He's wondering why he doesn't get his supper . . ."

"Come," Mattie whispered, tugging at his hand.

Her sombre violence constrained him: she seemed the embodied instrument of fate. He pulled the sled out, blinking like a night-bird as he passed from the shade of the spruces into the transparent dusk of the open. The slope below them was deserted. All Starkfield was at supper, and not a figure crossed the open space before the church. The sky, swollen with the clouds that announce a thaw, hung as low as before a summer storm. He strained his eyes through the dimness, and they seemed less keen, less capable than usual.

He took his seat on the sled and Mattie instantly placed herself in front of him. Her hat had fallen into the snow and his lips were in her hair. He stretched out his legs, drove his heels into the road to keep the sled from slipping forward, and bent her head back between his hands. Then suddenly he sprang up again.

"Get up," he ordered her.

It was the tone she always heeded, but she cowered down in her seat, repeating vehemently: "No, no, no!"

"Get up!"

"Why?"

"I want to sit in front."

"No, no! How can you steer in front?"

"I don't have to. We'll follow the track."

They spoke in smothered whispers, as though the night were listening.

"Get up! Get up!" he urged her; but she kept on repeating: "Why do you want to sit in front?"

"Because I—because I want to feel you holding me," he stammered, and dragged her to her feet.

The answer seemed to satisfy her, or else she yielded to the power of his voice. He bent down, feeling in the obscurity for the glassy slide worn by preceding coasters, and placed the runners carefully between its edges. She waited while he seated himself with crossed legs in the front of the sled; then she crouched quickly down at his back and clasped her arms about him. Her breath in his neck set him shuddering again, and he almost sprang from his seat. But in a flash he remembered the alternative. She was right: this was better than parting. He leaned back and drew her mouth to his . . .

Just as they started he heard the sorrel's whinny again, and the familiar wistful call, and all the confused images it brought with it, went with him down the first reach of the road. Half-way down there was a sudden drop, then a rise, and after that another long delirious descent. As they took wing for this it seemed to him that they were flying indeed, flying far up into the cloudy night, with Starkfield immeasurably below them, falling away like a speck in space . . . Then the big elm shot up ahead, lying in wait for them at the bend of the road, and he said between his teeth: "We can fetch it; I know we can fetch it——"

As they flew toward the tree Mattie pressed her arms tighter, and her blood seemed to be in his veins. Once or twice the sled swerved a little under them. He slanted his body to keep it headed for the elm, repeating to himself again and again: "I know we can fetch it"; and little phrases she had spoken ran through his head and danced before him on the air. The big tree loomed bigger and closer, and as they bore down on it he thought: "It's waiting for us: it seems to know." But suddenly his wife's face, with twisted monstrous lineaments, thrust itself between him and his goal, and he made an instinctive movement to brush it aside. The sled swerved in response, but he righted it again, kept it straight, and drove down on the black projecting mass. There was a last instant when the air shot past him like millions of fiery wires; and then the elm . . .

The sky was still thick, but looking straight up he saw a single star, and tried vaguely to reckon whether it were Sirius,[2] or—or— The effort tired him too much, and he closed his heavy lids and thought that he would sleep . . . The stillness was so profound that he heard a little animal twittering somewhere near by under the snow. It made a small frightened *cheep* like a field mouse, and he wondered languidly if it were hurt. Then he understood that it must be in pain: pain so excruciating that he seemed, mysteriously, to feel it shooting through his own body. He tried in vain to roll over in the direction of the sound, and stretched his left arm out across the snow. And now it was as though he felt rather than heard the twittering; it seemed to be under his palm, which rested on something soft and springy. The thought of the animal's suffering was intolerable to him and he struggled to raise himself, and could not because a rock, or some huge mass, seemed to be lying on him.[3] But he continued to finger about cautiously with his left hand, thinking he might get hold of the little creature and help it; and all at once he knew that the soft thing he had touched was Mattie's hair and that his hand was on her face.

He dragged himself to his knees, the monstrous load on him moving with him as he moved, and his hand went over and over her face, and he felt that the twittering came from her lips . . .

He got his face down close to hers, with his ear to her mouth, and in the darkness he saw her eyes open and heard her say his name.

"Oh, Matt, I thought we'd fetched it," he moaned; and far off, up the hill, he heard the sorrel whinny, and thought: "I ought to be getting him his feed . . ."

.   .   .   .

.   .   .   .

.   .   .   .

---

2. The Dog Star, which follows Orion; the brightest fixed star.
3. Sisyphus, King of Corinth, angered Zeus and was punished in Hades (Hell) by having to forever roll a rock uphill which continually fell back on him.

The querulous drone ceased as I entered Frome's kitchen, and of the two women sitting there I could not tell which had been the speaker.

One of them, on my appearing, raised her tall bony figure from her seat, not as if to welcome me—for she threw me no more than a brief glance of surprise—but simply to set about preparing the meal which Frome's absence had delayed. A slatternly calico wrapper hung from her shoulders and the wisps of her thin gray hair were drawn away from a high forehead and fastened at the back by a broken comb. She had pale opaque eyes which revealed nothing and reflected nothing, and her narrow lips were of the same sallow colour as her face.

The other woman was much smaller and slighter. She sat huddled in an arm-chair near the stove, and when I came in she turned her head quickly toward me, without the last corresponding movement of her body. Her hair was as gray as her companion's, her face as bloodless and shrivelled, but amber-tinted, with swarthy shadows sharpening the nose and hollowing the temples. Under her shapeless dress her body kept its limp immobility, and her dark eyes had the bright witch-like stare that disease of the spine sometimes gives.

Even for that part of the country the kitchen was a poor-looking place. With the exception of the dark-eyed woman's chair, which looked like a soiled relic of luxury bought at a country auction, the furniture was of the roughest kind. Three coarse china plates and a broken-nosed milk-jug had been set on a greasy table scored with knife-cuts, and a couple of straw-bottomed chairs and a kitchen dresser of unpainted pine stood meagrely against the plaster walls.

"My, it's cold here! The fire must be 'most out," Frome said, glancing about him apologetically as he followed me in.

The tall woman, who had moved away from us toward the dresser, took no notice; but the other, from her cushioned niche, answered complainingly, in a high thin voice: "It's on'y just been made up this very minute. Zeena fell asleep and slep' ever so long, and I thought I'd be frozen stiff before I could wake her up and get her to 'tend to it."

I knew then that it was she who had been speaking when we entered.

Her companion, who was just coming back to the table with the remains of a cold mince-pie in a battered pie-dish, set down her unappetising burden without appearing to hear the accusation brought against her.

Frome stood hesitatingly before her as she advanced; then he looked at me and said: "This is my wife, Mis' Frome." After another interval he added, turning toward the figure in the arm-chair: "And this is Miss Mattie Silver . . ."

. . . .

Mrs. Hale, tender soul, had pictured me as lost in the Flats and buried under a snow-drift; and so lively was her satisfaction on seeing me

safely restored to her the next morning that I felt my peril had caused
me to advance several degrees in her favour.

Great was her amazement, and that of old Mrs. Varnum, on learning
that Ethan Frome's old horse had carried me to and from Corbury Junction through the worst blizzard of the winter; greater still their surprise
when they heard that his master had taken me in for the night.

Beneath their wondering exclamations I felt a secret curiosity to know
what impressions I had received from my night in the Frome household,
and divined that the best way of breaking down their reserve was to let
them try to penetrate mine. I therefore confined myself to saying, in a
matter-of-fact tone, that I had been received with great kindness, and
that Frome had made a bed for me in a room on the ground-floor which
seemed in happier days to have been fitted up as a kind of writing-room
or study.

"Well," Mrs. Hale mused, "in such a storm I suppose he felt he
couldn't do less than take you in—but I guess it went hard with Ethan.
I don't believe but what you're the only stranger has set foot in that
house for over twenty years. He's that proud he don't even like his oldest
friends to go there; and I don't know as any do, any more, except myself
and the doctor . . ."

"You still go there, Mrs. Hale?" I ventured.

"I used to go a good deal after the accident, when I was first married;
but after awhile I got to think it made 'em feel worse to see us. And then
one thing and another came, and my own troubles . . . But I generally
make out to drive over there round about New Year's, and once in the
summer. Only I always try to pick a day when Ethan's off somewheres.
It's bad enough to see the two women sitting there—but *his* face, when
he looks round that bare place, just kills me . . . You see, I can look
back and call it up in his mother's day, before their troubles."

Old Mrs. Varnum, by this time, had gone up to bed, and her daughter and I were sitting alone, after supper, in the austere seclusion of the
horse-hair parlour. Mrs. Hale glanced at me tentatively, as though trying to see how much footing my conjectures gave her; and I guessed that
if she had kept silence till now it was because she had been waiting,
through all the years, for some one who should see what she alone
had seen.

I waited to let her trust in me gather strength before I said: "Yes, it's
pretty bad, seeing all three of them there together."

She drew her mild brows into a frown of pain. "It was just awful from
the beginning. I was here in the house when they were carried up—they
laid Mattie Silver in the room you're in. She and I were great friends,
and she was to have been my brides-maid in the spring . . . When she
came to I went up to her and stayed all night. They gave her things to
quiet her, and she didn't know much till to'rd morning, and then all of
a sudden she woke up just like herself, and looked straight at me out of

her big eyes, and said . . . Oh, I don't know why I'm telling you all this," Mrs. Hale broke off, crying.

She took off her spectacles, wiped the moisture from them, and put them on again with an unsteady hand. "It got about the next day," she went on, "that Zeena Frome had sent Mattie off in a hurry because she had a hired girl coming, and the folks here could never rightly tell what she and Ethan were doing that night coasting, when they'd ought to have been on their way to the Flats to ketch the train . . . I never knew myself what Zeena thought—I don't to this day. Nobody knows Zeena's thoughts. Anyhow, when she heard o' the accident she came right in and stayed with Ethan over to the minister's, where they'd carried him. And as soon as the doctors said that Mattie could be moved, Zeena sent for her and took her back to the farm."

"And there she's been ever since?"

Mrs. Hale answered simply: "There was nowhere else for her to go;" and my heart tightened at the thought of the hard compulsions of the poor.

"Yes, there she's been," Mrs. Hale continued, "and Zeena's done for her, and done for Ethan, as good as she could. It was a miracle, considering how sick she was—but she seemed to be raised right up just when the call came to her. Not as she's ever given up doctoring, and she's had sick spells right along; but she's had the strength given her to care for those two for over twenty years, and before the accident came she thought she couldn't even care for herself."

Mrs. Hale paused a moment, and I remained silent, plunged in the vision of what her words evoked. "It's horrible for them all," I murmured.

"Yes: it's pretty bad. And they ain't any of 'em easy people either. Mattie *was*, before the accident; I never knew a sweeter nature. But she's suffered too much—that's what I always say when folks tell me how she's soured. And Zeena, she was always cranky. Not but what she bears with Mattie wonderful—I've seen that myself. But sometimes the two of them get going at each other, and then Ethan's face'd break your heart . . . When I see that, I think it's *him* that suffers most . . . anyhow it ain't Zeena, because she ain't got the time . . . It's a pity, though," Mrs. Hale ended, sighing, "that they're all shut up there'n that one kitchen. In the summertime, on pleasant days, they move Mattie into the parlour, or out in the door-yard, and that makes it easier . . . but winters there's the fires to be thought of; and there ain't a dime to spare up at the Fromes.' "

Mrs. Hale drew a deep breath, as though her memory were eased of its long burden, and she had no more to say; but suddenly an impulse of complete avowal seized her.

She took off her spectacles again, leaned toward me across the bead-work table-cover, and went on with lowered voice: "There was one day, about a week after the accident, when they all thought Mattie couldn't live. Well, I say it's a pity she *did*. I said it right out to our minister once, and he was shocked at me. Only he wasn't with me that morning when she first came to . . . And I say, if she'd ha' died, Ethan might ha' lived; and the way they are now, I don't see's there's much difference between the Fromes up at the farm and the Fromes down in the grave-yard; 'cept that down there they're all quiet, and the women have got to hold their tongues."

BACKGROUNDS AND CONTEXTS

EDITH WHARTON

The Writing of *Ethan Frome*†

The conditions in which *Ethan Frome* originated have remained much more clearly fixed in my memory than those connected with any of my other stories, owing to the odd accident of the tale's having been begun in French. Early in the nineteen hundreds I happened to be spending a whole winter in Paris, and it occurred to me to make use of the opportunity to polish and extend my conversational French; for though I had spoken the language since the age of four I had never had occasion to practise it for any length of time, at least with cultivated people, having frequently wandered through France as a tourist, but never lived there for more than a few weeks consecutively. Accordingly, it was arranged that I should read and talk for so many hours a week with a young French professor; and soon after our studies began he suggested that before each of his visits I should prepare an "exercise" for him. [1]

I have never been able, without much mental anguish, to write anything but a letter or a story, and as stories come to me much more easily than letters, I timidly asked him if a story would "do," and, though obviously somewhat surprised at the unexpected suggestion, he acquiesced with equal timidity. Thus the French version of *Ethan Frome* began, and ploughed its heavy course through a copy-book or two; then the lessons were interrupted and the Gallic "Ethan" abandoned, I forget at what point in his career. The copy-book containing this earliest version of his adventures has long since vanished; [2] but a few years later Ethan's history stirred again in my memory, and I forthwith sat down and wrote it in English, reading aloud each evening what I had done during the day to a friend [3] as familiar as I was with the lonely lives in half-deserted New England villages, before the coming of the motor and the telephone. The legend that Henry James suggested my transposing the French "composition" into an English tale—a fable I have frequently come across of recent years—must be classed among the other inventions which honour me by connecting my name with his in the field of letters. I am not sure if he even saw the French beginning of the tale, but he certainly did not suggest its rewriting in English, and never read the story, or heard of it again, till it appeared in print in the latter language. [4]

While I am on the subject of literary fables, I might as well destroy

---

† Edith Wharton, "The Writing of *Ethan Frome*," *The Colophon: The Book Collectors' Quarterly* Part II, no. 4 (September 1932).
1. For a more detailed explanation of the French beginning, see excerpt from *A Backward Glance*, following pp. 78–80.
2. In fact, the manuscript resides at the Beinecke Library, Yale University.
3. Walter Berry (1859–1927), an international lawyer and old friend of Wharton.
4. See James's enthusiastic congratulatory letter, p. 85.

another which likewise concerns *Ethan Frome*. Not long since I read a thoughtful article on the making of fiction, in which the author advanced the theory that in a given case a certain perspective might be necessary to the novelist, and that one might conceivably write a better book about Main Street[5] if one lived as far away from it as Paris or Palermo; in proof of which *Ethan Frome* was cited as an instance of a successful New England story written by some one who knew nothing of New England. I have no desire to contest the theory, with which, in a certain measure, I am disposed to agree; but the fact is that *Ethan Frome* was written after a ten years' residence in the New England hill country where Ethan's tragedy was enacted, and that during those years I had become very familiar with the aspect, the dialect and the general mental attitude of the Ethans, Zeenas and Mattie Silvers of the neighbouring villages.[6] My other short novel of New England life, *Summer*,[7] which deals with the same type of people involved in a different tragedy of isolation, might, one would suppose, have helped to prove to the legend-makers that I knew something at first hand of the life and the people into whose intimacy I had asked my readers to enter with me on two successive occasions.

EDITH WHARTON

A Backward Glance†

* * * It was not until I wrote "Ethan Frome" that I suddenly felt the artisan's full control of his implements. When "Ethan Frome" first appeared I was severely criticized by the reviewers for what was considered the clumsy structure of the tale.[1] I had pondered long on this structure, had felt its peculiar difficulties, and possible awkwardness, but could think of no alternative which would serve as well in the given case; and though I am far from thinking "Ethan Frome" my best novel, and am bored and even exasperated when I am told that it is, I am still sure that its structure is not its weak point.

*   *   *

But the book to the making of which I brought the greatest joy and the fullest ease was "Ethan Frome". For years I had wanted to draw life

---

5. After Sinclair Lewis's *Main Street* (1920), controversial portrait of small-town American life, the phrase Main Street, as used here, encompassed a broad range of images of middle-class America.
6. Wharton kept a summer residence in the Berkshires of Massachusetts, 1902–1911.
7. Wharton's other novel of Berkshire small-town life, 1917.
† From Edith Wharton, *A Backward Glance* (New York: Appleton-Century, 1934), pp. 209, 293–96. Reprinted by permission of the Estate of Edith Wharton and the Watkins/Loomis Agency.
1. Refers to criticism of the frame employing the outside engineer-narrator.

as it really was in the derelict mountain villages of New England, a life
even in my time, and a thousandfold more a generation earlier, utterly
unlike that seen through the rose-coloured spectacles of my predeces-
sors, Mary Wilkins and Sarah Orne Jewett.[2] In those days the snow-
bound villages of Western Massachusetts were still grim places, morally
and physically: insanity, incest and slow mental and moral starvation
were hidden away behind the paintless wooden house-fronts of the long
village street, or in the isolated farm-houses on the neighbouring hills;
and Emily Brontë would have found as savage tragedies in our remoter
valleys as on her Yorkshire moors.[3]

*   *   *

"Ethan Frome" shocked my readers less than "Summer"; but it was
frequently criticized as "painful", and at first had much less success than
my previous books.[4] I have a clearer recollection of its beginnings than
of those of my other tales, through the singular accident that its first
pages were written—in French! I had determined, when we came to live
in Paris;[5] to polish and enlarge my French vocabulary; for though I had
spoken the language since the age of four I had never had much occasion to talk it, for any length of time, with cultivated people, having
usually, since my marriage, wandered through France as a tourist. The
result was that I had kept up the language chiefly through reading, and
the favourite French authors of my early youth being Bossuet, Racine,
Corneille and La Bruyère, most of my polite locutions dated from the
seventeenth century, and Bourget used to laugh at me for speaking "the
purest Louis Quatorze".[6] To bring my idioms up to date I asked Charles
Du Bos[7] to find, among his friends, a young professor who would come
and talk with me two or three times a week. An amiable young man was
found; but, being too amiable ever to correct my spoken mistakes, he
finally hit on the expedient of asking me to prepare an "exercise" before
each visit. The easiest thing for me was to write a story; and thus the
French version of "Ethan Frome" was begun, and carried on for a few

2. Sarah Orne Jewett (1849–1909), famous for her studies of rural life in Maine; Mary E. Wilkins
   Freeman (1852–1930), chronicler of rural life in Massachusetts.
3. Emily Brontë (1818–1848), English novelist of *Wuthering Heights* (1847), set on the Yorkshire
   moors among isolated farmers.
4. *Summer* (1917), also set in the Berkshires, was often compared to *Ethan Frome*, and Wharton
   herself referred to it, with its seduced and abandoned orphan heroine, as "hot Ethan."
5. R. W. B. Lewis in *Edith Wharton: A Biography* (New York: Scribner's, 1975), places the date
   of the exercise around 1907.
6. Jacques Bénigne Bossuet (1627–1704), French prelate known for his Christian *Discourse on
   Universal History*, 1681, and the unaffected, moving style of his sermons; Jean Racine (1639–
   1699) and Pierre Corneille (1606–1684), eminent French dramatists; Jean de La Bruyère
   (1645–1696), French satirist of society and manners. Paul Bourget (1852–1935), Wharton's
   friend, French novelist and critic, introduced her into French society and the French literary
   world. Bourget refers to Louis XIV (1638–1715), the "Sun King," famous for his palatial court
   at Versailles. He means that Wharton's French is very formal and archaic.
7. Charles du Bos, French critic and young follower of Bourget, translated Wharton's *House of
   Mirth* into French.

weeks. Then the lessons were given up, and the copy-book containing my "exercise" vanished forever. But a few years later, during one of our summer sojourns at the Mount, a distant glimpse of Bear Mountain brought Ethan back to my memory, and the following winter in Paris I wrote the tale as it now stands, reading my morning's work aloud each evening to Walter Berry,[8] who was as familiar as I was with the lives led in those half-deserted villages before the coming of motor and telephone. We talked the tale over page by page, so that its accuracy of "atmosphere" is doubly assured—and I mention this because not long since, in an article by an American literary critic, I saw "Ethan Frome" cited as an interesting example of a successful New England story written by some one who knew nothing of New England! "Ethan Frome" was written after I had spent ten years in the hill-region where the scene is laid, during which years I had come to know well the aspect, dialect, and mental and moral attitude of the hill-people. The fact that "Summer" deals with the same class and type as those portrayed in "Ethan Frome", and has the same setting, might have sufficed to disprove the legend—but once such a legend is started it echoes on as long as its subject survives.

EDITH WHARTON

[On *Ethan Frome*'s Dramatization]†

Not long ago, a friend, fulfilling one of the most sacred and cherished privileges of friendship, sent me the report of a lecture on American fiction in which the lecturer had done me the honour to include my name.

His reference to me (I quote from memory) was to the effect that *Ethan Frome* had some chance of surviving, though everything else I had written was destined to immediate oblivion. I took the blow meekly, bowed but not broken, and mindful that, though in my youth it would have been considered a discourtesy to fling such a verdict in the face of a faithful servant of English letters, other times (and especially other races) have introduced new standards of manners on my country.[1]

Perhaps the lecturer was as right as he thought himself; but I presently

8. Close friend of Wharton and an international lawyer (1859–1927). Wharton termed Berry her "soulmate." The cosmopolitan Berry grew up in Albany, New York, and knew New England well.
† Edith Wharton's Foreword to Owen Davis and Donald Davis, *Ethan Frome: A Dramatization of Edith Wharton's Novel* (New York: Scribner's, 1936).
1. In 1936 Wharton was considered an old-fashioned novelist of bygone manners in the heyday of modernism, naturalism, and proletarian fiction—the latter dismissed by Wharton as fiction of "the man with the dinner-pail."

extracted some comfort from the thought that Sainte Beuve, probably the most acute literary critic who ever lived, went hopelessly and almost invariably astray in trying to estimate the work of his contemporaries; and that Madame de Sévigné, herself one of the most enchanting of stylists, in speaking of the greatest poet of her day and country, replied to a questioner: "Racine? Oh, he'll disappear as quickly as the craze for coffee."[2]

There are times when it is comforting, and therefore perhaps permissible, to compare small things with great; and if I have broken through my lifelong rule of never noticing any comments on my work, it is because, in reading the dramatization of *Ethan Frome* by Owen and Donald Davis, I found myself thinking at every page: "Here at least is a new lease of life for 'Ethan.' "[3] And the discovery moved me more than I can say.

It has happened to me, as to most novelists, to have the odd experience, through the medium of reviews or dramatizations of their work, to see their books as they have taken shape in other minds: always a curious, and sometimes a painful, revelation. But I imagine few have had the luck to see the characters they had imagined in fiction transported to the stage without loss or alteration of any sort, without even that grimacing enlargement of gesture and language supposed to be necessary to "carry" over the footlights.

I should like to record here my appreciation of this unusual achievement, and my professional admiration for the great skill and exquisite sensitiveness with which my interpreters have executed their task; and to add that, if, as I am told, *their* interpreters, the personifiers of Ethan, of Zeena and Mattie, and the minor Starkfield figures, have reached the same level of comprehension, then my poor little group of hungry lonely New England villagers will live again for a while on their stony hillside before finally joining their forbears under the village headstones. I should like to think that this good fortune may be theirs, for I lived among them, in fact and in imagination, for more than ten years, and their strained starved faces are still near to me.

Ste-Claire le Château,
Hyères, January 1936.

---

2. Charles Augustin Sainte-Beuve (1804–1869), French literary critic; Madame de Sévigné (1626–1696), aristocratic French writer of letters who described court life and her reading, providing a famous picture of her times. Jean Racine (1639–1699), famous French tragedian.
3. The Owen and Donald Davis dramatization, staged by Guthrie McClintic, opened successfully in Philadelphia, January 1936, with Raymond Massey as Ethan, and ran over four months at the National Theater in New York.

Letters on *Ethan Frome* (1910–1912)†

Edith Wharton to Elizabeth Frelinghuysen Davis Lodge[1]

53 Rue de Varenne[2]
June 20 [1910]

* * *

I am hard at work on a short novel[3] which I have taken up since Teddy went to Switzerland,[4] & hope to have time to get well started while I am here alone. It has been impossible to work except spasmodically these last months, & more & more I find that Salvation is there, & there only.

* * *

Edith Wharton to Bernard Berenson[1]

53 Rue de Varenne
January 4 [1911]

* * *

I am driving harder and harder at that ridiculous nouvelle, which has grown into a large long-legged hobbledehoy of a young novel.[2] 20,000 long it is already, and growing. I have to let its frocks down every day,

---

† Reprinted with the permission of Charles Scribner's Sons, an imprint of Macmillan Publishing Company, The Estate of Edith Wharton, and the Watkins/Loomis Agency, from *The Letters of Edith Wharton* by R. W. B. Lewis and Nancy Lewis, editors. Copyright © 1988 by R. W. B. Lewis, Nancy Lewis, and William R. Tyler.
1. George Cabot ("Bay") Lodge, her husband, had died on August 21, 1909, at the age of thirty-six. [The "Bay" Lodges were American friends of Wharton. She met the aspiring poet "Bay"—son of Massachusetts senator Henry Cabot Lodge—in 1898. *Editor.*]
2. Wharton's Paris apartment [*Editor*].
3. *Ethan Frome.*
4. Wharton's husband, "Teddy," suffered from violent mood swings and increasingly serious mental instability. In early June he underwent treatment at the Kuranstalt Bellevue in Kreuzlingen, Switzerland, temporarily freeing Wharton from the exhausting problem of his care [*Editor*].
1. European art agent for wealthy American collectors and famous expert on Italian Renaissance painting who became Wharton's good friend [*Editor*].
2. *Ethan Frome.*

and soon it will be in trousers! However, I see an end, for I'm over the hard explanatory part, and the *vitesse acquise*[3] is beginning to rush me along. The scene is laid at Starkfield, Mass, and the nearest cosmopolis is called Shadd's Falls. It amuses me to do that *décor*[4] in the rue de Varenne.[5]

*   *   *

Edith Wharton to Bernard Berenson

Grand Hôtel des Thermes
Salsomaggiore[1]
May 16 [1911]

*   *   *

In your letter which awaited me at Milan was a question so flattering that I'm still wondering how it is that I failed to answer it. You asked if you might see the proofs[2] of my short-novel. If I had imagined that it could interest you I should have brought them with me; but I didn't. You know that, literally, *c'est le cas de dire*[3] that it's not "your size"; only an anecdote in 45,000 words! But it will begin its brief career in August Scribner, and appear later in a volumelet. So you won't have many months of suspense.

*   *   *

Edith Wharton to W. Morton Fullerton[1]

Salsomaggiore
September 22 [1911]

*   *   *

That was a good letter from Leyret.[2] Of course one lives by such things, & not by bread alone.[3] The disaster of my life was that for

---

3. "Gathering speed" *[Editor]*.
4. Setting *[Editor]*.
5. Her fashionable street in Paris *[Editor]*.
1. Wharton periodically underwent therapy for asthma and nervous tension at this Italian spa where she complained of boredom and lack of suitable companions. *[Editor]*.
2. Pages publisher sends to an author for final correction before publication. Refers to those for *Ethan Frome [Editor]*.
3. "It's no mistake to say" *[Editor]*.
1. Expatriate American journalist (1865–1952), friend of Henry James and Wharton, who became Wharton's lover approximately 1908–1910. *[Editor]*.
2. Henri Leyret (born 1864), author of a book about the Dreyfus case and other works on politics and government. [Presumably, Fullerton has had a letter of congratulations from Leyret, quite possibly having something to do with the famous Dreyfus case, which involved the false accusation of a French military officer and divided French society. Fullerton had covered the case for the *Times—Editor.*]
3. Wharton paraphrases Christ's words to the Devil, who tempted Christ to prove He was the Son of God by turning stones into bread. Christ replied: "Man shall not live by bread alone, but by every word that proceedeth out of the mouth of God." Matthew 4:4 *[Editor]*.

too long I was utterly starved of all that—& could not console myself with anything else. Apropos—I have just had a very good letter from H.J.,[4] who is staying in Scotland with my sister-in-law Minnie Jones, or rather with her cousin Mr. Cadwalader, for whom she plays hostess on his moor. Henry is in radiant good humour & spirits, & tells me that he has got hold of Ethan Frome in Scribner's, & that "it is going to be a triumph." I think it's the first unqualified praise I ever had from him, & it does me good, as Leyret's did you.—I wish though, he'd read the little story first "en volume."[5]

* * *

Edith Wharton to Mary Cadwalader Jones[1]

Grand Hôtel des Thermes
Salsomaggiore
September 23, 1911

* * *

I'm so pleased that you liked Ethan! He was written in the only quiet time I've had in the last distracted two years.

But I laughed "fit to bust" at your lending him to dear sweet Mrs. Winthrop. What a bewildered hour she must have had, digesting him.

* * *

Edith Wharton to W. Morton Fullerton

Villa "I Tatti"[1]
Settignano, Florence
October 16 [1911]

* * *

Thank you for the clipping about Ethan.—I have had another already, in the same strain, from a New York paper. They don't know *why* it's good, but they are right: it *is*. Vous verrez que je ferai encore mieux![2]

* * *

4. H. J. is Henry James. See excerpt from his letter, p. 85 *[Editor]*.
5. Wharton wishes Henry James had read the novel in the complete volume edition rather than the serialization in *Scribner's* magazine *[Editor]*.
1. Wharton's sister-in-law.
1. Bernard Berenson's home in Florence *[Editor]*.
2. "You'll see that I'll do even better" *[Editor]*.

Edith Wharton to Charles Scribner [1]

53 Rue de Varenne
November 27 [1911]

Dear Mr. Scribner,

Many thanks for your letter of Nov. 16th, telling me that you have deposited $1000. additional advance on "Ethan Frome."

I am somewhat puzzled by the figures you give regarding the number of copies sold. You say that at the date of writing 4200 copies have sold. I must have had a dozen letters from friends in New York & Boston, dated about Nov. 1st, & saying that the first edition was then sold out & the book absolutely unobtainable, & as I supposed you must certainly have printed 5000, your figures are naturally a surprise. What did the first edition consist of?—As far as it is possible to judge from reviews & from the personal letters constantly pouring in, "Ethan" is having a more immediate & general success than "The House of Mirth," [2] & this impression was corroborated for me the other day, by a friend who sailed about Nov 1st, & who told me that when she tried to get it at Brentano's they told her it was out of print & that they had more demand for it than for any novel published this autumn.—So you can understand my being surprised at the figures you give, & your making no mention of a second edition. [3]

*   *   *

Henry James [1] *to Edith Wharton*†

["It's a 'gem.' "]

Lamb House, Rye
25 October 1911

*   *   *

* * *—I exceedingly admire, sachez [2] Madame, *Ethan Frome.* A beautiful art & tone & truth—a beautiful artful *kept-downness*, & yet

1. Charles Scribner (1854–1930), Wharton's New York publisher *[Editor]*.
2. Wharton's 1905 bestseller *[Editor]*.
3. In reply, Charles Scribner wrote: "Nothing is more difficult to meet than the statement of an author's friends who report that a book is selling tremendously or cannot be had at the best bookstores. Retail clerks are very apt to say whatever they think a customer wishes to hear." He gave Wharton a week-by-week breakdown of sales in four Boston stores (300 copies in all), and in Brentano's, New York (283). By late February 1912, sales from *Ethan Frome* had reached nearly 7,000; but it would not be a true commercial success until the 1940s.
† Reprinted with permission of Charles Scribner's Sons, an imprint of Macmillan Publishing from *Henry James and Edith Wharton Letters: 1900–1915*, edited by Lyall H. Powers. Copyright © 1990 Lyall H. Powers.
1. Henry James (1843–1916), expatriate American author, became a good friend of Wharton's, visiting her both at The Mount (her estate in Lenox, Massachusetts), and in Paris. She frequently referred to him as "Dear Master" *[Editor]*.
2. "I want you to know."

effective cumulation. It's a "gem"—& excites great admiration here. Nous en causerons.[3]

*   *   *

THE *BERKSHIRE EVENING EAGLE*

["Fatal Coasting Accident"] †

Lenox[1] *High School Girl Dashed To Her Death*[2]

Four companions seriously injured.

Miss Hazel Crosby, who was steering, lost control of "Double Ripper"—fatal coasting accident in resort town.

Miss Hazel Crosby, a junior in the Lenox high school, was fatally and several companions seriously injured in a coasting accident in Lenox yesterday afternoon soon after 4 o'clock.

The young people were on a "double ripper" coasting sled, sweeping down a very steep hill at a tremendous rate of speed, when the fatality occurred. At the foot of the hill the sled veered and crashed into a lamp-post, fatally injuring Miss Crosby and fracturing the limbs of three others.

THE DEAD.

Miss Hazel Crosby, right leg fractured in three places, left leg in one place, lower jaw broken, internal injuries.

THE INJURED.

Miss Crissey Henry, serious concussion of the brain, bad injury to side of face, injured internally.

Miss Lucy Brown, thigh fractured between knee and hip, cut on face under chin, cut in back of head.

Miss Kate Spencer,[3] dislocation of right hip joint.

Mansuit Schmitt, contusions of head and body.

Miss Crosby was taken to the House of Mercy in this city last evening where she died at 11:30 o'clock. The fractures were reduced and everything possible was done for her, but the efforts of the skilled surgeons and doctors were without avail.

3. "We shall chat about that."
† From the *Berkshire Evening Eagle*, Pittsfield, Massachusetts, 12 March 1904. Reprinted with permission of the *Berkshire Eagle*.
1. Wharton and her husband built a substantial country home in Lenox, Massachusetts, and summered there from 1902 to 1911.
2. The probable connection between the tragic sledding accident and *Ethan Frome* is discussed on pp. 90–94.
3. Wharton knew Kate Spencer personally from her work at the Lenox library. See following pp. 90–93.

Miss Henry was taken to her home, and her condition was such that for a time her recovery was despaired of. Of those who survived the accident, she is the most seriously injured, but will recover.

SCENE OF ACCIDENT.

The scene of the accident is out a short distance from the Curtis hotel, in the center of Lenox. The hill leads from Egglestone monument through Stockbridge street in the direction of Stockbridge. The houses of Charles Lanier and W. D. Sloane are on this street.

Court House hill as it is called is exceedingly steep and for some time has been covered with sheet ice. It is in general use for coasting purposes and every afternoon sees a number of parties enjoying the sport at that point. It is the favorite coasting place for all the guests who go to the Curtis hotel for recreation and out of door sport in the wintertime, as owing to the ice, it is but little used by teams at this season of the year. The smooth condition of the road with but little snow upon it, affords superior advantages for the sport.

HIGH SPEED ATTAINED.

The road, from the coasters' viewpoint, was never in finer condition than it was yesterday. A speed almost unequaled in all the long history of coasting in Lenox was obtained, and the sport had been indulged in at intervals almost all day. It came to a close by the grim happenings that brought such disaster and sorrow to many homes and shrouded Lenox in gloom. On account of the peculiar circumstances attending the affair and the youth of the victims the accident was especially sad and distressing.

The five injured were but a part of the party who went from the high school building for coasting. They used a large sled, heavily built. Mansuit Schmitt, the only young man in the party, had been steering the sled on its course until the accident. Miss Crosby expressed a desire to guide the sled on one trip, and the permission was reluctantly granted. She took her position in front of the party of coasters.

A young sister of Schmitt was in the party just before the fatal slide was begun. She was invited to participate in the slide, but refused, stating that she was going on an errand and could not delay. As she bade them good-bye the five young people boarded the double ripper, and started on the coast which resulted in the death of one and injury of the other members of the party.

Despite the fact that the hill is one of the most popular coasting places in the town it is also very dangerous and numerous narrow escapes from accidents have been reported as taking place there. Just at the foot of the hill Hawthorne street branches off to the southwest. There are two entrances from Hawthorne street to Stockbridge street and the center of these entrances forms a triangle. In this triangle is located the lamp post with which the double ripper collided.

So far as can be learned, John Parsons is the only one who saw the accident. Soon after they passed him he heard a shout, presumably uttered by Miss Crosby who had lost control of the sled. It is just possible that one of the runners came in contact with a rut in the road causing the sled to sheer off, but there can be little certainty upon this point. Mr. Parsons turned just in time to witness the collision.

THE START.

The start was made at the brow of the hill, near the Egglestone monument where Schmitt pushed off, and in an instant the sled gained great momentum and fairly vanished from the view of the onlookers at the starting point. Shortly afterward a crash and shout were heard, and the spectators and residents living along the street hurried to the bend in the road.

There, at the foot of the hill, were all five members of the party, unconscious. The sled had crashed into a lamp post at the junction of Hawthorne and Stockbridge streets. Neither the post nor the sled was wrecked. Miss Crosby received the full force of the collision and it is a wonder that she was not instantly killed. Miss Crosby and Miss Spencer were lying close together when found and some distance beyond were the others in a human pile.

INJURED CARED FOR.

Miss Crosby and Miss Henry were carried into the residence of Edward Witherspoon at the Parsons place, and others were taken to the residence of John T. Parsons. Surgeons were telephoned for in all directions. From Lee, Dr. Hassett responded, and Drs. Charles H. Richardson, Henry Colt and L. C. Swift went from Pittsfield.

The interval between the accident and the arrival of the surgeons was one of high nerve tension in Lenox. Nearly everyone in the town hurried to the scene of the accident, and business in the little town was almost suspended. Rumors that at least two were killed were soon afloat, and added to the excitement.

From present indications, the accident was caused by Miss Crosby losing control of the sled at the bottom of the hill, where there is a sharp depression to the right in the road, and causing the sled to leave the track in the road and follow the sheet of ice which stood in the center of a triangle formed by Hawthorne street branch where it joins Stockbridge road.

The "double ripper" was owned by Herbert Spencer, a brother of one of the girls injured. Twice the four girls had coasted down the hill when young Schmitt put in an appearance. The boy then guided the bobs down the hill. While walking to the top of the hill the Crosby girl

requested that she be permitted to steer on the next slide. This request
was granted.

WHO VICTIMS ARE.

Miss Crosby was 18 years of age and was the daughter of Mr. and Mrs.
Louis Crosby, and, as already stated, a junior in the school. She was a
very bright pupil and a general favorite with everybody. She is survived,
besides her parents, by four sisters, Lewellyn, Edna, Patience and Constant, and by six brothers, Wyland, Harold, Karl, Howard, Sprague,
and Allids. Three of the brothers are members of the boys' choir of the
Episcopal church to which their parents belong. Hazel was the eldest
daughter. The family reside on Stockbridge street. Patience and Constant are twins. Mr. Crosby was formerly in the meat business but now
conducts a gardening business.

Miss Henry was attended by Dr. Hassett. She regained consciousness
today, but her condition is still quite serious. She bled quite freely from
the eyes and nose today. It is impossible to determine at this time
whether her skull is fractured. The family reside on West street. The
father is caretaker at the Winthrop, formerly the Robemon place. Miss
Henry is a sister of W. G. Henry, who is one of the permanent men at
the central fire station in this city. Miss Henry is in her junior year at
the high school.

Miss Spencer is a daughter of Mr. and Mrs. Ellery Spencer and the
family live on Fairview avenue. Miss Spencer was the only high school
senior in the party, the others being members of the junior class. Her
condition today was as comfortable as could be expected and her complete recovery is only a question of time.

The condition of Miss Lucy Brown today is very encouraging. She is
a daughter of Mr. and Mrs. Harry A. Brown of Cliffwood street.

Young Schmitt was delirious much of the time today. Although
apparently not seriously injured about the body his head appears to give
him some trouble. His condition is rather pitiable from the fact that
since the accident he has continually raved about it, giving vent to the
feeling that he was entirely responsible for the accident. The boy was a
member of the junior class at the high school and is very popular among
schoolmates. In addition to his school duties he acts as Lenox correspon-
dent for the Evening Journal.

HIGH SCHOOL PUPILS MEET.

A meeting of the Lenox high school pupils was held this afternoon to
take action anent[4] the accident. It is planned to send a floral tribute to
the funeral of Miss Crosby.

Mr. Crosby and Mrs. Arrowsmith, wife of Rev. Harold Arrowsmith,

---

4. "In regard to."

came to Pittsfield this morning and made arrangements for the removal of Miss Crosby's body to Lenox.

FUNERAL MONDAY.

The funeral is to be held Monday afternoon at 2:30 o'clock at the house and at 3 o'clock from the church. Rev. Mr. Arrowsmith is to conduct the services.

SCOTT MARSHALL

[Edith Wharton and Kate Spencer] †

The recent release of the film version is an opportune moment to re-examine one aspect relating to Wharton's writing of *Ethan Frome*: the real-life sledding accident in 1904 in Lenox, Massachusetts,[1] which is generally believed to have served as the "inspiration" for the final suicide run that Ethan and Mattie make on a sled near the end of the story. In *Edith Wharton* (1975), R. W. B. Lewis summarized this as follows:

> One event external to her life also contributed to the climax of *Ethan Frome*. In March 1904 there had been a disastrous sledding accident at the foot of Courthouse Hill in Lenox (Schoolhouse Hill in the novella). Four girls and a boy, all about eighteen and all but one juniors in Lenox High School, had gone coasting after school on a Friday afternoon. They made several exuberant runs down the mile-long slope, a descent on which a tremendous momentum can be achieved. On their last flight the young people's "double ripper" sled crashed into the lamppost at the bottom of the hill. One of the girls, Hazel Crosby, suffered multiple fractures and internal injuries; she died that evening. Lucy Brown had her thigh fractured and her head gashed, and was permanently lamed. Kate Spencer's face was badly scarred. (p. 308)

The 1904 sledding accident has increasingly been acknowledged as a formative part of the story. When the novella was republished in paperback in 1987 by Viking Penguin Classics with an introduction by Doris Grumbach, it also contained footnotes and an appendix by Sarah Higginson Begley. Begley included a full reprint of the coverage of the accident from the March 12, 1904 edition of *The Berkshire Evening Eagle*: "Lenox High School Girl Dashed To Her Death—Four Companions Seriously Injured—Miss Hazel Crosby, Who Was Steering, Lost

† From *Edith Wharton Review* 10.1 (Spring 1993): 20–21. Reprinted by permission of the author, the Estate of Edith Wharton, and the Watkins/Loomis Agency.
1. Newspaper coverage of the sledding accident is reprinted in this volume, pp. 86–90.

Control of "Double Ripper"—Fatal Coasting Accident in Resort Town."

From 1902 through 1911 Edith Wharton's principal home was her country estate, The Mount, in Lenox. Although she was travelling in Europe with her husband Teddy at the time of the March accident, it has been assumed by literary scholars that Wharton must have heard of or read about the accident and that she then transformed it into her fiction a few years later.

Wharton—as usual—was quite secretive about her sources and inspirations on *Ethan Frome* and she is never known to have mentioned the local real-life sledding accident to any one, not even in letters to friends. In her 1922 introduction to the Modern Student's Library edition of *Ethan Frome*, and in her autobiography, *A Backward Glance* (1934), she concentrated instead on her need to reproduce the rural landscape as she had seen it (as opposed to the "rose-coloured spectacles" of preceding women writers, *ABG*, p. 293) and of the decaying villages inhabited by "sad, slow-speaking people" (*ABG*, p. 153) which she had seen during her automobile explorations of the countryside. But she refused to say more: "So much for the origin of the story; there is nothing else of interest to say of it, except as concerns its construction" (M.S.L. edition of *EF*, p. v–vi).

What has not been generally known is that Wharton was personally acquainted with one of the injured victims of the 1904 accident, Kate Spencer, and that their friendship developed during the period when *Ethan Frome* was conceived and written.

Catherine (Kate) Spencer was born on December 26, 1887, the daughter of Alice Peck and Ellery Spencer. At the time of the accident, Kate—the only high school senior of the five on the sled—lived with her family on Fairview Avenue in Lenox. According to the 1904 newspaper account in *The Berkshire Evening Eagle*, she suffered the "dislocation of [her] right hip joint" in the accident. In addition, Lewis in *Edith Wharton* states that her "face was badly scarred." Lewis then links Kate Spencer with Ethan by pointing out that "Ethan Frome, when the narrator meets him at the opening of the tale, walks painfully with a lameness that checked 'each step like the jerk of a chain'; [and] there is an angry red gash across his forehead" (p. 308).

In 1902 Wharton became a volunteer Associate Manager (at times also called Assistant Manager) of the Lenox Library; she continued this work until her move to France in late 1911. By 1905 Kate Spencer, according to the library's annual reports, was working there as Assistant Librarian on a staff of three (Librarian, Assistant Librarian and 2nd Assistant Librarian). The two women came to know each other through their regular work at the library.

On July 7, 1909 Wharton, who was staying at Queen's Acre in Windsor, England with Howard Sturgis (see Lewis, p. 260–61), wrote to Spencer in Lenox:

I am so surprised, & so sorry, to hear of your decision to leave the
library; & so especially regretful to learn that your doing so is owing
to ill health. I had no idea that you had not been well, & only hope
that rest & change will soon bring about such improvement that
we shall see you at your post again. It has been a great advantage to
the managers to have you & Miss White [the Librarian] in charge
of the library, & we have all appreciated your courtesy & willing-
ness to do your share of the work, & the pleasant spirit in which
you did it . . ."

Wharton concluded by sending Spencer "my sincerest sympathy, &
best hopes for your recovery, & for your return to the library . . ." The
letter was forwarded from Lenox to Spencer at a bungalow by the sea on
Staten Island, where she may have gone for rest and medical treatment.

In addition to the letter, the collection of the Lenox Library includes
several gift tags for Christmas presents [year(s) unknown] in Wharton's
handwriting: "For Miss Spencer from Mrs. Wharton." One can only
speculate on the gifts—possibly books—that Wharton sent to the ailing
young woman.

Wharton's acquaintance with Kate Spencer coincides with the origins
of *Ethan Frome* as a brief exercise written in French to improve her
proficiency in that language. Both Lewis in *Edith Wharton* (p. 296) and
Cynthia Griffin Wolff in *A Feast of Words: The Triumph of Edith Wharton* (p. 161) date that effort to around 1907. The novella as we know it
was begun not much more than a year after Wharton's surviving letter
to Spencer.

If Wharton did indeed draw on her personal acquaintance with Spencer and the 1904 accident for her fiction, it should be noted that she
had also found similar material in the tragic death of her good friend
Ethel Cram in Lenox in July 1905. Cram, who had just been named as
Associate Manager of the Lenox Library (to serve alongside Wharton),
was returning home in a carriage from the library when a passing motor-
car caused the horse to shy and her niece, who was driving, to drop the
reins. An experienced horsewoman, Cram reached for the reins to
regain control, but was kicked in the head by the horse and fell from the
carriage. She remained comatose for several months—hovering between
life and death—and thereby inspiring the situation that Wharton deline-
ated for Bessy Amherst in *The Fruit of the Tree* (1907).

As for Kate Spencer, little is known following her contact with Edith
Wharton at the Lenox Library. One wonders about her reaction to the
sledding incident as it was described in *Ethan Frome*, as well as the
resulting injuries for Ethan and Mattie, when the novella first appeared.
Spencer never married and lived for the rest of her life in Lenox, for
many years sharing a home with her brother, Edmund (1886–1953),
who served as the town Postmaster from 1923–1934. In 1954—at the
time of a production of the play *Ethan Frome* by Owen and Donald

Davis at the nearby Stockbridge Playhouse—*The Berkshire Eagle* ran an article recalling the 50th anniversary of the 1904 sledding accident. It was noted that: "Miss Spencer lives on Tucker Street and still suffers from facial injuries received in the accident" (August 26, 1954).

Kate Spencer died on February 18, 1976 and was buried in the cemetery of the Church on the Hill in Lenox. Nearby are the graves of two other participants in that terrible accident in 1904: Hazel Crosby, who was killed that day at age 18, and Lucy Brown, who lived until 1960. Only a few steps away also lie the graves of Teddy Wharton, his mother and his sister. All rest peacefully in the shadow of the white Congregational Church, which closely resembles its counterpart in Starkfield, as described in *Ethan Frome* by Edith Wharton.

R. W. B. LEWIS

[*Ethan Frome* Biographically] †

Ethan Frome, which ran in *Scribner's* from August through October and was published in book form at the end of September, was in good part the product of Edith Wharton's personal life during the previous few agitated years.[1] Into no earlier work of fiction, not even *The House of Mirth*,[2] had she poured such deep and intense private emotions. *Ethan Frome* in this regard was a major turning point, whether or not it was also the very finest of her literary achievements. Edith had hitherto reserved her strongest feelings for poetry; henceforth, they would go into her novels and stories. The experience of writing the fictively conceived 1908 journal[3] had served her well. From this moment forward, and with obvious exceptions, Edith Wharton's fictional writings began to comprise the truest account of her inward life.

One event external to her life also contributed to the climax of *Ethan Frome*. In March 1904 there had been a disastrous sledding accident at the foot of Courthouse Hill in Lenox (Schoolhouse Hill in the novella).[4] Four girls and a boy, all about eighteen and all but one juniors in Lenox High School, had gone coasting after school on a Friday afternoon. They made several exuberant runs down the mile-long slope, a descent on which a tremendous momentum can be achieved. On their last flight the young people's "double-ripper" sled crashed into the lamppost at the

---

† From R. W. B. Lewis, *Edith Wharton: A Biography*, pp. 308–11. Copyright © 1975 by Harper and Row, Publishers, Inc. Reprinted by permission of HarperCollins Publishers, Inc., the Estate of Edith Wharton, and the Watkins/Loomis Agency.
1. Refers to her husband's worsening mental illness.
2. Wharton's 1905 bestselling novel of New York society life.
3. Wharton's journal, covering the period of her affair with American expatriate journalist Morton Fullerton, is housed at the Lilley library in Bloomington, Indiana.
4. See account of the accident in Lenox, pp. 86–90.

bottom of the hill. One of the girls, Hazel Crosby, suffered multiple fractures and internal injuries; she died that evening. Lucy Brown had her thigh fractured and her head gashed, and was permanently lamed. Kate Spencer's face was badly scarred.

Ethan Frome, when the narrator meets him at the opening of the tale, walks painfully with a lameness that checked "each step like the jerk of a chain"; there is an angry red gash across his forehead. The story that Ethan eventually unfolds for his visitor, and that the latter pieces together from other sources, goes back nearly thirty years to events leading up to a sledding catastrophe.

In her description of the bleak village of Starkfield and the allusions to nearby places like Bettsbridge, Corbury Flats, and Corbury Junction, Edith Wharton was drawing upon her memory of Plainfield and Lenox, of the Berkshire scenes she had so frequently passed through on the drives to Ashfield[5] and back. She was re-creating the spell that the New England landscape had laid upon her, its dark somber beauty, its atmosphere (for her) of the haunted and tragic.

The treatment both of setting and character shows Edith Wharton in perfect command of the methods of literary realism;[6] in its grim and unrelenting way, *Ethan Frome* is a classic of the realistic genre. At the same time, it is Edith Wharton's most effectively American work; her felt affinities with the American literary tradition were never more evident. A certain Melvillian[7] grandeur went into the configuration of her tragically conceived hero. Despite her early disclaimers, the spirit of Nathaniel Hawthorne pervades the New England landscape of the novella and lies behind the moral desolation of Ethan Frome—a desolation as complete in its special manner as that of his namesake, Hawthorne's Ethan Brand.[8] The sense of deepening physical chill (the French translation was called *Hiver*)[9] that corresponds to the inner wintriness is similarly Hawthornian in nature. The role of the inquisitive city-born narrator is deployed with a good deal of the cunning and artistry of Henry James.[1]

But the great and durable vitality of the tale comes at last from the personal feelings Edith Wharton invested in it, the feelings by which she

---

5. To visit Charles Eliot Norton (1827–1908), professor of the history of fine art at Harvard, and his daughter, Sara, Wharton's lifelong friend.   /
6. American realism, which dominated the literary scene from after the Civil War until well into the nineteenth century, is notable for its emphasis on regionalism, particularly apparent in the New England landscapes of *Ethan Frome*.
7. Herman Melville (1819–1891) was famous for his great tragic hero, Captain Ahab, in *Moby-Dick*.
8. Nathaniel Hawthorne (1804–1864), New England author of bleak moral allegories. "Ethan Brand" (1851) is his short story of a man convinced he has committed the "unpardonable sin," intellectual pride.
9. "Winter."
1. American expatriate author (1843–1916), noted for narrative technique and psychological subtlety of point of view. Lewis is placing Wharton squarely within the American literary tradition to counter arguments that she was a francophile expatriate novelist of manners, divorced from her native literary tradition.

lived her narrative. *Ethan Frome* portrays her personal situation, as she had come to appraise it, carried to a far extreme, transplanted to a remote rural scene, and rendered utterly hopeless by circumstance. As she often did, Edith shifted the sexes in devising her three central characters. Like Edith Wharton, Ethan Frome is married to an ailing spouse a number of years older than he, and has been married for about the same length of time as Edith had been tied to Teddy.[2] Ethan sometimes wonders about Zeena's sanity, and he daydreams about her death, possibly by violence (one recalls "The Choice").[3] He looks about frantically for some avenue to freedom, but his fate is conveyed to him in Edith's regular image for her own condition: "The inexorable facts closed in on him like prison-warders handcuffing a convict. . . . He was a prisoner for life."

The relationship between Ethan and Mattie Silver contains memories of Morton Fullerton[4] (even the names echo faintly) and passages transposed from the 1908 journal. Ethan and Mattie go star charting together; he feels that for the first time in his life he has met someone who can share his sensitiveness to natural beauty. During their one evening together, he with his pipe and Mattie with her sewing, Ethan lets himself imagine—as Edith had done on a winter evening in the Rue de Varenne[5]—that their evenings would always be so. But in the savage quarreling between Ethan and Zeena, in the latter pages of the story, we hear something of the bitter recriminations Edith and Teddy had begun to visit upon each other.[6] And in the denouement—where the bountifully healthy and vindictive Zeena commands a household that includes Mattie as a whining invalid and Ethan as the giant wreck of a man—we have Edith Wharton's appalling vision of what her situation might finally have come to.

It was quickly recognized by reviewers that *Ethan Frome* was one of Edith Wharton's finest achievements, though some of them found the concluding image too terrible to be borne. The entire tale, said a writer in *The New York Times*, was an exercise in subtle torture. A library guide declared the book too pessimistic to be recommended to the general reader, and the critic in *The Bookman*—confusing Edith Wharton's judgment on life with her personal attitudes—could not forgive her her cruelty toward both her characters and her readers. But there was a great deal of praise, and almost every reviewer had admiring words for the story's construction and style.[7]

Gratifying letters poured in on Edith. Dr. Kinnicutt told her prophetically that *Ethan Frome* was "a classic that will be read and re-read with

2. Wharton married in 1885.
3. 1908 Wharton short story in which a wife wishes her husband dead and her lover dies instead.
4. The American expatriate journalist with whom Wharton had an affair.
5. Wharton's Paris street.
6. Teddy Wharton's deteriorating condition, his speculation with Wharton's fortune, and his sexual affairs had brought matters to a head in their marriage.
7. See "Contemporary Reviews," pp. 113–125.

pleasure and instruction," and was astonished at what she had been able to do in the midst of her "pressing anxieties." James expressed total admiration. He had been jovially skeptical about the narrator's opening remark: "I had been sent by my employers . . ." the notion of dear Edith being sent anywhere by anyone, he commented, boggled belief. But when he finished the story he found, with his usual critical exactness, that it contained "a beautiful art and tone and truth—a beautiful artful kept-downness."[8] Others, if less eloquent, were equally warm in their enthusiasm.

Ethan Frome was Edith Wharton's sixteenth book in thirteen years. Between *The Greater Inclination*[9] in 1899 and *Ethan Frome* in 1911, there had been only one year, 1906, when she failed to produce at least one volume; and she made up for it by bringing out a novella, a full-length novel, a book of short stories, and a collection of travel sketches in the next twenty-four months. Nor would her phenomenal energy flag in the years to come. The war was an inevitable interruption, but beginning with *The Age of Innocence* in 1920, she continued to appear at the rate of a volume a year until her death. Of all these manifold and varied writings, *Ethan Frome* has been much the most widely read and admired.

It was not, however, an immediate commercial success. In some small circles, especially in England, the novella was recognized almost at once as a work that approached greatness; but it did not otherwise exert a very broad appeal. It was not until the 1930s—surprisingly, given the public's aversion to literary realism during the Depression years—that the sales suddenly picked up, and a long-running dramatic version was produced on Broadway.[1] It has since become a standard classroom text, Edith Wharton's one sure contribution—though *The House of Mirth* and *The Age of Innocence* are being given increasing attention—to surveys of American literature. *Ethan Frome* has also been translated twice into French, half a dozen times into Italian, and into Swedish, Russian, and Japanese.

Edith was dismayed and resentful at the slowness of the sales in 1911. She fell to bickering with Scribners[2] in a manner reminiscent of earlier days, but this time with more fateful consequences. Soon after publication she told Charles Scribner that the book seemed to be having an immediate success and asked for a second advance of one thousand dollars, taking the occasion to remark that the volume had been "*very* badly printed. . . . I have never seen so many defective letters and various typographical untidiness in any book you have published for me, and I

---

8. See James's letter, p. 85.
9. Wharton's first collection of short stories.
1. Dramatized by Owen and Donald Davis, staged by Guthrie McClintic, with Raymond Massey as Ethan, ran four months at the National Theater in New York in 1936.
2. Wharton's letter to Charles Scribner is reprinted on p. 85.

think a protest ought to be made." Scribner, who had pointed out that shorter books never did as well as full-length novels, reported that as of mid-November, *Ethan Frome* had sold a little over four thousand copies, as much as her two most recent collections of short stories had sold since publication.

Edith expressed puzzlement over the figures: friends in Boston and New York had told her the first edition had sold out and the book was unobtainable; a bookseller at Brentano's observed that "they had more demand for it than any novel published this season." "Nothing," Scribner replied patiently, "is more difficult to meet than the statement of an author's friends who report that a book is selling tremendously or cannot be had at the best bookstores. Retail clerks are very apt to say whatever they think a customer wishes to hear." He enclosed a week-by-week breakdown of sales in four Boston stores (300 in all) and in Brentano's (283). By late February 1912 sales of *Ethan Frome* had reached nearly seven thousand, and it was "still in active demand."

When it became evident that *Ethan Frome* was not to be a major commercial success, Mrs. Wharton reverted to the charge that it had been sparsely advertised, and trusted that her next novel, *The Custom of the Country*,[3] would be given much better publicity. Scribners contended that they had in fact spent more than they could afford for a book of its small price, and promised the new work would be pressed hard.

E. H. VAN DEUSEN, M.D.

Observations on a Form of Nervous Prostration †

*   *   *

* * *It [the nervous prostration seen in some mental patients] is also traceable to depressing emotions, grief, domestic trouble, prolonged anxiety and pecuniary embarrassment; * * *[Some of] its leading symptoms are general *malaise*, . . . muscular atonicity, changing the expression of the countenance . . . with accompanying tendency to irritability, mental depression, . . . melancholia. . . .

*   *   *

The exhaustion consequent upon protracted attendance at a sick bed, with loss of sleep and irregular meals, solicitude as to the final issue, and, in case of a fatal termination, the shock of the bereavement, is a cause.

3. Scribner's, 1913.
† From *The American Journal of Insanity* 25 [Utica, New York] (1868–9): 445, 446, 447, 450–51.

*   *   *

The early married life of the wives of some of our smaller farmers seems especially calculated to predispose to this condition. Transferred to an isolated farm-house, very frequently from a home in which she had enjoyed a requisite measure of social and intellectual recreation, she is subjected to a daily routine of very monotonous household labor. Her new *home*, if it deserve the name, is, by a strict utilitarianism, deprived of everything which can suggest a pleasant thought: not a flower blooms in the garden; books she has, perhaps, but no time to read them. Remote from neighbors, as in sparsely settled districts, for weeks together, she sees only her husband and the generally uneducated man who shares his toil.

The urgency of farm work necessitates hurried, unsocial meals, and as night closes in, wearied with his exertions, the farmer is often accustomed to seek his bed at an early hour, leaving his wife to pass the long and lonely evening with her needle. Whilst the disposal of his crops, and the constant changes in the character of farm labor afford her husband sufficient variety and recreation, her daily life, and especially if she have also the unaided care of one or two ailing little children, is exhausting and depressing to a degree of which but few are likely to form any correct conception. From this class come many applications for the admission of female patients.

*   *   *

It is a well recognized fact in mental pathology, that in the asthenic [1] the earliest marked morbid psychical symptom is distrust. It is true that this is usually preceded by irritability and other modifications of temper and disposition—grave symptoms always—which should promptly receive the attention both of physicians and friends, but, as before remarked, the first clearly marked morbid sentiment is distrust. If the sufferer be an individual of deep religious feelings, to whom there is but the one only, great and vital interest, there is distrust of God's promises, morbid views of personal relations to the church, and to society—in fine, what is improperly termed "religious melancholy." If the acquisition of gain and the possession of broad acres have been the great object of life, there are torturing apprehensions of poverty; the poor-house stares the patient in the face and pauperism is his inevitable fate. Title deeds are filled with flaws, his notes are forgeries, and even gold and silver to him are worthless. If the conjugal relations have been peculiarly close and tender, there are the tortures of jealousy. In a few cases the morbid feeling has been general in its application.

*   *   *

1. Debilitated patient *[Editor]*.

CARROLL SMITH-ROSENBERG

The Hysterical Woman: Sex Roles and Role Conflict in Nineteenth-Century America †

* * *

Yet hysteria is also a socially recognized behavior pattern and as such exists within the larger world of cultural values and role relationships. For centuries hysteria has been seen as characteristically female—the hysterical woman the embodiment of a perverse or hyper-femininity.[1] Why has this been so? Why did large numbers of women "choose" the character traits of hysteria as their particular mode of expressing malaise, discontent, anger, or pain?[2] To begin to answer this question, we must explore the female role and role socialization. Clearly not all women were hysterics; yet the parallel between the hysteric's behavior and stereotypic femininity is too close to be explained as mere coincidence. To examine hysteria from this social perspective means necessarily to explore the complex relationships that exist between cultural norms and individual behavior, between behavior defined as disease and behavior considered normal.

* * *

So far this discussion of role socialization and stress has emphasized primarily the malaise and dissatisfaction of the middle-class woman. It is only a covert romanticism, however, that permits us to assume that lower-class and farm women, because their economic functions within the family were more vital than those of their decorative and economi-

---

† From Carroll Smith-Rosenberg, *Disorderly Conduct: Visions of Gender in Victorian America* (New York: Knopf, 1985). Reprinted by permission of Alfred A. Knopf, Inc.

1. The argument can be made that hysteria exists among men and therefore is not exclusively related to the female experience; the question is a complex one. There are, however, four brief points concerning male hysteria that I would like to make. First, to this day hysteria is still believed to be principally a female "disease" or behavior pattern. Second, the male hysteric is usually seen by physicians as somehow different. Today it is a truism that hysteria in males is found most frequently among homosexuals; in the nineteenth century, men diagnosed as hysterics almost exclusively had a lower socioeconomic status than their physicians—immigrants, especially "new immigrants," miners, railroad workers, blacks. Third, since it was defined by society as a female disease, one may hypothesize that there was some degree of female identification among the men who assumed a hysterical role. Lastly, we must recall that a most common form of male hysteria was battle fatigue and shell shock. I should like to thank Erving Goffman for the suggestion that the soldier is in a position analogous to women's regarding autonomy and power.

2. The word "choose," even in quotation marks, is value-laden. I do not mean to imply that hysterical women consciously chose their behavior. I feel that three complex factors interacted to make hysteria a real behavioral option for American women: first, the various experiences that caused a woman to arrive at adulthood with significant ego weaknesses; second, certain socialization patterns and cultural values that made hysteria a readily available alternate behavior pattern for women; and third, the secondary gains conferred by the hysterical role in terms of enhanced power within the family. Individual cases presumably represented their own peculiar balance of these factors, all of which will be discussed in this essay.

cally secure urban sisters, escaped their sense of frustration, conflict, or confusion. Normative prescriptions of proper womanly behavior were certainly internalized by many poorer women. The desire to marry and the belief that a woman's social status came not from the exercise of her own talents and efforts but from her ability to attract a competent male protector were as universal among lower-class and farm women as among middle- and upper-class urban women. For some of these women—as for their urban middle-class sisters—the traditional female role proved functional, bringing material and psychic rewards. But for some it did not. The discontinuity between the child and adult female roles, along with the failure to develop substantial ego strengths, crossed class and geographic barriers—as did hysteria itself. Physicians connected with almshouses, and, later in the century, with urban hospitals and dispensaries, often reported hysteria among immigrant and tenement-house women.[3]

* * *

Depression also appears as a common theme. Hysterical symptoms not infrequently followed a death in the family, a miscarriage, some financial setback which forced the patient to become self-supporting; or they were seen by the patient as related to some long-term, unsatisfying life situation—a tired schoolteacher, a mother unable to cope with the demands of a large family.[4] Most of these women took to their beds because of pain, paralysis, or general weakness. Some remained there for years.

* * *

Any general description of the personal characteristics of the well-to-do hysteric emphasized her idleness, self-indulgence, deceitfulness, and "craving for sympathy." Petted and spoiled by her parents, waited upon

---

3. William A. Hammond, *On Certain Conditions of Nervous Derangement* (New York: G. P. Putnam's Sons, 1881), p. 42; S. Weir Mitchell, *Lectures on the Diseases of the Nervous System, Especially in Women*, 2nd ed. (Philadelphia: Lea Brothers & Co., 1885), pp. 110, 114; Charles K. Mills, "Hysteria," in *A System of Practical Medicine by American Authors*, ed. William Pepper, assisted by Louis Starr, vol. V, "Diseases of the Nervous System" (Philadelphia: Lea Brothers & Co., 1883), p. 213; Charles E. Lockwood, "A Study of Hysteria and Hypochondriasis," *Transactions of the New York State Medical Association* XII (1895): 340–51. E. H. Van Deusen, superintendent of the Michigan Asylum for the Insane, reported that nervousness, hysteria, and neurasthenia were common among farm women and resulted, he felt, from the social and intellectual deprivation of their isolated lives (Van Deusen, "Observations on a Form of Nervous Prostration," *American Journal of Insanity* XXV [1869]: 447). Significantly, most English and American authorities on hysteria were members of a medical elite who saw the wealthy in their private practices and the very poor in their hospital and dispensary work. Thus the observation that hysteria occurred in different social classes was often made by the very same clinicians.
4. See W. Symington Brown, *A Clinical Handbook on the Diseases of Women* (New York: William Wood & Company, 1882); Charles L. Dana, "A Study of the Anaesthesias of Hysteria," *American Journal of the Medical Sciences* (October 1890): 1; William S. Playfair, *The Systematic Treatment of Nerve Prostration and Hysteria* (Philadelphia: Henry C. Lea's Son & Co., 1883), p. 29.

hand and foot by servants, she had never been taught to exercise self-control or to curb her emotions and desires.[5] Certainly she had not been trained to undertake the arduous and necessary duties of wife and mother. As one late-nineteenth-century physician lectured:

> Young persons who have been raised in luxury and too often in idleness, who have never been called upon to face the hardships of life, who have never accustomed themselves to self-denial, who have abundant time and opportunity to cultivate the emotional and sensuous, to indulge the sentimental side of life, whose life purpose is too often an indefinite and self-indulgent idea of pleasure, these are the most frequent victims of hysteria.[6]

Sound education, outside interests such as charity and good works, moral training, systematic outdoor exercise, and removal from an overly sympathetic family were among the most frequent forms of treatment recommended. Mothers, consistently enough, were urged to bring up daughters with a strong sense of self-discipline, devotion to family needs, and dread of uncontrolled emotionality.[7]

Emotional indulgence, moral weakness, and lack of willpower characterized the hysteric in both lay and medical thought. Hysteria, S. Weir Mitchell warned, occurred in women who had never developed habitual restraint and "rational endurance"—who had early lost their power of "self rule."[8] "The mind and body are deteriorated by the force of evil habit," Charles Lockwood wrote in 1895; "morbid thought and morbid impulse run through the poor, weak, unresisting brain, until all mental control is lost, and the poor sufferer is . . . at the mercy of . . . evil and unrestrained passions, appetites and morbid thoughts and impulses."[9]

* * *

As might be expected, conscious anger and hostility marked the response of a good many doctors to their hysterical patients. One New York neurologist called the female hysteric a willful, self-indulgent, and narcissistic person who cynically manipulated her symptoms. "To her distorted vision," he complained, "there is but one commanding personage in the universe—herself—in comparison with whom the rest of mankind are nothing." Doctors admitted that they were frequently

5. Robert B. Carter, *On the Pathology and Treatment of Hysteria* (London: John Churchill, 1853), p. 140; J. Leonard Corning, *A Treatise on Hysteria and Epilepsy* (Detroit: George S. Davis, 1888), p. 70; Mills, "Hysteria," p. 218.
6. George Preston, *Hysteria* (1897), p. 36.
7. See, for example, Mitchell, *Diseases of the Nervous System*, p. 170; Rebecca B. Gleason, M.D., of Elmira, New York, quoted by M. L. Holbrook, *Hygiene of the Brain and Nerves and the Cure of Nervousness* (New York: M. L. Holbrook & Company, 1878), pp. 270–71.
8. S. Weir Mitchell, *Fat and Blood* (Philadelphia: J. B. Lippincott, 1881), pp. 30–31.
9. Lockwood, "Hysteria and Hypochondriasis," pp. 342–43; virtually every authority on hysteria echoed these sentiments.

tempted to use such terms as "willful" and "evil," "angry" and "impatient" when describing the hysteric and her symptoms.[1] Even the concerned and genteel S. Weir Mitchell, confident of his remarkable record in curing hysteria, described hysterical women as "the pests of many households, who constitute the despair of physicians, and who furnish those annoying examples of despotic selfishness, which wreck the constitutions of nurses and devoted relatives, and in unconscious or half-conscious self-indulgence destroy the comfort of everyone about them." He concluded by quoting Oliver Wendell Holmes's acid judgment that "a hysterical girl is a vampire who sucks the blood of the healthy people about her."[2]

Hysteria as a chronic, dramatic, and socially accepted sick role could thus provide some alleviation of conflict and tension, but the hysteric purchased her escape from the emotional and—frequently—from the sexual demands of her life only at the cost of pain, disability, and an intensification of woman's traditional passivity and dependence. Indeed, a complex interplay existed between the character traits assigned women in Victorian society and the characteristic symptoms of the nineteenth-century hysteric: dependency, fragility, emotionality, narcissism. (Hysteria has, after all, been called in that century and this a stark caricature of femininity.) Not surprisingly, the hysteric's peculiar passive aggression and her exploitative dependency often functioned to cue a corresponding hostility in the men who cared for her or lived with her. Whether fathers, husbands, or physicians, they reacted with ambivalence and in many cases with hostility to her aggressive and never-ending demands.

II

* * *

The effect of hysteria upon the family and traditional sex-role differentiation was disruptive in the extreme. The hysterical woman virtually ceased to function within the family. No longer did she devote herself to the needs of others, acting as self-sacrificing wife, mother, or daughter: through her hysteria she could and in fact did force others to assume those functions. Household activities were reoriented to answer the hysterical woman's importunate needs. Children were hushed, rooms darkened, entertaining suspended, a devoted nurse recruited. Fortunes might be spent on medical bills or for drugs and operations. Worry and concern bowed the husband's shoulders; his home had suddenly become a hospital and he a nurse. Through her illness, the bedridden woman came to dominate her family to an extent that would have been consid-

---

1. F. C. Skey, *Hysteria* (New York: A. Simpson, 1867), p. 63.
2. Mitchell, *Diseases of the Nervous System*, p. 266; Mitchell, *Fat and Blood*, p. 37.

ered inappropriate—indeed, shrewish—in a healthy woman. Taking to one's bed, especially when suffering from dramatic and ever-visible symptoms, might also have functioned as a mode of passive aggression, especially in a milieu in which weakness was rewarded and in which women had since childhood been taught not to express overt aggression. Consciously or unconsciously, they had thus opted out of their traditional role.

*   *   *

To understand hysteria's place within the broader social experience of America's women, we must not only look at stress and dysfunction within the hysteric's own psychic background, but at the relation between hysterical character formation and female role socialization. To do so, I propose that we examine the roles male society sought to impose on America's daughters (and on their mothers) in the elaborate child-rearing literature that began to appear during the first third of the nineteenth century.

There is evidence in children's books, child-rearing manuals, marriage guides, and books of etiquette that women were sharply discouraged from expressing competitive inclinations or asserting mastery in such "masculine" areas as physical skill, strength, and courage, or in academic, scientific, or commercial pursuits. Rather they were encouraged to be coquettish, entertaining, nonthreatening, and nurturing. Male religious writers and educators forbade overt anger and violence as unfeminine and vulgar and they did not reward curiosity, intrusiveness, exploratory behavior, in women. Indeed, when such characteristics conflicted with the higher feminine values of cleanliness, deportment, unobtrusiveness, or obedience, they were criticized or punished. Yet these same habits of mind are now deemed essential to the development of autonomy in children and are thought to be a key to learning, especially in the areas of science and mathematics. While most children's literature asserted that boys were "brave, active and lively, Strength swelleth in their bones and labor is their delight all day long . . . ," girls were taught that their greatest happiness lay in an unending routine of caring for the needs of others.[3]

*   *   *

There is, I believe, a suggestive parallel between the hysterical woman of the nineteenth century and a masochistic female personality as

3. I base these statements on an ongoing study of children's literature in which I am engaged. The American Antiquarian Society's collection of eighteenth- and nineteenth-century children's books is particularly rich. See also Charles Carpenter, *History of American School Books* (Philadelphia: University of Pennsylvania Press, 1963), and Nigel Temple, ed., *Seen and Not Heard: A Garland of Fancies for Victorian Children* (London: Hutchinson & Co. Ltd., 1970), which offers a pleasant sample of nineteenth-century children's literature.

described by Karen Horney in 1934.[4] The masochistic female personality, Horney argued, suffered from "free floating anxiety," a deep-rooted sense of inferiority, and an absence of adequate aggression. By "aggression" Horney meant the ability to take initiative, to make efforts, to carry things through to completion, and to form and express autonomous views. All of these constitute important ego functions. Insecure, afflicted with anxieties, the masochistic woman demanded constant attention and expressions of affection, which she sought to secure by appealing to pity. She displayed inferiority feelings, weakness, and suffering. Such a self-image and pattern of object relations necessarily "generated hostile feelings [in the masochistic woman], but feelings which the masochistic woman was unable to express directly because they would have jeopardized her dependency relationships." "Weakness and suffering, therefore," Horney observed, "already serving many functions, now also act as a vehicle for the indirect expression of hostility."

Though both men and women develop masochistic personalities, Horney hypothesized that far larger numbers of women than men would do so in cultures in which women more than men (1) "Manifest[ed] . . . inhibitions in the direct expression of demands and aggressions; (2) regard[ed] . . . [themselves] as weak, helpless, or inferior and implicitly or explicitly demand[ed] considerations and advantages on this basis; (3) [became] emotionally dependent on the other sex; (4) show[ed] . . . tendencies to be self-sacrificing, to be submissive, to feel used or to be exploited, to put responsibilities on the other sex; (5) use[d] . . . weakness and helplessness as a means of wooing and subduing the other sex."[5]

In essence, then, many nineteenth-century women reached maturity with major ego weaknesses and with narrowly limited compensatory ego strengths, all of which implies a relationship between this pattern of socialization and the adoption of hysterical behavior by particular individuals. It seems plausible to suggest that a certain percentage of nineteenth-century women, faced with stress developing out of their own peculiar personality needs or because of situational anxieties, might well have defended themselves against such stress by regressing toward the childish hyper-femininity of the hysteric. The discontinuity between the roles of courted woman and pain-bearing, self-sacrificing wife and mother, the realities of an unhappy marriage, the loneliness and chagrin of spinsterhood may all have made the petulant infantilism and narcissistic self-assertion of the hysteric a necessary alternative to women who felt unfairly deprived of their promised social role and who had few strengths with which to adapt to a more trying one. Indeed, society had

4. Karen Horney, "The Problem of Feminine Masochism," in Horney, *Feminine Psychology*, ed. Harold Kelman (New York: W. W. Norton, 1967), pp. 214–44. See also her essays, "The Overvaluation of Love" and "The Neurotic Need for Love," in Horney, *Feminine Psychology*.
5. Horney, "Feminine Masochism," pp. 229 and passim.

structured this regression by consistently reinforcing those very emotional traits characterized in the stereotype of the female and caricatured in the symptomatology of the hysteric. At the same time, the nineteenth-century female hysteric also exhibited a significant level of hostility and aggression—rage—which may have led in turn to her depression and to her self-punishing psychosomatic illnesses. In all these ways, then, the hysterical woman can be seen as both product and indictment of her culture.

* * *

CARROLL D. WRIGHT

From *The Working Girls of Boston* †

[Introduction by Leon Stein and Philip Taft]

In 1877 Carroll D. Wright, a pioneer social statistician, was appointed director of the Massachusetts Bureau of Statistics of Labor, the first bureau of labor statistics in the country. From its founding in 1873, controversy enmeshed the bureau.

Massachusetts was the chief industrial state in the nation. Seeking facts, the bureau probed, inquired, pryed. Suspecting the motives for the prying, even hinting that the bureau was a tool of the workers, employers resisted and made the job of gathering facts and figures a difficult one. At the same time, workers were suspicious of Wright's impartiality.

Nevertheless Wright, the persistent professional, gathered his data and published his tables, charts and figures with his eye only on the facts. Despite opposition, he held his post for fifteen years. In that time he also organized the National Convention of Chiefs and Commissioners of Bureaus of Statistics of Labor, through which he spread and encouraged the professional use of data-gathering in the labor-management field.

Wright carried his investigations into the shop, the factory, the office. He studied wage rates, living costs, industrial conflicts as well as the secondary consequence of the industrial situation—housing, crime, illiteracy, poverty, broken homes.

* * *

In connection with the workroom and its surroundings is disclosed the fact that girls are very frequently called upon to climb four, five, six,

† *The Working Girls of Boston* (New York: Arno, 1969), pp. 69, 70, 71, 75; 92; 109.

and even seven long flights of stairs in order to reach their work. The girls themselves in many instances make special mention of, as termed by them, this "hardship," and complain very much of having to climb stairs. Freight elevators, where used, are forbidden, in most cases, to help, while in some instances where their use for passenger service is permitted, a "danger" sign is posted, and they are used at the risk of the employés. In one case reported, the use of elevator by employés is allowed only at certain hours, and if any are tardy a few moments, they forfeit the privilege, and must mount the stairs, this being especially hard on one girl troubled with heart-disease, in whose favor no exception is made. One girl, lame from infancy, says that in climbing stairs she is placed at a great disadvantage, her workroom being "high up."

Some evidence is also furnished as to the matter of escapes in case of fire. A few report wide stairs, easy exits, and fire-escapes, while others say their workrooms are up three to six flights, with no fire-escapes, and in one case, with poor entrance, and narrow and dark passage ways not wide enough for two abreast, some 250 to 300 persons being employed in the building, up three if not more flights.

Effect of Work on Health.

Long hours, and being obliged to stand all day, are very generally advanced as the principal reasons for any lack or loss of health occasioned by the work of the girls. The nature of the work is mentioned as a cause for decline, which together with the other causes described will be found to be prevalent in all the various branches of their work.

* * *

In Trade, a bookkeeper was found who had ruined her eyes, by bringing her books home nights and working until twelve and one o'clock. Among the saleswomen, "standing all day" is generally reported as being very trying on their health and strength. In one store, no stools are provided, the girls being obliged to go to one end of the store to sit down. The employer does not countenance help sitting down while customers are in the store, and as they are generally busy all day, there is little or no time when the store is vacant, the result being, practically, that the girls stand all day. Another girl says she works on outside counter, and owing to people constantly passing no stools can be used, and she finds the work very tiresome.

The new cash system requiring a constant raising of the arm is a great strain upon the girls, is very exhausting, and gives them a pain in the side; one girl reports many saleswomen out sick on this account.

A good many saleswomen consider their work very hard, and that it has a bad effect on their health; in one instance, a girl says she has paid out over $500 in doctor's bills during the past few years. In one store, it is very unsatisfactory in this respect; no talking is allowed, only half enough time is given for dinner, and being obliged to walk home at night, the girl is completely exhausted; on Saturday she brings dinner and supper.

In the busy season, the work is particularly trying. One girl says she gets pretty well tired out during this time (six months), and although there is not much chance to increase help, she thinks they might pay extra during the busy season.

In bakeries the strain of long hours and standing is especially felt by the salesgirls, while in other branches of business the health of many girls is so poor as to necessitate long rests, one girl being out a year on this account. Another girl in poor health was obliged to leave her work, while one other reports that it is not possible for her to work the year round, as she could not stand the strain, not being at all strong. A girl, who had worked in one place for three years, was obliged to leave on account of poor health, being completely run down from badly venti-lated workrooms, and obliged to take an eight months' rest; she worked a week when not able, but left to save her life. She says she has to work almost to death to make fair compensation (now $12 per week).

* * *

It is in evidence from other sources that in a few stores, and in some of considerable size, the water-closet accommodations are very defi-cient, in one instance 60 women being obliged to use one closet. The evil effects of waiting for the use of a closet common to so large a num-ber is apparent. Many of these women are constantly under the care of physicians for some disease growing out of the condition of things described. In such cases a little expense on the part of the proprietors would result in a happier and a healthier body of workers, and the outlay would be returned over and over again.

Some day law *must* compel men who are so negligent of the natural wants of their employés to adopt conveniences which through their own selfishness and foolishness they now withhold.

* * *

The average weekly income from all sources whatever for 544 girls was $5 per week or less, while 435 received a total average weekly income of from $5 to $10, there being only 53 receiving a total average weekly income of over $10 per week. *Brought into specific averages, we find that the average weekly income for the year was in personal service $5.25, on trade $4.81, in manufactures $5.22, or the general average for all involved for the whole year was $5.17 per week. This latter figure must stand as the total average weekly income from all sources, earnings, assistance, and other work, of the working girls of Boston.* It should be remembered that the average weekly earnings from occupation only, distributed over the whole year, was but $4.91; the total average yearly income from all sources was $269.07; for the different departments, $273.02 in personal service, $250.63 in trade, and $271.41 in manufactures.

Wages and earnings are affected by various causes, many of which are disclosed through the personal testimony of the girls themselves.

A good deal of complaint is made in regard to the low wages quite generally paid to working girls in all the various occupations in which they were found employed. The cause of complaint, especially under "Trade," is ascribed to the fact that girls living "at home," with little or no board to pay, work for very low wages. This is considered a great hardship to the lone working girl who is entirely dependent upon her own resources. The mothers in some cases have said that it takes more than the girls earn to feed and clothe them, and some of the girls have been taken from their work and are now idle on that account. In the large stores, employés are reported as hired at the lowest figures possible, and it is said, that wages in the future are likely to be even less.

*   *   *

From the recapitulation just given, and the recapitulation of the tables on wages and earnings, we get at the real economic condition of the working girls. By an analysis of the recapitulation of principal expenses, it will be seen that these items of expense are not common to all; for instance, of the 1,032 girls, 959 paid out something for food and lodging, the average yearly expense for each being $166.31; 1,013 spent on an average $67.75 for clothing; only a very small percentage of the

RECAPITULATION.—*Principal Expenses; Savings and Debt.*

CLASSIFICATION.	PERSONAL SERVICE.		TRADE.		MANUFACTURES.		ALL OCCUPATIONS.	
	Number.	Yearly Average.	Number.	Yearly Average.	Number.	Yearly Average.	Number.	Yearly Average.
Principal Expenses.								
Food and lodging, .	78	$165 01	113	$144 43	768	$169 66	959	$166 31
Clothing, . . .	83	65 18	120	80 08	810	66 19	1,013	67 75
Medical attendance, .	8	13 88	14	22 00	117	25 65	139	24 60
Fuel, ...	4	12 50	7	8 71	70	8 50	81	8 72
Washing, . . .	4	27 50	10	24 50	79	19 82	93	20 66
Car fares, . . .	8	20 88	28	26 11	138	22 06	174	22 66
Support of others, .	9	72 67	6	68 00	61	66 48	76	67 33
Other expenses, . .	56	41 61	72	36 11	520	42 17	648	41 45
Total yearly expenses,	83	261 43	123	246 20	826	263 53	1,032	261 30
Savings and Debt.								
Savings, . . .	13	80 69	11	63 82	96	71 95	120	72 15
Debt, ...	4	21 75	5	31 40	21	40 67	30	36 60

whole number were under any expense for medical attendance, fuel, washing, car fares, or support of others, while 648 reported other expenses not classified. These principal expenses not being common to all, it is therefore impossible to give a yearly average for each of the 1,032 girls for each of these items in detail; but the $261.30, given as the average of all expenses for the year, represents the actual average yearly expense for each of the 1,032 girls involved.

The margin of annual income over annual expense is very small; from an annual income of $269.07, the average for all the girls, there must be paid out a yearly expense of $261.30, leaving a margin for everything outside of the absolute necessaries of life of $7.77.

CRITICISM

Contemporary Reviews

NEW YORK TIMES BOOK REVIEW

["Three Lives in Supreme Torture"] †

Mrs. Wharton prefers to present life in its unsmiling aspects, to look at it with the eye of the tragic poet, not with the deep sympathy, smiling tenderness, and affectionate tolerance of the greatest novelists. Thus she never shows life as it is, as the great novelists do, but as an aspect or view of life—the reflex of life on the writer if you will—which colors all things with some mastering mood of him or her.

The present grim tale of a bud of romance ice-bound and turned into a frozen horror in the frigid setting of a New England Winter landscape is conceived in the remorseless spirit of the Greek tragic muse. The rigidity of the bleak Puritan outlook on life does duty for the relentless Fates.[1] It is a powerful and skillful performance and seems to recreate a life and an atmosphere essentially the same as that which breathes in the romances of Hawthorne.[2] That atmosphere is, no doubt, the true emanation of the soul of New England—that New England, warped by the dour theology of the cruel and fanatic age that planted it, which was Hawthorne's own, and which now has retired to such frozen fastnesses as the lonely and starved village among the barren hills in which Mrs. Wharton places her story.

The story itself is one which will hardly bear even indication of what it is without an effect of marring it. It deals with a gaunt, tall farmer and his wife and another woman—a young girl, the wife's poor relation, who is, like them, an inmate of the desolate farmhouse perched bleakly

---

† From the *New York Times Book Review* (8 October 1911): 603.

1. *Ethan Frome* was often compared to Greek tragedy. The first Puritans seceded from the Church of England under Elizabeth I, protesting excesses and wishing to "purify" the church, thence their name. However, their own rigidity and excessive suppression of pleasure and art have made the name "Puritan" synonymous with cold, stern discipline and a dour attitude. Puritanism, brought to New England by the earliest settlers, became highly influential in social thought and political policy in the United States. Here, the reviewer likens Puritanism, with its fatalistic doctrine of Determinism, i.e. salvation or damnation predetermined at birth, to Greek fatality. In Greek mythology, the three Fates were old women who controlled man's destiny: one spun the thread of life, one measured it, and the third cut it.

2. New England author (1804–1864) who often set his moral allegories in the 1600 world of his Puritan ancestors.

in the midst of its barren acres. The man is one of those—found in all
starved communities—who have been chained to the soil by the duty of
caring for a family of stricken elders—a very incarnation of the tragedy
of youth and strength wasted in the service of useless age. The wife is,
as a wife, an accident. She is a whining slattern[3] who hugs her imaginary ailments to her flat and barren breast and spends the scant substance wrung from the grudging northern earth upon quacks and patent
nostrums.[4] That, also, is a common type in starved and hopeless rural
communities.

The girl is a pretty, gentle creature whose worldly efficiency has been
tried and found wanting in the hard tasks of the shop girl in some busy
little New England mill town, a human reed bruised in the wind. On
the face of it it is a very sordid triangle. Actually, Mrs. Wharton has
been able to invest the girl with such sweetness, such delicacy, such
innocence, such child-likeness, to endow her with such simplicity and
such wistfulness; the man himself is so utterly simple, so starved of joy;
and both are so helpless in the toils of bitter circumstance that the effect
is anything but sordid.

Moreover, the whole drama is enacted for the reader under the spell
of a sure foreknowledge that tragedy is coming swift-footed to end the
hardly more than glimpsed hope of happiness for the doomed pair who
dwell apart in that house and watch for little comforts like faint candle
beams beneath closed doors. A brief interlude of smiles and tears and
shy glances and a mad moment of stolen kisses—and then the end. All
that is crushed beneath the horror of a stretch of long, ruined years.
Retribution sits at the poor man's fireside in the shape of two haggard
and witchlike figures—the gaunt wife and the wreck of the girl that was.

It is a cruel story. It is a compelling and haunting story. But it is a
story which a bald telling, without the art which has thrown the crude
material of the plot into due dramatic perspective and given it poetic
atmosphere, could easily make absurd, or even revolting. The mere saying that Mrs. Wharton has brought about the catastrophe by sending
two of her principal characters coasting down an icy hill and "smashing
them up" for life—but not killing them—against a great tree near the
bottom, conveys an impression of clumsiness and brutality which only
the actual reading of the story will avail to dispel. Mrs. Wharton has, in
fact, chosen to build of small, crude things and a rude and violent event
a structure whose purpose is the infinite refinement of torture. All that
is human and pitiful and tender in the tale—and there is much—is
designed and contrived to sharpen the keen edge of that torture. And the
victims lie stretched upon the rack for twenty years.

The author of *The House of Mirth*,[5] which lacked much of being

3. Untidy woman.
4. Quack medicines.
5. Wharton's 1905 bestselling novel of wealthy New York socialites.

either a great novel or a true one, and which lacked also not a little of being a really convincing drama, in spite of the element of truth and the wide popular appeal which has caused it to stand forth in the public mind as Mrs. Wharton's most conspicuous achievement, has accomplished in this story something very much finer and stronger. There is in it much of the keen concentrated effectiveness which the author has more than once obtained in her short stories. If *Ethan Frome* is not a great novel—it is, indeed, hardly long enough to be called a novel at all, though it far oversteps short-story limits—it is, at least, an impressive tragedy.

There are writers who are both great novelists and great dramatists; that is, who reflect life with singular completeness and faithfulness at the same time that they give the overpowering impression of a shaping and designing destiny governing the fortunes of their leading personages and driving to an inevitable conclusion. Such a novelist, for instance, was George Meredith,[6] from whom the modern makers of fiction borrow so much consciously and unconsciously. There are writers, again, who are merely novelists—who send their creatures to school, to life, not without smiles and tears and pangs to see them suffer. Such a novelist was Thackeray.[7] And there are dramatists who do not write for the theatre and so pass as novelists. It seems to this reviewer that Mrs. Wharton belongs properly to the last classification and that *Ethan Frome* is the proof of it.

OUTLOOK

["Artistic Workmanship"] †

* * *[T]he somber repression of mirth, the denial of normal human instincts, and the monotonous tone of gray . . . pervade Mrs. Wharton's short long story *Ethan Frome*. The background is an old, dilapidated farm-house framed by a bleak New England landscape, and the tragedy gains a penetrating pathos from the bareness of its surroundings and the sense of futility which issues from it; the incidents would be a mere group of fortuitous happenings, so insignificant that they would lack the dignity of a malicious fate, if it were not for the touch of patient loyalty with which Ethan Frome bears its dreary burden at the end. As a piece of artistic workmanship it would be hard to overstate the quality of this story; it is conceived and executed with a unity of insight, structural

6. English novelist (1828–1909) who fought sentimental excesses.
7. William Makepeace Thackeray (1811–1863), best known for the social satire of his famous novel *Vanity Fair*.
† From *Outlook* 99 (21 October 1911): 405.

skill, and feeling for style which lies only within the reach of an artist who, like Guy de Maupassant,[1] knows every resource of the art. It is to be hoped that when Mrs. Wharton writes again she will bring her great talent to bear on normal people and situations.

THE NATION

["As One Writes of Home"] †

More than ten years ago Mrs. Wharton published a short story called "The Duchess at Prayer."[1] Since that time we have cherished an estimate of her powers which no intermediate accession to her repertory has raised, nor even, to speak truth, quite justified. Practised, cosmopolitan, subtle, she has seemed, on the whole, to covet most earnestly the refinements of Henry James.[2] In spite of her habit of a franker approach, her consistent rating of matter above manner, and the gravitation—we should hesitate to say transfer—of her interest from exotic to native themes; we might have been reasonably content to rank her as the greatest pupil of a little master, were it not for the appearance of *Ethan Frome*. This startling fulfillment recalls not only the promise of the early story, but its revelation of a more potent influence—the inspiriting example of a greater novelist to whom Mr. James's *devoirs* have been paid in the phrase, "The master of us all."[3] Exactly how much the inception and execution of "The Duchess at Prayer" owed to Balzac's "La grande Bretèche"[4] is beyond our present point, which is, specifically, that the excellence of Mrs. Wharton's work in this case outstripped the charge of imitation, and allied her with that company of splendid talents whom neither magnificence nor the catastrophes of passion can abash.

There is certainly no imitative strain in *Ethan Frome*. The style is assured and entirely individual, the method direct and firm in its grasp upon substantial fact. Yet here is the companion-piece to the "Duchess," a variation upon the same theme of triumphant malice and tor-

1. (1850–1893). French short-story writer and novelist noted for realism of detail and attention to style.
† From *The Nation* 93 (26 October 1911): 396–7. This article is reprinted from *The Nation* magazine.© The Nation Company, Inc.
1. Wharton's early medieval romantic short story published in *Scribner's* in 1900, in which the Duchess's lover is buried alive by her husband underneath a heavy statue.
2. American expatriate writer (1843–1916), friend of Wharton, and highly influential in her early work in terms of psychological realism and international theme. James was often reproached for an overly analytical, obscure, mannered style.
3. James meant French novelist Honoré de Balzac (1799–1850), considered the founder of literary realism.
4. Balzac's short story of an illicit love affair which employs a double narrator.

tured love, evoking the same emotions. And here as there the genius of a place presides, and the scene and the hour conspire to meet the racial temper.[5] But there is this great difference: in the place of sumptuous memories, decaying under the sultry oppression of Italian noon, she was, at heart, a stranger; whereas she writes now of New England as one writes of home, plainly, and with a wealth of understanding and familiar allusion. Even the arrangement of the narrative is designed to fit the life described and its probabilities rather than to satisfy any precious scruples. A winterbound stranger in an out-of-the-way Massachusetts hamlet recognizes in the limping figure of Ethan Frome the "ruin of a man," and apprehends some singular misfortunes behind his obvious plight. The sparse comment of a community respectful of privacies and little indulgent of curiosity yields but scanty information. Out of the native's penury come at length hours of enforced companionship, the daily rides to the station during which "Frome drove in silence, the reins loosely held in his left hand, his brown, seamed profile, under the helmet-like peak of the cap, relieved against the banks of snow."

"It was that night," explains the visitor, "that I found the clue to Ethan Frome, and began to put together this vision of his story." Such an approach could not be improved, forbearing, as it does, to violate the seal of silence; nor could, we think, the conclusion of village confidences be spared, with its ultimate breaking down of reserve between the initiated, its natural cadence of secret curiosity, and its softening echo of unavailing human sympathy.

Surely, the melancholy spirit that haunts the remoter byways of rural New England has entered into this chronicle; over all its scenes breathe the benumbing and isolating rigors of her winters, a sense of invisible fetters, a consciousness of depleted resources, a reticence and self-contained endurance that even the houses know how to express, retired from the public way, or turned sideways to preserve a secluded entrance. Yet it is with a softly-breathed strain of native romance that the drama opens. As well try to transplant arbutus from its native habitat as to dissociate this exquisite burgeoning of passion from its homely circumstances and the inflexible trammels[6] of a local speech meant for taciturnity rather than expression. Thriving on meagre opportunities and pleasures—the coasting, the picnic, the walk home from the "church sociable"—and on the sharing of frugal household cares, the love between the young farmer and the little dependent who inefficiently "helped" in his home, spread like a secret flowering too innocent and too fragrant to escape the wife's malicious eye. The brave and fragile figure of Mattie Silver is not an idealized one, although this is the type

5. Italian temper, as *Ethan Frome* meets the New England.
6. Impediments or hindrances.

of New England girlhood whose modesty and touch of fairy grace have been the subject of much poetry.

The wife who stands for fate in this drama is a curious and repugnant figure. She introduces the same vein of close-mouthed malignity which darkens local history. The helpless fear and loathing she inspires in her husband is the essence of supernatural terror without its obsolete husk of ignorance. By showing this instance of a hypochondriac roused by jealousy out of a "sullen self-absorption" and transformed into a mysterious alien presence, an evil energy secreted from the long years of silent brooding, Mrs. Wharton touches on a very radical identity. We realize that the same gloating satisfaction that made the wife smile upon the parting lovers, had something to do with her capabilities as a nurse. Her pleasure at the sight of pain she had inflicted—was it, perchance, from such an evil spring that her strength was drawn for the long years of drudgery between two cripples?

No hero of fantastic legend was ever more literally hag-ridden than was Ethan Frome. The profound irony of his case is that it required his own goodness to complete her parasitic power over him. Without his innate honesty and his sense of duty he could have escaped her demands and her decrees, refused the money for her nostrums[7] and "doctor books," followed the vision of a new free life "out West." In his submission to obligation and in his thwarted intellectual aspirations he typifies the remnant of an exceptional race whose spiritual inheritance has dwindled amid hard conditions until all distinction is forfeited except that of suffering; but which still indicates its quality, if only by its capacity for suffering.

The wonder is that the spectacle of so much pain can be made to yield so much beauty. And here the full range of Mrs. Wharton's imagination becomes apparent. There is possible, within the gamut of human experience, an exaltation of anguish which makes a solitude for itself, whose direct contemplation seals the impulse of speech and strikes cold upon the heart. Yet sometimes in reflection there is revealed, beneath the wringing torment, the lineaments of a wronged and distorted loveliness. It is the piteous and intolerable conception which the Greeks expressed in the medusa head[8] that Mrs. Wharton has dared to hold up to us anew, but the face she shows us is the face of our own people.

---

7. Quack medicines.
8. In Greek mythology, the angry goddess Athena turned Medusa's hair into serpents and made her face so horrible it turned beholders to stone.

THE *HARTFORD DAILY COURANT*

["Not a Study of Life or Character or Locality"] †

* * *

There is an artistic subtlety in the way Mrs. Wharton tells how she got the story of the isolated Fromes.

Mrs. Hale's "finer sensibility and a little more education" had enabled her to "judge with detachment" her neighbors in Starkfield. After all, it was not she, but Ethan himself in an hour of detachment who told the gruesome story to Mrs. Hale's lodger, Mrs. Hale furnishing the atmosphere or background—which Mrs. Wharton does not transcribe very well—in a "delicately shaded version of the Starkfield chronicle." In fact so far from this being a typical New England story it might have happened (although it probably did not happen) anywhere—"even in a community rich in pathological instances." It is not within the bounds of belief or sympathy, even in a novel, that a fairly well-to-do small farmer, of a cold and reserved nature, such as was Ethan Frome's until his "accident," should have manifested sentimentality for the cousin and help of his sickly or hypochondriac wife by "neglecting the mill that he might help her about the house and scrub the kitchen floor," or plan with her clumsy (and ineffectual) double suicide because the wife sent the girl away. The novel in spite of much admirable phrasing is not a study of life or character or locality. It is an unflinching tragedy of banalities, dyspepsia and spinal injury—purely physical.

SATURDAY REVIEW

["Things Too Terrible . . . To Be Told"] †

* * *

Almost we are afraid to say that *Ethan Frome* is not a novel; for Mr. Wells is at this moment insisting that such criticism is as foolish as Mr. Trotter's contention that a dramatic exercise by Mr. Shaw is not a play.[1] It is a novel in that it unfolds completely to our view the lives of its few people; but it is a short story in that the mood is throughout the same; and that the interest is from first to last fastened upon the one terrible incident of the story's climax. Also it is a short story because the story is

---

† From the *Hartford Daily Courant* (30 October 1911): 17.
† From *Saturday Review* [England] 112 (18 November 1911): 650.
1. Refers to critical arguments about form, one critic protesting that the unconventional Irish dramatist George Bernard Shaw (1856–1950), who experimented with dramatic form and incorporated many of his social and political ideas into his drama, was not writing plays.

short—it can be read easily at a sitting. For many reasons it is worth reading. The writing is singularly beautiful. It has passed through flame of the author's imagination. Yet, having read the story, we wish we had not read it. The error is in the end. There are things too terrible in their failure to be told humanly by creature to creature. Ethan Frome driving down with the girl he loved to death—here there is beauty and a defiance of the misery of circumstance which may sadden, but uplift, the reader. But these lovers could not die. They must live horribly on, mutilated and losing even the nobility of their passion in the wreck of their bodies. Had Mrs. Wharton allowed her creatures to die as they intended *Ethan Frome* would be high indeed among our shorter tales—high as [George Meredith's] *The Tale of Chloë.*[2] She has marred her work with no motive we can discover. With Mrs. Wharton it could not have been the mere craving for the exaggerated terror which in art must always defeat itself. The end of Ethan Frome is something at which we cover the eyes. We do not cover the eyes at the spectacle of a really great tragedy.

FREDERIC TABER COOPER

["Art for Art's Sake"] †

It is hard to forgive Mrs. Wharton for the utter remorselessness of her latest volume, *Ethan Frome,* for nowhere has she done anything more hopelessly, endlessly grey with blank despair. Ethan Frome is a man whose ambitions long ago burned themselves out. He early spent his vitality in the daily struggle of winning a bare sustenance from the grudging soil of a small New England farm. An invalid wife, whose imaginary ailments thrived on patent medicines, doubled his burden. And then, one day, a pretty young cousin, left destitute, came to live on the farm, and brought a breath of fragrance and gladness into the gloom. Neither Ethan nor the cousin meant to do wrong; it was simply one of those unconscious, inevitable attachments, almost primitive in its intensity. It never was even put into words, until the day when Ethan's wife, perhaps because of a smouldering jealousy, perhaps because the motive she gave was the true one, namely that the girl was shiftless and incompetent, sent her out into the world to shift for herself. It is while driving her over to the railway station that Ethan consents to the girl's wish that just once more he will take her coasting down a long hill that is a favourite coasting place throughout the neighbourhood. It is a long, steep, breathless rush, with a giant tree towering up near the foot, to be

2. George Meredith (1828–1909), English novelist and poet.
† From the *Bookman* 34 (November 1911): 312.

dexterously avoided at the last moment. It is while he holds the girl close to him on the sled, that a ghastly temptation comes to Ethan and he voices it: How much easier, instead of letting her go away, to face unknown struggles, while he remained behind, eating his heart out with loneliness—how much easier merely to forget to steer! One shock of impact, and the end would come. And to this the girl consents. And neither of them foresees that not even the most carefully planned death is inevitable, and that fate is about to play upon them one of its grimmest tricks, and doom them to a lifelong punishment, she with a broken back, he with a warped and twisted frame, tied beyond escape to the slow starvation of the barren farm, and grudgingly watched over by the invalid wife, scarcely more alive than themselves. Art for art's sake is the one justification of a piece of work as perfect in technique as it is relentless in substance.

BOOKMAN (LONDON)

["Inevitability of a Great Greek Tragedy"] †

Mrs. Wharton has more than satisfied one's expectation, and her art has never been shown to greater advantage than in this story of Ethan Frome, the young Massachusetts farmer. It is a tragedy, almost unendurably poignant, but justified by its inevitableness. From his youth Fate dealt hardly with Ethan. His father died, leaving him a bleak unproductive farm, and a failing saw-mill. After a lingering illness, his mother also died. That was in the Fall; had it been in the Spring his future might have been different, but Ethan dared not face the winter alone in this "New England farmhouse that made the landscape lonelier." Then he took his first step toward the abyss: he asked Zeena, the tall, uncomely, raw-boned woman who had nursed his mother, to be his wife. From that time his life was a martyrdom, for Zeena soon showed her real character as a sickly, querulous neurotic. Then came the next stroke of Destiny. To save expense, for the poverty at the farm was grinding, Mattie Silver, the penniless young cousin of Zeena, was invited to live with them. As the girl served without pay her cousin suggested that on the rare occasions, when there was an entertainment in the village, Mattie should go to it, so that she should not feel too sharp a contrast between the life she had left and the isolation of the farm. On these occasions, Ethan, although at first he had inwardly demurred at the extra toil imposed on him, was accustomed to fetch home his wife's cousin. Soon he found himself wishing that the village

† From the *Bookman* (London) 41 (January 1912): 216.

might give all its nights to revelry. Gradually the wife's suspicions are aroused; a hired girl is employed, and Mattie must go. Poverty makes Ethan helpless; money might have saved two lives, if not three, but there is none. So the blow falls in the last act that is to consign the three to a living death. It is a beautiful, sad, but intensely human story, working out to its final conclusion with all the inevitability of a great Greek tragedy. [1]

ELIZABETH SHEPLEY SERGEANT

Idealized New England †

"What a terrible book," I said, "what a supremely cruel book!"

"A tragic masterpiece," she contradicted, "a landmark in American literature. Against that iron New England background Mrs. Wharton's few figures have an almost Euripidean quality." [1]

"But the Greeks never made their audiences writhe," I protested. "Could you write choruses to 'Ethan Frome,' melodious choruses to be chanted by tranquil, veiled women and offering some alleviation to the bitter lot of man? [2] No," I went on with heat, "you'll find only jibbering fiends to break Ethan's agony. The story is a fine example of what hate can accomplish as creative inspiration; and of the difference between observation and understanding."

"Come now," she said, "that sounds like local prejudice. You should be sufficiently disaffected by New York and Europe to perceive the depleted side of your native states." [3]

"Have I not seen the industrious Swede and the inscrutable Finn absorbing the land cleared by my ancestors' vitality?"

"Well then! And you care so much for the French classic manner [4]— how can you fail to appreciate the rapidity, the suppressions, the sharp yet delicate shadings of this poignant New England drama?"

"Ah, but that's just why the book wounds me so. My acquired literary sense, which Mrs. Wharton pricks to admiration on every page, here conflicts with something far more real and subconscious—the knowledge I was born with of the kind of people, the kind of place, yes and

---

1. Contemporary critics often mentioned the fatality of *Ethan Frome*, comparing it to Greek tragedy.
† Reprinted with permission from *New Republic* 3 (8 May 1915): 20–21.
1. Euripides (480?–406? B.C.), Greek tragic playwright.
2. In Greek drama, the chorus was a body of actors who commented on the action, often representing society and placing the tragic action into a larger perspective.
3. Born in Massachusetts, Sergeant was for many years a resident of Paris and published *French Perspectives* in 1916.
4. As above, refers to Sergeant's knowledge of the French, and, obliquely, to Wharton's residence in France also.

the kind of drama of weakened will she is so relentlessly describing. And I tell you that in spite of the *vraisemblance*[5] of the surface, she has got them all wrong. She has nowhere dug down into the subsoil."

"You don't mind quarreling with the authorities," she remarked. "Of course you read Mr. Herrick on Mrs. Wharton in THE NEW REPUBLIC?"[6]

"Yes, it was precisely that article which sent me back to the sources. No doubt Mrs. Wharton is more psychologist than social historian; no doubt, as he said, her real interest is in the subtler and more universal sort of spiritual conflicts. But I can't admit that the conflict between love and duty in 'Ethan Frome' is less conditioned by special environment, than, for example, Lily Bart's struggle."[7]

"You will grant that men tied to wives older than themselves, ill, ugly and querulous, are doomed in every quarter of the globe to fall in love with girls like blackberries who put red ribbons in their hair."

"Certainly. But Ethan and his wife Zeena, and her young cousin, Mattie Silver, are not generalized types. Would Mr. Herrick accept them as they stand, for Ohio or Illinois? They are New England country people of old stock living in a lonely snowed-in hill town in the Berkshires. Mrs. Wharton's deliberate purpose is to show what life in Starkfield really means to a man who has been there too many winters; to show the grim New England skeleton that the summer resident usually fails to discover during his pleasant months in the elm shaded village—unless he happens upon a degenerate chore-boy, or sees a poor little girl in short skirts carrying her shame to school under a cape."

"True, and the New England writers have largely ignored the skeleton. The 'idyll' has been done to death, like the conscience. I commend Mrs. Wharton for finding a new subject in an overworked field."

"So do I, but if 'Ethan Frome' is a New England tale in the same sense as Miss Brown's or Mrs. Freeman's stories or 'The Country of the Pointed Firs'—and this is just the point I am venturing to make against Mr. Herrick—then surely one is justified in asking, as he does about the New York novels, whether the author has been fair to her subject.[8] Do Zeena's false teeth click true, do Ethan and Mattie make love in Starkfield fashion, would they have taken the fatal coast that brought about the intolerable horror of their lives?"

"Ugh," said my friend, "those false teeth—what a sure realistic note!

---

5. "Realism."
6. Refers to Robert Herrick's essay, "Mrs. Wharton's World," 13 February 1915, pp. 40–42, in which he praises *Ethan Frome* above her satires of society and her sociological novel, *The Fruit of the Tree*, because he finds in *Ethan Frome* the "spiritual interest" and universality, lacking or deemphasized in the others.
7. Lily Bart is the doomed heroine of Wharton's 1905 bestseller of life in society, *The House of Mirth*.
8. Alice Brown (1857–1948) and Mary Wilkins Freeman, 1852–1930, were both known for vivid portraits of rural New England life. *The Country of the Pointed Firs* (1896), Sarah Orne Jewett (1849–1909), also depicts rural New England.

I can never forget the glass by the bed, into which the wife dropped them when she blew out the candle at night in the terrible gray, cold room."

"Of course you can't. Neither could Mrs. Wharton. You both look at Starkfield with the eyes of the sophisticated stranger who arrives there in a blizzard, and stumbles through the drifts into Ethan's run-down 'place.' You notice the superficial things that would make you miserable. Ethan suffered in all sorts of ways, but not from false teeth: he was brought up on them! His mother had them; his cousins and neighbors had them; he probably admired Mattie less because she hadn't 'had her molars out'!"

"Well, I waive the teeth," said she with a shudder. "Let's take the coasting parties and the church sociable. Surely Mrs. Wharton has those in key?"

"In the unconsciously contemptuous key of the person who has a box at the opera. How should cosmopolitans understand what such diversions mean to Starkfield folks? They have all sorts of consolations if you only knew. Even when winter breaks and the teams sink up to their axles in mud, they have things to live for and look for—pussy-willows, for instance. Laugh if you like! Do you remember 'Miss Tempy's Watchers'[9] and the one thorny quince tree she 'kind of expected into bloomin' ' every spring?"

"You mean that because of its very repressions, its very barrenness, and physical deprivations, New England life still produces a sort of flower—"

"Pale as snowdrops, hidden in dead leaves like hepaticas and arbutus; yet precious to those who know where to look for it. That is the sort of flower Ethan's and Mattie's love was, but they could never have expressed it to each other."

"Mrs. Wharton lets them express it so little," she objected.

"Ah, but a word, a touch would have spoiled it for them. I think Ethan, dim and weakened descendant of rugged forefathers that he was, would have had the spirit to drive his Mattie to the station when his wife sent her packing. But he would not have dreamed of stopping for that preposterous coast for death. It was just Mrs. Wharton's own sense of the blankness and emptiness, the lack of beauty and passion in Starkfield lives, that made her construct that tremendous fourth act for her lovers and condemn them to its gruesome, long-drawn epilogue."

"You think they would have driven on silently to the station and parted with a dumb handshake and a look?"

"Sustained by something they did not understand, something they half rebelled against and yet could not possibly foreswear."

"Then Ethan's real tragedy would have been that he had nothing real, tangible, to cling to—only an idea, a feeling, a dream to carry him

9. Sarah Orne Jewett's short story set in a small New Hampshire town.

through those slow gray years when Zeena continued to flourish on patent medicines?"

"Exactly. The real New England tragedy, as Mrs. Wharton herself realized at bottom, is not that something happens but that nothing does. Yet if Ethan was tender to Zeena instead of strangling her complaining voice in her lanky throat, it was because when he was out alone in the pasture lot and heard the hermit thrush singing in the pines he knew he had been right. The image of his girl was warm in his heart then and undefiled, like Martha's memory of her 'lady.' "[1]

"Miss Jewett again! It isn't fair. She had a natural love of light and sun, an aversion to the shadow and cruelty and ugliness of life which Mrs. Wharton has the courage to face and to probe."

"Is that the essential point of difference? I don't think so. There are chapters in Miss Jewett's works—in 'Deephaven' for example—and passages in her letters which show her full knowledge of the shadow even though she did not often linger there. For that matter, almost any of her stories if told from outside in rather than from inside out might be sordid and grim. That's the bearing of our whole argument, isn't it? Take the 'The Queen's Twin.'[2] What was she? To most people a poor, cracked old creature, the victim of a silly delusion. It needed the feeling heart of Mrs. Todd to realize that she was, in fact as in fancy, the sister soul of royalty, a woman with a shining destiny."

"You evidently think the only creative truth is that perceived by love. I believe any strong passion is worth recording."

"Possibly. Indifference could not have written 'Ethan Frome.' But if Mrs. Wharton had realized Ethan as Miss Jewett did the Queen's Twin, as she herself loved and understood her most significant creation, Lily Bart, we should get some shock of those deep-down unwritable things which are the vital parts of novels as they are of human beings. We should get life, not a literary copy of it."

"It's no use," said my friend, "to argue on her own soil with the descendant of a band of hopeless idealists who see the hardest facts in a sort of Platonic glow.[3] I am afraid I must still read and admire 'Ethan Frome.' "

"Wait till you are old. That is a New England counsel, but just wait! Then the 'Queen's Twin,' and the 'Dunnet Shepherdess'[4] will still be full of living human poetry and truth and the salt-sweet scent of high coast pastures, and 'Ethan Frome' will be rotting in his grave."

1. "Martha's Lady," a short story by Sarah Orne Jewett of a servant's memory of a beloved mistress over a lifetime.
2. Sarah Orne Jewett short story.
3. Plato (427?–347 B.C.), Greek philosopher, sought unity behind the changing impressions of material reality; thus a Platonic glow involves the concept of a realm of pure ideas.
4. Another Jewett story of New England.

Modern Criticism

LIONEL TRILLING

The Morality of Inertia †

* * *

We can never speak of Edith Wharton without some degree of respect. She brought to her novels a strong if limited intelligence, notable powers of observation, and a genuine desire to tell the truth—a desire which in some part she satisfied. But she was a woman in whom we cannot fail to see a limitation of heart, and this limitation makes itself manifest as a literary and moral deficiency of her work, and of *Ethan Frome* especially. It appears in the deadness of her prose, and more flagrantly in the suffering of her characters. Whenever the characters of a story suffer, they do so at the behest of their author—the author is responsible for their suffering and must justify his cruelty by the seriousness of his moral intention. The author of *Ethan Frome*, it seemed to me as I read the book again to test my memory of it, could not lay claim to any such justification. Her intention in writing the story was not adequate to the dreadful fate she contrived for her characters. She indulges herself by what she contrives—she is, as the phrase goes, "merely literary." This is not to say that the merely literary intention does not make its very considerable effects. There is in *Ethan Frome* an image of life-in-death, of hell-on-earth, which is not easily forgotten: the crippled Ethan, and Zeena, his dreadful wife, and Mattie, the once charming girl he had loved, now bedridden and querulous with pain, all living out their death in the kitchen of the desolate Frome farm—a perpetuity of suffering memorializes a moment of passion. It is terrible to contemplate, it is unforgettable, but the mind can do nothing with it, can only endure it. * * *In the context of morality, there is nothing to say about *Ethan Frome*. It presents no moral issue at all.

* * *

† Excerpts from "The Morality of Inertia" in A *Gathering of Fugitives*, copyright © 1956 by Lionel Trilling and renewed 1984 by Diana Trilling, reprinted by permission of Harcourt Brace & Company.

Edith Wharton was following where others led. Her impulse in conceiving the story of Ethan Frome was not, however, that of moral experimentation. It was, as I have said, a purely literary impulse, in the bad sense of the word "literary." Her aim is not that of Wordsworth in any of his stories of the suffering poor,[1] to require of us that we open our minds to a realization of the kinds of people whom suffering touches. Nor is it that of Flaubert in *Madame Bovary*,[2] to wring from solid circumstances all the pity and terror of an ancient tragic fable. Nor is it that of Dickens or Zola,[3] to shake us with the perception of social injustice, to instruct us in the true nature of social life and to dispose us to indignant opinion and action. These are not essentially literary intentions; they are moral intentions. But all that Edith Wharton has in mind is to achieve that grim tableau of which I have spoken, of pain and imprisonment, of life-in-death. About the events that lead up to this tableau, there is nothing she finds to say, nothing whatever. The best we can conclude of the meaning of her story is that it might perhaps be a subject of discourse in the context of rural sociology—it might be understood to exemplify the thesis that love and joy do not flourish on poverty-stricken New England farms. If we try to bring it into the context of morality, its meaning goes no further than certain cultural considerations—that is, to people who like their literature to show the "smiling aspects of life," it may be thought to say, "This is the aspect that life really has, as grim as this"; while to people who repudiate a literature that represents only the smiling aspects of life it says, "How intelligent and how brave you are to be able to understand that life is as grim as this." It is really not very much to say.

And yet there is in *Ethan Frome* an idea of considerable importance. It is there by reason of the author's deficiencies, not by reason of her powers—because it suits Edith Wharton's rather dull intention to be content with telling a story about people who do not make moral decisions, whose fate cannot have moral reverberations. The idea is this: that moral inertia, the *not* making of moral decisions, constitutes a large part of the moral life of humanity.

This isn't an idea that literature likes to deal with. Literature is charmed by energy and dislikes inertia. It characteristically represents morality as positive action. The same is true of the moral philosophy of the West—has been true ever since Aristotle[4] defined a truly moral act by its energy of reason, of choice. A later development of this tendency said that an act was really moral only if it went against the inclination

---

1. William Wordsworth (1770–1850), English romantic poet who idealized the primitive life for its simplicity and innocence [Editor].
2. Gustave Flaubert's *Madame Bovary* (1856) is a meticulously detailed tragedy of an ordinary but highly romantic woman who commits adultery and then suicide [Editor].
3. Both English novelist Charles Dickens (1812–1870) and French novelist Émile Zola (1840–1902) wrote to expose social injustice [Editor].
4. Greek philosopher (384–322 B.C.) [Editor].

of the person performing the act: the idea was parodied as saying that one could not possibly act morally to one's friends, only to one's enemies.

Yet the dull daily world sees something below this delightful preoccupation of literature and moral philosophy. It is aware of the morality of inertia, and of its function as a social base, as a social cement. It knows that duties are done for no other reason than that they are said to be duties; for no other reason, sometimes, than that the doer has not really been able to conceive of any other course—has, perhaps, been afraid to think of any other course. Hobbes said of the Capitol geese that saved Rome by their cackling that they were the salvation of the city, not because they were they but there.[5] How often the moral act is performed not because we are we but because we are there! This is the morality of habit, or the morality of biology. This is Ethan Frome's morality, simple, unquestioning, passive, even masochistic. His duties as a son are discharged because he is a son; his duties as a husband are discharged because he is a husband. He does nothing by moral election. At one point in his story he is brought to moral crisis—he must choose between his habituated duty to his wife and his duty and inclination to the girl he loves. It is quite impossible for him to deal with the dilemma in the high way that literature and moral philosophy prescribe, by reason and choice. Choice is incompatible with his idea of his existence; he can only elect to die.

Literature, of course, is not wholly indifferent to what I have called the morality of habit and biology, the morality of inertia. But literature, when it deals with this morality, is tempted to qualify its dullness by endowing it with a certain high grace. There is never any real moral choice for the Félicité of Flaubert's story "A Simple Heart."[6] She is all pious habit of virtue, and of blind, unthinking, unquestioning love. There are, of course, such people as Félicité, simple, good, loving— quite stupid in their love, not choosing where to bestow it. We meet such people frequently in literature, in the pages of Balzac, Dickens, Dostoevsky, Joyce, Faulkner, Hemingway. They are of a quite different order of being from those who try the world with their passion and their reason; they are by way of being saints, of the less complicated kind. They do not really exemplify what I mean by the morality of inertia. Literature is uncomfortable in the representation of the morality of inertia or of biology, and overcomes its discomfort by representing it with the added grace of that extravagance which we denominate saintliness.

But the morality of inertia is to be found in very precise exemplifica-

---

5. Thomas Hobbes (1588–1679), English philosopher, called the father of materialism for his theory that all events, even of the mind, can be reduced to some species of physical motion [Editor].
6. French writer Gustave Flaubert's short story of a servant girl known for her faith and endless self-denial [Editor].

tion in one of Wordsworth's poems. Wordsworth is preeminent among the writers who experimented in the representation of new kinds and bases of moral action—he has a genius for imputing moral existence to people who, according to the classical morality, should have no moral life at all. And he has the courage to make this imputation without at the same time imputing the special grace and interest of saintliness. The poem I have in mind is ostensibly about a flower, but the transition from the symbol to the human fact is clearly, if awkwardly, made. The flower is a small celandine, and the poet observes that it has not, in the natural way of flowers, folded itself against rough weather:

> But lately, one rough day, this Flower I passed
> And recognized it, though in altered form,
> Now standing as an offering to the blast,
> And buffeted at will by rain and storm.

> I stopped, and said with inly-muttered voice,
> It doth not love the shower nor seek the cold;
> This neither is its courage nor its choice,
> But its necessity in being old.

Neither courage nor choice, but necessity: it cannot do otherwise. Yet it acts as if by courage and choice. This is the morality imposed by brute circumstance, by biology, by habit, by the unspoken social demand which we have not the strength to refuse, or, often, to imagine refusing. People are scarcely ever praised for living according to this morality—we do not suppose it to be a morality at all until we see it being broken.

This is morality as it is conceived by the great mass of people in the world. And with this conception of morality goes the almost entire nega-tion of any connection between morality and destiny. A superstitious belief in retribution may play its part in the thought of simple people, but essentially they think of catastrophes as fortuitous, without explana-tion, without reason. They live in the moral universe of the Book of Job.[7] In complex lives, morality does in some part determine destiny; in most lives it does not. Between the moral life of Ethan and Mattie and their terrible fate we cannot make any reasonable connection. Only a moral judgment cruel to the point of insanity could speak of it as any-thing but accidental.

* * *

---

7. In the Old Testament, Job suffers great losses and physical pain because of a wager between God and the Devil. Thus, his story has always raised the question: Why do men suffer without purpose? [Editor].

CYNTHIA GRIFFIN WOLFF

[The Narrator's Vision] †

* * *Ethan Frome is about its narrator.
The novel begins with him, begins insistently and obtrusively.

> I had the story, bit by bit, from various people, and, as generally happens in such cases, each time it was a different story.
> If you know Starkfield, Massachusetts, you know the post-office. If you know the post-office you must have seen Ethan Frome drive up to it, drop the reins on his hollow-backed bay and drag himself across the brick pavement to the white colonnade; and you must have asked who he was.
> It was there that, several years ago, I saw him for the first time; and the sight pulled me up sharp.

We must ask why Wharton would begin thus, assaulting us with the narrator's presence in the very first word. It is a decidedly unusual way to open a fiction. Only two like it come readily to mind: *Wuthering Heights* and "Bartleby the Scrivener." Wharton has informed us that she was consciously indebted to Brontë's work when she wrote *Ethan Frome*;[1] and her preoccupation at the time with the techniques of Hawthorne suggests that she may have had Melville's tale in mind as well. What does all of this suggest? First of all, an extraordinarily literary self-consciousness. Second, a focus on the narrator (for however intricate Brontë's story is, however compelling Melville's vision, it is the *narrator's reaction* that must be deemed the ultimate "subject" in both fictions).

Bearing this fact in mind, let us rush momentarily ahead—to that point in the novel where the "real subject" is generally assumed to begin. An astounding discovery awaits us: the man whom we come to know as the young Ethan Frome is *no more than a figment of the narrator's imagination*. Wharton's method of exposition leaves no doubt. We are not permitted to believe that the narrator is recounting a history of something that actually happened; we are not given leave to speculate that he is passing along a confidence obtained in the dark intimacy of a cold winter's night. No: the "story" of Ethan Frome is introduced in unmistakable terms. "It was that night that I found the clue to Ethan Frome, and began *to put together this vision* of his story . . ." (emphasis mine). Our narrator is a teller of terrible tales, a seer into the realms of demen-

---

† From Cynthia Griffin Wolff, *A Feast of Words: The Triumph of Edith Wharton*, © 1994 by Cynthia Griffin Wolff. Reprinted by permission of Addison-Wesley Publishing Company, Inc.
1. *Wuthering Heights*, Emily Brontë's novel of the Yorkshire moors; "Bartleby the Scrivener," short story of Wall Street by Herman Melville. See Wharton's reference to Emily Brontë in *A Backward Glance*, p. 79 [*Editor*].

tia. The "story" of Ethan Frome is nothing more than a dream vision, a brief glimpse into the most appalling recesses of the narrator's mind. The overriding question becomes then—not who is Ethan Frome, but who in the world is this ghastly guide to whom we must submit as we read the tale.

The structure demands that we take him into account. Certainly *he* demands it. It is *his* story, ultimately his "vision" of Ethan Frome, that we will get. His vision is as good as any other (so he glibly assures us at the beginning—for "each time it was a different story"), and therefore his story has as much claim to truth as any other. And yet, he is a nervous fellow. The speech pattern is totally unlike Wharton's own narrative style—short sentences, jagged prose rhythms, absolutely no sense of ironic control over the language, no distance from it. Yes, the fellow is nervous. He seems anxious about our reaction and excessively eager to reassure us that had *we* been situated as *he* was, catching a first horrified glimpse of Ethan Frome, we "must have asked who he was." Anyone would. Frome is no mere bit of local color. He is, for reasons that we do not yet understand, a force that compels examination; "the sight pulled me up sharp." (It would pull all of you up sharp, and all of you would have done as I did.)

Certain elements in Wharton's story are to be taken as "real" within the fictional context: Ethan Frome is badly crippled; he sustained his injuries in a sledding accident some twenty-four years ago; he has been in Starkfield for most of his life, excepting a short visit to Florida, living first with his parents and then with his querulous, sickly wife Zeena; there is a third member of the household, his wife's cousin, Miss Mattie Silver; she too was badly crippled in the same sledding accident that felled Ethan. To these facts the various members of the town will all attest—and to *nothing more*. Everything that the reader can accept as reliably true can be found in the narrative frame; everything else bears the imprint of the narrator's own interpretation—as indeed even the selection of events chronicled in the frame does—and while that interpretation *might* be as true as any other, we dare not accept it as having the same validity as the bare outline presented above. Even at the end of the narrator's vision, in the concluding scene with Mrs. Hale, Wharton is scrupulously careful not to credit the vision by giving it independent confirmation.[2]

2. Critics of *Ethan Frome* have consistently missed the point of its structure, even though Wharton went to considerable lengths to call this feature of the novel to the public's attention. John Crowe Ransom's remarks are typical of the dissatisfaction with Wharton's "clumsy" method. "We are allowed to anticipate the reporter who is gathering the story, and then we go back and see him make slight detective motions at gathering it; but we are forced to conclude that he did not gather it really; that, mostly, he made it up. Why a special reporter at all? And why such a peculiar chronological method? These are features which picture to me, if it is not impertinent, the perturbation of an author wrestling with an unaccustomed undertaking, uneasy of conscience, and resorting to measures. Forgetting the Preface, and the exterior or developing story, we attend strictly to Ethan's story . . ." See "Characters and Character: A

At this point the narrator himself is still probing. He has now spent a long winter's night in the Frome household, where no one outside the family has set foot for many years, and he is an object of some interest. He responds to that interest by attempting to use it to gain information. "Beneath their wondering exclamations I felt a secret curiosity to know what impressions I had received from my night in the Frome household, and divined that the best way of breaking down their reserve was to let them try to penetrate mine. I therefore confined myself to saying, in a matter-of-fact tone, that I had been received with great kindness, and that Frome had made a bed for me in a room on the ground-floor which seemed in happier days to have been fitted up as a kind of writing-room or study." Despite this tactic, the narrator elicits nothing that he has not already known. Mrs. Hale agrees that " 'it was just awful from the beginning. . . . It's a pity . . . that they're all shut up there'n that one kitchen.' " And these fervent platitudes fall so far short of assuring the narrator that he has touched upon the truth that even as they come tumbling inconsequently from her lips, he withdraws into himself. "Mrs. Hale paused a moment, and I remained silent, plunged in the vision of what her words evoked." Her words, vague generalities—driving the narrator back into his own "vision."

If we return now to the opening of the story, we must remind ourselves that the status of the narrator is doubly significant: we are surely meant to credit the information that is given to us in the frame as "true" (and the contrast between the validity of the contents of the frame and the unreliability of the contents of the internal story is clearly signaled by the recurrence of that key word, vision); however, since it, too, is reported by the narrator who has thrust himself before us in the first word of the first sentence, we must recognize that it is biased information and that evaluations and judgments have been built even into the language and choice of incident which make it up. Wharton does not do what Conrad[3] often did, open with a reliable omniscient narrator only to introduce her talkative character when the "facts" have already been established. Instead she forces us to traffic only with the narrator from the beginning; if we are to do that effectively, we must weigh his introduction as carefully as we measure his vision, for only by doing so can we understand, finally, why the vision is so important.

The obsessive anxiety of the narrator's opening statements reveals his need to assure us that we would have reacted just as he did. He wants to

Note on Fiction," *American Review*, VI (January 1936), 273–74. Of course it is just the decision to *ignore* the "exterior or developing story" that has marred so many readings of *Ethan Frome*. Blake Nevius corrects those critics who misquote the narrator (reading "version" for "vision"); Nevius calls it to our attention, in fact, that the inner story is the narrator's "vision," but he makes no more than the linguistic correction. He does not see its significance.
3. Polish-born British novelist (1857–1924), famous for his experimentation with point of view [*Editor*].

elicit our confidence; perhaps he also wants to reassure himself that he
is part of our company.

Many of his preliminary remarks about Ethan have a double thrust,
carrying the strong implication that he is (or seems) one way, but that
he might be (or might at one time have had the option of being) quite
dramatically different. It is, indeed, striking how often the narrator's
conjuration of Ethan manages to conflate *two* images. "He was the most
striking figure in Starkfield, though he was but the ruin of a man. It was
not so much his great height that marked him, for the 'natives' were
easily singled out by their lank longitude from the stockier foreign breed:
it was the careless powerful look he had, in spite of a lameness checking
each step like the jerk of a chain." For clarity's sake we must dissect
fantasy from fact: Ethan is tall, as are most natives, and he walks with a
pronounced limp; yet these simple attributes have been elevated by the
narrator's language—"the most striking figure in Starkfield," "but the
ruin of a man," "careless powerful look," "each step like the jerk of a
chain." Ethan Frome becomes, in the eyes of the teller of his tale, an
emblem of vanquished heroism, defeated strength, and foreclosed
potentiality—not merely a crippled man, but Manhood brought low.
" 'It was a pretty bad smash-up?' I questioned Harmon, looking after
Frome's retreating figure, and thinking how gallantly his lean brown
head, with its shock of light hair, must have sat on his strong shoulders
before they were bent out of shape."

The contrast preys upon the narrator's mind, and he finds himself
compelled to pry into the matter. Relentlessly he questions those taciturn New Englanders, and he gets a series of enigmatic and taciturn
replies. "Harmon drew a slab of tobacco from his pocket, cut off a wedge
and pressed it into the leather pouch of his cheek. 'Guess he's been in
Starkfield too many winters. Most of the smart ones get away.' 'Why
didn't *he?*' 'Somebody had to stay and care for the folks. There warn't
ever anybody but Ethan. Fust his father—then his mother—then his
wife.' " [4] Too many winters. The phrase becomes a key to the puzzle.
"Though Harmon Gow developed the tale as far as his mental and moral
reach permitted there were perceptible gaps between his facts, and I had
the sense that the deeper meaning of the story was in the gaps. But one
phrase stuck in my memory and served as the nucleus about which I
grouped my subsequent inferences: 'Guess he's been in Starkfield too
many winters.' "

The narrator offers this phrase to us as a central clue to Ethan's

4. Some critics have made much of Ethan's care-taking obligations. Lionel Trilling, "The Morality of Inertia," [See above, pp. 126–129] in *Great Moral Dilemmas*, ed. Robert M. MacIver
   (New York: Harper and Brothers, 1956), is one. Few, however, focus on the fact that care-
   taking obligations might have been discharged in any number of ways, that Ethan might have
   sold the farm and moved his parents to Florida (where he had a job once). That is, very few
   critics have noticed the *willed* quality of Ethan Frome's static hell.

dilemma and to his own investigation; then abruptly, the distance between those two narrows. The narrator becomes implicated in Ethan's fate, and his investigation must be presumed to include himself as well. "Before my own time there was up I had learned to know what that meant. . . . When winter shut down on Starkfield, and the village lay under a sheet of snow perpetually renewed from pale skies, I began to see what life there—or rather its negation—must have been in Ethan Frome's young manhood. . . . I found myself anchored at Starkfield . . . for the best part of the winter." Was the speaker interested in Ethan Frome's history before he (like Ethan) had been constrained to spend a winter at Starkfield? There is no way, really, of knowing, for the entire tale is told retrospectively (and of course, the narrator is insistent—perhaps too insistent—that *anyone* would have felt an interest in the man, the interest that he felt immediately upon seeing him).

Who is the narrator? A busy man—we see the energy that he pours into his quest—a man of affairs: "I had been sent up by my employers on a job connected with the big power-house at Corbury Junction, and a long-drawn carpenters' strike had so delayed the work that I found myself anchored at Starkfield." Nothing else would have brought such a man up here. Even marooned as he is in this desolate spot, he does what he can to keep his routines regular: he hires Denis Eady's horses to take him daily over to Corbury Flats where he can pick up a train, and when Eady's horses fall sick, he hires Ethan Frome. The man has a visionary side; we have already seen it in the language of his opening remarks. But surely he is at heart an active man, a man who is part of the larger world, a man who keeps his options open, a man who bears no essential similarity to these poor folk among whom he has been thrust. Spending one winter in Starkfield will surely mean nothing to such a man. "During the early part of my stay I had been struck by the contrast between the vitality of the climate and the deadness of the community"—the observation of a confident outsider.

And yet, slowly, something within him begins to succumb to this insidious environment. "Day by day, after the December snows were over, a blazing blue sky poured down torrents of light and air on the white landscape, which gave them back in an intenser glitter. One would have supposed that such an atmosphere must quicken the emotions as well as the blood; but it seemed to produce no change except that of retarding still more the sluggish pulse of Starkfield. When I had been there a little longer, and had seen this phase of crystal clearness followed by long stretches of sunless cold; when the storms of February had pitched their tents about the devoted village and the wild cavalry of March winds had charged down to their support; I began to understand why Starkfield emerged from its six months' siege like a starved garrison capitulating without quarter. . . . I felt the sinister force of Harmon's phrase: 'Most of the smart ones get away.' " And as he begins to "feel" the force of the phrase—and of the environment which sucks his confidence and his independence away from him—and as his tale draws closer and closer to that crucial moment of transition when we move into the "vision," a peculiar thing begins to happen to his language. The brave assertion of heroic contingencies falters; what he limns now is capitulation, and at the heart of the experience is an unavoidable and dreadful image—"cold" and "starved."

Doggedly, the narrator persists in his quest. He sounds the finer sensibility of Mrs. Ned Hale, who rises only to the platitude that she seems fated to reiterate without explanation: " 'Yes, I knew them both . . . it was awful. . . .' "

And yet, it is not entirely clear what *would* satisfy him. He does not want facts alone; he wants something less tangible, something deeper. "No one gave me an explanation of the look in his face which, as I persisted in thinking, neither poverty nor physical suffering could have put there." He wants an explanation for his own inferences and his own suppositions—we might call them the projections of his own morbid imagination. Harmon Gow, who is more loquacious, can be prodded to speak. The "facts" as he sees them look only to those causes which the narrator has already rejected as insufficient, poverty and physical suffering. But the language in which he speaks, language which the narrator records more completely than any other utterance in the frame, addresses itself to the deeper meaning and heightens the horror of the narrator's speculations by reinforcing those images of starvation: " 'That Frome farm was always 'bout as bare's a milkpan when the cat's been round; and you know what one of the old water-mills is wuth nowadays. When Ethan could sweat over 'em both from sun-up to dark he kinder choked a living out of 'em; but his folks et up most everything, even then, and I don't see how he makes out now. . . . Sickness and trouble: that's what Ethan's had his plate full up with, ever since the very first helping.' "

The narrator's next description of Ethan—drawn during their initial intimate contact as Frome drives him for the first time to the railroad junction—brings all of these themes together. The sight of Frome still calls up visions of ancient heroism and strength; but superimposed upon these images and ultimately blotting them out is a picture of Ethan Frome as the embodiment of some deep mortal misery. Not poverty, merely; not hard work, merely. But something intrinsic to human existence, something imponderable and threatening—something that might swallow up everything else. "Ethan Frome drove in silence, the reins loosely held in his left hand, his brown seamed profile, under the helmet-like peak of the cap, relieved against the banks of snow like the bronze image of a hero. He never turned his face to mine, or answered, except in monosyllables, the questions I put, or such slight pleasantries as I ventured. He seemed a part of the mute melancholy landscape, an incarnation of its frozen woe, with all that was warm and sentient in him fast bound below the surface; but there was nothing unfriendly in his silence. I simply felt that he lived in a depth of moral isolation too remote for casual access, and I had the sense that his loneliness was not merely the result of his personal plight, tragic as I guessed that to be, but had in it, as Harmon Gow had hinted, the profound accumulated cold of many Starkfield winters." And, as we have already observed, this is a winter of the soul that the narrator must now share.

We can see the narrator attempting to assert a distance between himself and this foreboding figure; but in the palpable cold of the region of Starkfield, all things seem to contract. Instead of discovering reassuring distinctions, the narrator finds disconcerting and unexpected similarities. "Once I happened to speak of an engineering job I had been on the previous year in Florida, and of the contrast between the winter landscape about us and that in which I had found myself the year before; and to my surprise Frome said suddenly: 'Yes: I was down there once, and for a good while afterward I could call up the sight of it in winter. But now it's all snowed under.' . . . Another day, on getting into my train at the Flats, I missed a volume of popular science—I think it was on some recent discoveries in bio-chemistry—which I had carried with me to read on the way. I thought no more about it till I got into the sleigh again that evening, and saw the book in Frome's hand. 'I found it after you were gone,' he said. . . . 'Does that sort of thing interest you?' I asked. 'It used to.' . . . 'If you'd like to look the book through I'd be glad to leave it with you.' He hesitated, and I had the impression that he felt himself about to yield to a stealing tide of inertia; then, 'Thank you—I'll take it.' "

The winter landscape reduces the world and obliterates casual surface distinctions. The snow-covered fields lie about the two men, "their boundaries lost under drift; and above the fields, huddled against the white immensities of land and sky, one of those lonely New England farm-houses that make the landscape lonelier." Unknown affinities emerge when everything that fleshes out man's daily existence is taken away—like the ice-age rocks that unpredictably thrust their noses through the frozen ground during winter heaves—shared mortal problems and shared mortal pain. A man must confront himself in such a world, and the narrator is brought to this terrible task in his journey with Ethan Frome. Frome is his Winterman, his shadow self, the man he might become if the reassuring appurtenances of busy, active, professional, adult mobility were taken from him.

The narrator is a man of science; he knows the meaning of cold. Cold is an absence, a diminishment, a dwindling, and finally a death. Everything contracts in the cold. The "place" of the novel is defined by this contraction: from the world to Starkfield; from Starkfield to the thickening darkness of a winter night, "descending on us layer by layer";

from this "smothering medium" to the "forlorn and stunted" farmhouse that is a castrated emblem of its mutilated owner. This relentless constriction of place accompanies a slow shedding of adult personae and leads finally to a confrontation with the core of self that lives beneath these and that would emerge and engulf everything else should the supporting structures of the outside world be lost, somehow. To this point is the narrator reduced—to the edge of nothingness: without identity, without memory, without continuity, without time. All these are outside and beyond. Now there is only the farmhouse. The two men enter it, enter into a small, dark back hallway. The movement is inescapably de-creative, and it is captured in a perverse and grotesque inversion of the terms of birth. They move through the hall to the door of a small, warm room. Slowly, the door is opened, and as it opens, the narrator, who is poised on the threshold, starts to "put together this vision" of Frome's story. The fantasy begins.

The fantasy begins with an involuntary echo of the narrator's own world: Ethan Frome, a young man striding through the clear atmosphere of a winter night, "as though nothing less tenuous than ether intervened between the white earth under his feet and the metallic dome overhead. 'It's like being in an exhausted receiver,' he thought"—an association that is plausible in the young Ethan Frome, who had been, so the fantasy postulates, at a technological college at Worcester, but which is much more probably related to the consciousness of the storyteller, who has been sent to Starkfield to work on a power plant. Perhaps the principal thrust of the image is to assert the similarities between the two. They are surely placed similarly. The story brings Ethan to the church where Mattie Silver has gone to dance. He waits for her—poised just outside and looking in—and his position recapitulates the modalities of the narrator's own placement in the framing story, the cold without and the warmth within. However, the implication here is inverted: in young Ethan's life the warmth of the dance represents gaiety, freedom, and love.

The motif of the threshold renders one of the most significant themes of the novel. The narrator's vision begins while he is poised at the edge of the kitchen with the door beginning to swing open. The long fantasy is spun out; it concludes with the terrible, abortive sledding accident, and we return to the framing world of the narrator. "The querulous drone ceased as I entered Frome's kitchen. . . ." The entire fantasy has been formulated in the instant that marks the passage from hall to kitchen—that timeless eternity of hesitation upon the threshold. In its essential formulation, the story is about that transition (or the failure to make it). The narrator's fantasy about young Ethan begins by placing him at the juncture of two worlds. Over and over again he is pictured thus. Ethan and Mattie return to the farmhouse, and they are greeted at the threshold by Zeena. "Against the dark background of the kitchen she stood up tall and angular, one hand drawing a quilted counterpane to her flat breast, while the other held a lamp. The light, on a level with her chin, drew out of the darkness her puckered throat and the projecting wrist of the hand that clutched the quilt, and deepened fantastically the hollows and prominences of her high-boned face under its ring of crimping-pins." The next night, after Zeena has gone, the vision is reenacted with Mattie: "So strange was the precision with which the incidents of the previous evening were repeating themselves that he half expected, when he heard the key turn, to see his wife before him on the threshold; but the door opened, and Mattie faced him. She stood just as Zeena had stood, a lifted lamp in her hand, against the black background of the kitchen. She held the light at the same level, and it drew out with the same distinctness her slim young throat and the brown wrist no bigger than a child's. Then, striking upward, it threw a lustrous fleck on her lips, edged her eyes with velvet shade, and laid a milky whiteness above the black curve of her brows." Since these threshold scenes with Zeena and Mattie are the only two significant passages that have been preserved from the Black Book *Ethan*,[5] we must infer that Wharton chose to use them again because *only these* were appropriate to the story as it is told by the narrator, for only these echo his own spatial position and his own psychological dilemma.

*   *   *

* * *There is more than a little accuracy in the narrator's obsessive claim—"you must have asked who he was." We all harbor a "Winterman": it is always tempting to cast aside the complexities and demands of adulthood. Within every one of us there lurks a phantom self, not our "real" self, not the self that the world sees, but a seductive shade who calls us to passivity and dependency in a sweet, soft voice. Here is the greatest danger—to relax, to let go, to fall pell-mell, tumbling, backward and down. The horror of the void.

Such is the world we enter as the door to Ethan Frome's kitchen begins to swing slowly open: a world of irrecoverable retreat.

Central to such a world is an inability to communicate: its habitants are inarticulate, mute; and like the patient farm animals they tend to, they are helplessly bound by their own incapacities. The narrator has already experienced Ethan's parsimonious conversation, and his vision repeatedly returns to it. Ethan, walking with Mattie, longing to tell her of his feelings, admiring her laughter and gaiety: "To prolong the effect he groped for a dazzling phrase, and brought out, in a growl of rapture: 'Come along.' " Again and again Ethan "struggled for the all-expressive word"; and again and again he fails to find utterance.

Speech is the bridge that might carry Ethan Frome to a world beyond

5. Wharton's earlier French draft of *Ethan Frome* [Editor].

Starkfield, the necessary passport to wider activities and larger horizons. Without it, he is literally unable to formulate plans of any complexity because all such determinations are beyond his limited powers of conceptualization and self-expression. Because he cannot think his problems through in any but the most rudimentary way, he is as helpless as a child to combat the forces that bind him. It is not that he does not feel deeply, for he does. However, one mark of maturity is the ability to translate desire into coherent words, words into action; and Ethan Frome is incapable of all such translations. "Confused motions of rebellion stormed in him. He was too young, too strong, too full of the sap of living to submit so easily to the destruction of his hopes. Must he wear out all his years at the side of a bitter querulous woman? Other possibilities had been in him, possibilities sacrificed, one by one, to Zeena's narrow-mindedness and ignorance. . . . All the healthy instincts of self-defence rose up in him against such waste." Still, he cannot concoct his own plans. All thoughts of another life must come to him ready-made. He gropes among the meager scraps of his experience: there is the "case of a man over the mountain," a man who left his wife and went West. His eye falls on a newspaper advertisement, and he reads "the seductive words: 'Trips to the West: Reduced Rates.' " But these solutions are no better than clothes bought through a mail-order catalogue: they do not fit his situation; they hang loosely on his lank frame, bearing only the general outline of the garment he desires; he must do the finishing work himself, must tailor the garment to fit. And he cannot do such work (how had that other man done it, anyway? how could *he*, Ethan Frome, scrape together enough money to make such a move?). Imprisonment is not inevitably inherent in the external conditions of his world. The example of the other fellow demonstrates as much. But Frome does not have any set of categories available to him that can explain how escape is possible.

It is not too much to say that the entire force of Ethan's life has been exerted merely to hold him at the level of primitive communication he does manage; and the balance of his life, even as he leads it, is precarious and dangerous. A more fully developed capacity to express himself might open avenues of escape. Any further dwindling of his limited abilities would lead in the opposite direction, propelling him down pathways that are both terrifying and fascinating. Further to lose the power of expression would be a diminishment of self; but though loss of self is an appalling specter, there is at the same time a sensuous attraction in the notion of annihilation—of comforting nothingness.

Why had he married Zeena in the first place, for example? Left with his mother after his father's death, Ethan had found that "the silence had deepened about him year by year. . . . His mother had been a talker in her day, but after her 'trouble' the sound of her voice was seldom heard, though she had not lost the power of speech. Sometimes, in the long winter evenings, when in desperation her son asked her why she didn't 'say something,' she would lift a finger and answer: 'Because I'm listening.' . . . It was only when she drew toward her last illness, and his cousin Zenobia Pierce came over from the next valley to help him nurse her, that human speech was heard again in the house. . . . After the funeral, when he saw her preparing to go away, he was seized with an unreasoning dread of being left alone on the farm; and before he knew what he was doing he had asked her to stay there with him." Yet Ethan's own habitual tendency to silence is not relieved by Zeena's presence. The deep muteness of his nature seems to have a life of its own, spinning outside of him and recreating itself in his environment. After a year or so of married life, Zeena "too fell silent. Perhaps it was the inevitable effect of life on the farm, or perhaps, as she sometimes said, it was because Ethan 'never listened.' The charge was not wholly unfounded. When she spoke it was only to complain, and to complain of things not in his power to remedy; and to check a tendency to impatient retort he had first formed the habit of not answering her, and finally of thinking of other things while she talked."

He knows that his silence (so like the silence of his mother who had been "listening" to unearthly voices) is but a short step from pathology. He fears that Zeena, too, might turn "queer"; and he knows "of certain lonely farm-houses in the neighborhood where stricken creatures pined, and of others where sudden tragedy had come of their presence." But his revulsion from silence is ambivalent, for beyond insanity, there is another vision—the close, convivial muteness of death. Ethan feels its attractions each time he passes the graveyard on the hill. At first the huddled company of gravestones sent shivers down his spine, but "now all desire for change had vanished, and the sight of the little enclosure gave him a warm sense of continuance and stability." On the whole, he is more powerfully drawn to silence than to speech. Over and over again, the arrangements of his life reinforce that silence. If his consciousness recoils from it in terror, some deeper inclination perversely yearns toward it.

It is always easier for Ethan to retreat from life into a "vision" (the word is echoed within the fantasy in a way that inescapably reinforces the narrator's deep identification with him). If Ethan is not able to talk to Mattie during that walk home from church, the deprivation is more than compensated for by his imagination. "He let the vision possess him as they climbed the hill to the house. He was never so happy with her as when he abandoned himself to these dreams. Half-way up the slope Mattie stumbled against some unseen obstruction and clutched his sleeve to steady herself. The wave of warmth that went through him was like the prolongation of his vision." The force of such visions is indescribable; it is the appeal of passivity, the numbing inertia that renders Frome impotent in the face of real-world dilemmas. Like a man who has become addicted to some strong narcotic, Frome savors emotional indolence as if it were a sensual experience. In the evening he spends alone with Mattie he is ravished by it. They sit and talk, and "the commonplace nature of what they said produced in Ethan an illusion of long-established intimacy which no outburst of emotion could have given, and he set his imagination adrift on the fiction that they had always spent their evenings thus and would always go on doing so. . . ." In truth he is not listening to Miss Mattie Silver with any greater attention than he gives to Zenobia; he is listening to the mermaid voices within himself. Afterwards, the vision lingers. "He did not know why he was so irrationally happy, for nothing was changed in his life or hers. He had not even touched the tip of her fingers or looked her full in the eyes. But their evening together had given him a vision of what life at her side might be, and he was glad now that he had done nothing to trouble the sweetness of the picture." As always, the uncompromised richness of the dream is more alluring than the harsher limitations of actual, realized satisfactions.

In electing passivity and a life of regression, Ethan Frome has chosen to forfeit the perquisites of manhood. The many images of mutilation throughout the story merely reinforce a pattern that has been fully established well before the sledding accident. Ethan flees sexuality just as he has fled self-assertion. When he loses his mother, he replaces her almost without a perceptible break in his routines, and the state of querulous sickliness to which Zeena retreats after a year of marriage might plausibly be seen as a peevish attempt to demand attention of some sort when the attentions more normal to marriage have not been given. It is not Zenobia's womanliness that has attracted Ethan: "The mere fact of obeying her orders . . . restored his shaken balance." Yet the various components of this wife-nurse soon grate upon Ethan Frome's consciousness. "When she came to take care of his mother she had seemed to Ethan like the very genius of health, but he soon saw that her skill as a nurse had been acquired by the absorbed observation of her own symptoms." Ethan and Zeena have been brought together by their mutual commitment to the habits of care-taking; now they have become imprisoned by them.

At first, Ethan's affection for Mattie seems to have a more wholesome basis. However we soon realize that the sensual component in that relationship is of a piece with the sensuality of death. It thrives on exclusions and cannot survive in the rich atmosphere of real-world complexities. Ethan features Mattie as someone who can participate in his visions, and he does not allow the banality of her actual personality to flaw that supposition. One evening they stand watching the blue shadows of the hemlocks play across the sunlit snow. When Mattie exclaims: " 'It looks just as if it was painted!' it seemed to Ethan that the art of definition could go no farther, and that words had at last been found to utter his secret soul. . . ." His imagination can remedy the deficiencies of genuine conversation; if worse comes to worst, he can ignore genuine conversation altogether (as he has in his relationship with Zeena) and retreat to the more palatable images of his fancy.

By far the deepest irony is that Ethan's dreams of Mattie are not essentially different from the life that he has created with Zeena; they are still variations on the theme of dependency. Mattie "was quick to learn, but forgetful and dreamy. . . . Ethan had an idea that if she were to marry a man she was fond of the dormant instinct would wake, and her pies and biscuits become the pride of the country; but domesticity in the abstract did not interest her." The fantasies here are doubly revealing. As always he substitutes make-believe for reality—loving his vision of Mattie rather than Mattie herself. However, even when Ethan is given full rein, even when he can make any imaginary semblance of Mattie that he wants, he chooses a vision that has no sexual component. He does not see her as a loving wife to warm his bed in the winter. No. She is, instead, a paragon of the kitchen, a perfect caretaker, someone who can fill his stomach—not satisfy his manhood. She is, in short, just what he had imagined Zeena might be. And there is no reason, even at the beginning of the tale, to suppose that Mattie Silver would be any better in the role than Zeena.

Ethan and Mattie are never pictured as man and woman together; at their most intimate moments they cling "to each other's hands like children." At other times, they envision a life in which they exchange the role of caretaker and protector: if Mattie might become the best cook in the county; Ethan longs " 'to do for you and care for you. I want to be there when you're sick and when you're lonesome.' " When they finally do come together in their momentous first kiss, even that physical contact is described in terms that remove it from the world of adult passion and reduce it to the modalities of infancy: "He had found her lips at last and was drinking unconsciousness of everything but the joy they gave him."

The sled ride is a natural climax to all of the themes that have been interwoven throughout the story. It is, or ought to be, a sexual culmination—the long, firm sled; the shining track opening up before them; the swift, uneven descent, now plunging "with the hollow night opening out below them and the air singing by like an organ," now bounding dizzily upward only to plunge again with sudden exultation and rapture past the elm until "they reached the level ground beyond, and the speed of the sled began to slacken." The description of their long, successful first ride gives some intimation of the possibilities before them. Nevertheless, the language does not remain fixed; the vision is not steady. By this time the story has achieved such a palpable air of veracity that the reader is apt to accept this language as a more or less adequate description of what "really happened." Of course it is not. Even at this point—

especially at this point—we must recollect that Ethan's world and all of the decisions in it (all the language that renders those decisions) is no more than the narrator's vision. We have finally reached the heart of that vision—the ultimate depths of the shadow world in which the narrator has immersed himself—and the inescapable implications of it crowd about us like the shades that gather dusk together and enfold the world in night.

The story becomes a veritable dance around the notion of vision. Ethan's eyesight is keen. " 'I can measure distances to a hair's breadth—always could,' " he boasts to Mattie. And she echoes his thought: " 'I always say you've got the surest eye. . . .' " Yet tonight "he strained his eyes through the dimness, and they seemed less keen, less capable than usual." Other visions are competing against his clear-eyed view. The couple discovers that each has ached throughout the long six months before, dreaming of the other, dreams defying sleep. This, too, is a climax; for the mingling of their love-fancies becomes the most explicit bond between them. It is a more compelling vision even than the long, smooth, slippery track before them, a vision that is compounded by the potent imagery of Mattie's despair. " 'There'll be that strange girl in the house . . . and she'll sleep in my bed, where I used to lay nights and listen to hear you come up the stairs. . . .' " Vision calls to vision, and Ethan, too, succumbs to the stealing softness of his own dreams. "The words were like fragments torn from his heart. With them came the hated vision of the house he was going back to—of the stairs he would have to go up every night, of the woman who would wait for him there. And the sweetness of Mattie's avowal, the wild wonder of knowing at last that all that had happened to him had happened to her too, made the other vision more abhorrent, the other life more intolerable to return to. . . ."

It is Mattie who suggests death (though her plea has the urgency of a lingering sexual appeal): " 'Ethan! Ethan! I want you to take me down again!' " And he resists her—as he has always resisted any action.

In the end, he is seduced by the vision; her words do not even penetrate. "Her pleadings still came to him between short sobs, but he no longer heard what she was saying. Her hat had slipped back and he was stroking her hair. He wanted to get the feeling of it into his hand, so that it would sleep there like a seed in winter." Not the violence of passion, but the loving, soothing release of sleep. Never has the silence been more profound (her words lost entirely into the cold and empty ether—that exhausted receiver of sky inverted over earth). The close conviviality of the grave has overwhelmed his imagination at last: "The spruces swathed them in blackness and silence They might have been in their coffins underground. He said to himself: 'Perhaps it'll feel like this . . .' and then again: 'After this I sha'n't feel anything. . . .' " The indivisible comfort of nothingness.

The delicate balance has swung finally to the side of retreat; time and space rush forward, and Ethan Frome lapses back into the simplicities of childhood, infancy. Words will not suffice to reach him now. Nothing does, save one sound—"he heard the old sorrel whinny across the road, and thought: 'He's wondering why he doesn't get his supper. . . .' " Food—and then sleep—the very oldest memories, the persistent, original animal needs, nothing more. Mattie urges him, but he responds only to the "sombre violence" of her gesture as she tugs at his hand. Slowly they take their places. But then, Ethan stops. " 'Get up! Get up!' " he urges the girl. "But she kept on repeating: 'Why do you want to sit in front?' 'Because I—because I want to feel you holding me,' he stammered, and dragged her to her feet." This is how he must go, cradled in the embrace of her arms.[6]

The ride begins. Down the hill—no farewell but the gentle neighing of the sorrel. Down and down again, a "long delirious descent [in which] it seemed to him that they were flying indeed, flying far up into the cloudy night, with Starkfield immeasurably below them, falling away like a speck in space." " 'We can fetch it' "; he repeats the refrain as the sled wavers and then rights itself toward the looming elm. "The air shot past him like millions of fiery wires, and then the elm. . . ."

Afterwards, there seems nothing left but silence; silence at first, and then "he heard a little animal twittering somewhere near by under the snow. It made a small frightened *cheep* like a field mouse. . . . He understood that it must be in pain. . . . The thought of the animal's suffering was intolerable to him and . . . he continued to finger about cautiously with his left hand, thinking he might get hold of the little creature and help it; and all at once he knew that the soft thing he had touched was Mattie's hair and that his hand was on her face." He has come to the very verge, but he has not managed to go over. His own final threshold remains uncrossed. He has not quite died. He has only been reduced, irretrievably reduced, to the sparse simplicities of animal existence.

Having plunged thus far from the world of adult possibilities, having brought Mattie and Zeena with him, he is doomed, after all, to wait for the end—possibly to wait for a long time. The last words of the vision measure the level of reality to which he has consigned himself. "Far off, up the hill, he heard the sorrel whinny, and thought: 'I ought to be getting him his feed. . . .' " Thus the vision concludes, and the narrator steps finally through the kitchen door into the unchanging world of Ethan Frome, his wife, and Miss Mattie Silver. The condition of static misery that he infers, the life that has been Frome's scant portion, is an

---

6. Kenneth Bernard, "Imagery and Symbolism in *Ethan Frome*," *College English*, XXIII (December 1961), has remarked incisively on a number of metaphorical patterns in the novel. Bernard is the only critic to note that Frome wishes to die cradled in Mattie's arms—that, in effect, he regresses at the crucial moment.

inevitable consequence of those dark impulses that lead past madness to the edge of oblivion.

We leave the narrator reflecting upon the tale he has told. It is not "true" except as an involuntary expression of his own hidden self; nevertheless, this purgatory of the imagination becomes ominously insistent, and the "self,"; having had life breathed into it, grows stronger even as the narrator assembles his story. Mrs. Hale's banal chatter falls upon deaf ears: he heeds her no more than Ethan has heeded Zeena or Mattie; and like Ethan, he has a parsimonious way with conversation. "Mrs. Hale paused a moment, and I remained silent, plunged in the vision of what her words evoked." Insidiously, the vision possesses him.

* * *

* * *Within *Ethan Frome* the narrator lapses into a vision (the tale of Ethan which is, as we have seen, a terrified expression of the narrator's latent self—his *alter ego*, his "Winterman"). The *novel*, *Ethan Frome*, focuses on the narrator's problem: the tension between his public self and his shadow self, his terror of a seductive and enveloping void.

* * *

ELIZABETH AMMONS

[*Ethan Frome* as Fairy Tale]†

* * *

Although finally highly realistic both in its liberal social criticism and its more sweeping psychological implications, *Ethan Frome* is designed to read like a fairy tale. It draws on archetypes of the genre—the witch, the silvery maiden, the honest woodcutter—and brings them to life in the landscape and social structure of rural New England. To tell the story Wharton introduces an unnamed, educated city-dweller, who has had to piece the narrative together; all he can offer about Ethan, he announces at the end of his preface, is:

this vision of his story . . . .
. . . .
. . . .
. . . .

Short ellipses often appear in Wharton's fiction, but this ellipsis is excessive, and it exists to help establish genre. It trails off for three printed lines

†From *Edith Wharton's Argument with America* by Elizabeth Ammons (Athens: University of Georgia Press, 1980), pp. 61–77. Copyright © 1980 by the University of Georgia Press, Athens, Georgia. Reprinted by permission of the publisher.

to emphasize that, while Ethan's story will appear real and we can believe that the tragedy did happen, the version here is a fabrication. It is an imagined reconstruction of events organized in part out of shared oral material and shaped for us into one of many possible narratives. As the narrator says in his opening statement: "I had the story bit by bit, from various people, and, as generally happens in such cases, each time it was a different story." This tale, in other words, belongs to a community of people (ourselves now included) and has many variants. Also important is Wharton's selection of the word "vision." Not a documentary term, "vision" prepares us for the fact that Ethan's story, with its vivid use of inherited symbols and character types, will seem a romance or fairy tale.

Wharton's plot, as in most fairy stories, is simple. After seven miserable years married to sickly Zeena, a woman seven years his senior, Ethan Frome (who is twenty-eight) falls in love with twenty-one-year-old Mattie Silver. She is the daughter of Zeena's cousin and works as the childless couple's live-in "girl." When Zeena banishes Mattie because she knows that Ethan and the girl have fallen in love, the young lovers try to kill themselves by sledding down a treacherous incline into an ancient elm. The suicide attempt fails, leaving Ethan lame and Mattie a helpless invalid. The narrator reconstructs this story when he visits Starkfield twenty-four years after the event; Ethan is fifty-two and the three principals are living together, Zeena taking care of Mattie and Ethan supporting them both.

Although the pattern is very subtly established, the numbers that accumulate in Wharton's story bring to mind natural cycles: fifty-two (the weeks of the year); twenty-four (the hours of the day and a multiple of the months of the year); seven (the days of the week) with its echoes in the multiples twenty-one, twenty-eight, thirty-five; three (among other things, morning, afternoon, night). The implication here of generation and natural order ironically underlines Wharton's awful donnée.[1] Expressed figuratively: in the frozen unyielding world of Ethan Frome, there is no generative natural order; there is no mother earth. There is only her nightmare reverse image, the witch, figured in Zeena Frome.[2]

Specifically, a network of imagery and event in *Ethan Frome* calls up the fairy tale *Snow-White*. The frozen landscape, the emphasis on sevens, the physical appearance of Mattie Silver (black hair, red cheeks, white skin), her persecution by witchlike Zeena (an older woman who takes the girl in when her mother dies and thus serves as a stepmother to her), Mattie's role as housekeeper: all have obvious parallels in the

---

1. Usually, the point of departure for a narrative; here, suggests underlying theme [Editor].
2. As Elizabeth Janeway remarks, "the witch is the shadow and opposite of the loving mother" (*Man's World, Woman's Place: A Study in Social Mythology* [New York: Dell, 1971], p. 126; see also pp. 119, 127–29). Mother is warm, the witch is cold. Mother is soft, the witch is bony. Mother gives, the witch takes away. And so the antitheses run all through the dichotomy, young/old, beautiful/ugly, fertile/barren, and so forth. Viewed in these terms, both Zeena and the earth itself in *Ethan Frome* serve as mother-antitheses.

traditional fairy tale about a little girl whose jealous stepmother tries to keep her from maturing into a healthy, marriageable young woman. Although Wharton is not imitating this well-known fairy tale—rather, she draws on familiar elements of *Snow-White* as touchstones for a new, original fairy tale—still, for many readers, without their even realizing it, the implicit contrast between Zeena's victory in *Ethan Frome* and the stepmother's defeat in *Snow-White* no doubt contributes to the terror of Wharton's story. Most fairy tales reassure by teaching that witches lose in the end. Children and heroines (Snow-Whites) do not remain the victims of ogres. Someone saves them. Here is part of the horror of *Ethan Frome*: Wharton's modern fairy tale for adults, while true to traditional models in the way it teaches a moral about "real" life at the same time that it addresses elemental fears (e.g., the fear of death, the fear of being abandoned), does not conform to the genre's typical denouement. The lovers do not live happily ever after. The witch wins.

Zeena's face alone would type her as a witch. Sallow-complexioned and old at thirty-five, her bloodless countenance is composed of high protruding cheekbones, lashless lids over piercing eyes, thin colorless hair, and a mesh of minute vertical lines between her gaunt nose and granite chin. Black calico, with a brown shawl in winter, makes up her ordinary daytime wear, and her muffled body is as fleshless as her face. Late one night Ethan and Mattie return from a church dance to the dreary house where a "dead cucumber-vine dangled from the porch like the crape streamer tied to the door for a death." They are met by Zeena: "Against the dark background of the kitchen she stood up tall and angular, one hand drawing a quilted counterpane to her flat breast, while the other held a lamp. The light, on a level with her chin, drew out of the darkness her puckered throat and the projecting wrist of the hand that clutched the quilt, and deepened fantastically the hollows and prominences of her high-boned face." Confronting the youthful couple at midnight in her kitchen, "which had the deadly chill of a vault," Ethan's spectral wife, complete with stealthy, destructive cat, appears the perfect witch of nursery lore.

Mattie Silver, in contrast, seems a fairy maiden, a princess of nature in Ethan's eyes. Her expressive face changes "like a wheat-field under a summer breeze," and her voice reminds him of "a rustling covert leading to enchanted glades." When she sews, her hands flutter like birds building a nest; when she cries, her eyelashes feel like butterflies. Especially intoxicating is her luxuriant dark hair, which curls like the tendrils on a wildflower and is "soft yet springy, like certain mosses on warm slopes." By candlelight her hair looks "like a drift of mist on the moon." Simone de Beauvoir, quoting Michel Carrouges, provides in general terms a nearly perfect description of Mattie's psychomythic significance for Ethan: "Woman is not the useless replica of man, but rather the enchanted place where the living alliance between man and nature is brought about. If she should disappear, men would be alone, strangers lacking passports in an icy world. She is the earth itself raised to life's summit, the earth become sensitive and joyous; and without her, for man the earth is mute and dead.[3] Zeena's colors are those of the dead earth—black, grey, brown; Mattie's are blood red and snowy white. She sleeps under a red and white quilt, wears a crimson ribbon and a cherry red "fascinator," and has rosy lips and a quick blush. A vision of her face lingers with Ethan one morning: "It was part of the sun's red and of the pure glitter on the snow." Passion and purity mingle in Ethan's image of Mattie, making her more valuable to him (but no more attainable) than the precious metal her last name specifies.

The imagery Ethan associates with Mattie Silver is frankly sexual: visions of secret natural glens and nooks, lush dainty vegetation with dewy tendrils, mysterious mists. And his imagination turns to nature and the fairy world because the desired sexual experience is for him bound up in a masculine fantasy of possessing woman like some secret place the explorer dreams of claiming for himself. In one of the book's many sexual images anticipating the near-fatal sledding accident, Ethan calms Mattie, who is distraught because the red glass pickle dish (one of the story's obvious symbols) which she borrowed from Zeena's pitiful hoard of unused wedding gifts has gotten broken during their intimate supper. "His soul swelled with pride as he saw how his tone subdued her. . . . Except when he was steering a big log down the mountain to his mill he had never known such a thrilling sense of mastery." But Ethan is an unsophisticated and conscientious man; he does not want to "ruin" Mattie, nor spoil his romantic fantasy by turning their relationship into a furtive backstairs affair. Therefore he never makes love to her. Instead he dreams of getting a divorce from Zeena and marrying Mattie. He remembers a couple like themselves who did just that, moved to the West and now "had a little girl with fair curls, who wore a gold locket and was dressed like a princess." But the fairy tale Ethan lives, in contrast to the one he fantasizes, has a barren conclusion.

Hurting young people and depriving them of hope and joy is the fairy-tale witch's job, and Zeena does not shirk the task. She constantly finds fault with Mattie, and for seven years she has tortured her youthful husband with whining complaints about her various ailments. She even haunts Ethan. Her ugly visage takes fleeting possession of Mattie's on the blissful evening the lovers play house together, and her name, like a hex, throws "a chill between them." Nor will her loyal cat give them peace. The sly beast acts as Zeena's stand-in, leaping out of her rocker and setting it in eerie motion during the romantic supper the couple enjoys in her absence. In the middle of the supper the animal knocks

3. Michel Carrouges, "Les Pouvoirs de la femme," Cahiers du Sud (no. 292), quoted in Simone de Beauvoir, The Second Sex (New York: Alfred A. Knopf, 1952; rpt. Bantam, 1961), p. 130.

Zeena's prized pickle dish to the floor and thus guarantees Mattie's banishment, which in turn precipitates the lovers' suicide attempt and the fairy tale's macabre denouement.

The ghastly conclusion Ethan must live with is worse than if Mattie had gone away, married someone else, or even died. The suicide attempt transforms Mattie into a mirror image of Zeena. The narrator enters the Frome house late one winter night twenty-four years after Mattie and Ethan tried to kill themselves, and he can barely tell the two women apart. The girl of Ethan's dreams now sits droning in a chair "which looked like a soiled relic of luxury." "Her hair was as gray as her companion's, her face as bloodless and shrivelled . . . with swarthy shadows sharpening the nose and hollowing the temples. . . . Her dark eyes had the bright witch-like stare that disease of the spine sometimes gives."

The end of *Ethan Frome* images Zeena Frome and Mattie Silver not as two individual and entirely opposite female figures but as two virtually indistinguishable examples of one type of woman: in fairy-tale terms, the witch; in social mythology, the shrew. Mattie, in effect, has become Zeena. Shocking as that replicate image may at first seem, it has been prepared for throughout the story. Mattie and Zeena are related by blood. They live in the same house and wait on the same man, and they came to that man's house for the same purpose: to take the place of an infirm old woman (Zeena takes over for Ethan's mother, Mattie for his wife). The two women, viewed symbolically, do not contrast with each other as Justine Brent and Bessy Amherst do in *The Fruit of the Tree*[4] nor amplify each other as Anna Leath and Sophy Viner will in *The Reef*; rather, one follows the other, walks down her road. Mattie comes to live in Zeena's house, falls in love with Zeena's husband, makes friends with Zeena's cat, tends Zeena's plants, breaks Zeena's wedding dish. She greets Ethan from Zeena's kitchen door, standing "just as Zeena had stood, a lifted lamp in her hand, against the black background of the kitchen." It is Zeena's terrible face that obscures Ethan's perception of Mattie when the young woman rocks in the old woman's chair on the evening they spend together, and the same hideous apparition blinds Ethan just before he and Mattie crash their sled into the tree. Zeena's identity and fate stalk Mattie until, in the end, she too becomes a witch, a miserable gnarled old woman.

As a fairy story, *Ethan Frome* terrifies because it ends askew. Incredibly, the witch triumphs. Mattie Silver becomes Zeena's double rather than Ethan's complement.

Edith Wharton said of *Ethan Frome*, "It was the first subject I had ever approached with full confidence in its value, for my own purpose, and a relative faith in my power to render at least a part of what I saw in

4. Wharton's 1907 novel [Editor].

it."[5] Her critics have not been as confident about what the story means—or *if* it means; Lionel Trilling, for example, has stated outright (and with evident irritation): "It presents no moral issue at all."[6] But as is sometimes the case, a much earlier critic did grasp Wharton's purpose. In *Voices of Tomorrow: Critical Studies of the New Spirit in Literature*, published in 1913 (just two years after *Ethan Frome*), Edwin Bjorkman declares of the painfulness of Wharton's story:

> This one redeeming factor asserts itself subtly throughout the book, though Mrs. Wharton never refers to it in plain words. It is this: that, after all, the tragedy unveiled to us is social rather than personal. . . . If it had no social side, if it implied only what it brought of suffering and sorrow to the partakers in it, then we could do little but cry out in self-protective impatience: "Sweep off the shambles and let us pass on!" . . . Ethan and Matt and Zeena [are not presented] as individual sufferers. They become instead embodiments of large groups and whole strata; and the dominant thought left behind by the book is not concerned with the awfulness of human existence, but with the social loss involved in such wasting of human lives.

Bjorkman begins his next paragraph emphatically: "*Ethan Frome* is to me above all else a judgment on that system which fails to redeem such villages as Mrs. Wharton's Starkfield."[7]

Wharton's subsequent critics have not matched for passion or accuracy this early critical appraisal, and perhaps the problem has to do with our forgetting what life was like for many people, and particularly women, in rural America before the First World War. Wharton's usual subject was the upper- or upper-middle-class woman. Given her own station in life, she naturally understood her own type of situation best. Nevertheless, as early as her first published fiction, "Mrs. Manstey's View" in 1891, and *Bunner Sisters* a year later, Edith Wharton showed a desire to deal with the problems of poor women. One could argue that some of her attempts are inept, marred by condescension and even snobbishness; but the charge cannot be leveled at *Ethan Frome*. In it,

---

5. Edith Wharton, Introduction to *Ethan Frome* (New York: Charles Scribner's Sons, 1922), vii. [Reprinted in this volume, pp. xi–xiii—*Editor.*]
6. Lionel Trilling, "The Morality of Inertia," *A Gathering of Fugitives* (London: Secker and Warburg, 1957), p. 33. [Excerpted in this volume, pp. 126–129—*Editor.*]
7. Edwin Bjorkman, *Voices of Tomorrow: Critical Studies of the New Spirit in Literature* (New York and London: Mitchell Kennerley, 1913), pp. 296–97. Bjorkman also sees that romantic love, in addition to economics, is an important theme in the story but, oddly—given how attuned he is to the social criticism of the story, he misses Wharton's point about love; he gathers that she implies marriage to Mattie as the answer to Ethan's problems when, in Bjorkman's opinion, "Romantic love, as idealized for us by our sentimental-minded forefathers, has long gone into bankruptcy." He declares: "Had Zeena died and Matt married Ethan—well, it is my private belief that inside of a few years life on that farm would have been practically what it was before Matt arrived, with Matt playing the part of Zeena II—different, of course, and yet the same" (pp. 301, 303). His "private belief," of course, is not really private at all, but the result of Wharton's construction of her tale.

as in *Summer* six years later, Edith Wharton's sympathies are fully engaged, and the moral she argues is clean and true.

That moral—Wharton's social criticism—emerges directly from her fairy tale. *Ethan Frome* maintains that witches are real. There are women whose occupation in life consists of making other people unhappy. *Ethan Frome* includes three. Ethan's mother, housebound and isolated for years on a failing farm, lived out her life an insane, wizened creature peering out her window for passersby who never came and listening for voices that only she could hear. Her frightening silence oppressed Ethan until Zeena joined the household to care for her. But then Zeena too fell silent. Ethan

> recalled his mother's growing taciturnity, and wondered if Zeena were also turning "queer." Women did, he knew. Zeena, who had at her fingers' ends the pathological chart of the whole region, had cited many cases of the kind while she was nursing his mother; and he himself knew of certain lonely farm-houses in the neighbour-hood where stricken creatures pined, and of others where sudden tragedy had come of their presence. At times, looking at Zeena's shut face, he felt the chill of such forebodings. At other times her silence seemed deliberately assumed to conceal far-reaching intentions, mysterious conclusions drawn from suspicions and resentments impossible to guess.

Zeena's hypochondria, her frigidity, her taciturnity broken only by querulous nagging, her drab appearance—these make her an unsympathetic character. They also make her a typically "queer" woman of the region, a twisted human being produced by poverty and isolation and deadening routine. (She gives the housework to Mattie, and why not? Few jobs are more lonely or monotonous, plus the girl provides another presence in the vacant house and one on whom Zeena can vent her frustrations.) Mattie Silver is merely spared the gradual disintegration into queerness that Ethan has witnessed in Zeena and his mother. The accident, like magic, swiftly transforms the girl into a whining burdensome hag.

In reality, Mattie had no future to lose. Ethan asks for assurance that she does not want to leave the farm, and "he had to stoop his head to catch her stifled whisper: 'Where'd I go, if I did?' " There is nowhere for her to go. She has no immediate family and no salable skills; all she can do is trim a hat, recite one poem, and play a couple of tunes on the piano. She tried stenography and bookkeeping, both of which exhausted her, and working on her feet all day as a clerk in a department store did not bring her strength back. As Anna Garlin Spencer, Edith Wharton's contemporary, points out in a study published one year after *Ethan Frome*, laws to protect the health of women workers existed but were inadequate and seldom enforced. In *Woman's Share in Social Culture* (1912) she explains that even young women who worked only during the unmarried years between fourteen and twenty often lost their health permanently. "The fact is that because young women must all work for pay between their school life and their marriage in the case of the poverty-bound, the poorest-paid and many of the hardest and most health-destroying of employments are given to them as a monopoly." For instance:

> in the canning factories 2,400 rapid and regular motions a day in tin-cutting for the girls employed. . . . In the confectionery business, 3,000 chocolates "dipped" every day at a fever heat of energy. In the cracker-making trade, the girls standing or walking [all day] not six feet from the ovens. . . . In the garment trades the sewing machines speeded to almost incredible limits, the unshaded electric bulbs and the swift motion of the needle giving early "eye-blur" and nerve strain. . . . In department stores . . . where five or six hundred girls are employed nineteen to thirty seats may be provided; but to use even these may cost the girl her position.[8]

The Woman's Book, more than a decade and a half earlier, had pointed out exactly the same abuse:

> Now that some laws exist for the protection of shop-girls an attempt is made to see that they are enforced. Violations are frequently discovered. In one large shop where the law has been obeyed to the extent of putting in the one seat required for every six girls, a fine was imposed upon any girl found sitting on it.[9]

Mattie's physical inability to hold onto her job as a department-store girl is realistic. And factory work would be no better, as Edith Wharton knew from firsthand observation because she had toured industrial mills in North Adams, Massachusetts, early in the century in her research for The Fruit of the Tree.

Ethan thinks of Mattie "setting out alone to renew the weary quest for work. . . . What chance had she, inexperienced and untrained, among the million bread-seekers of the cities? There came back to him miserable tales he had heard at Worcester, and the faces of girls whose lives had begun as hopefully as Mattie's. . . ." (final ellipsis Wharton's). Mattie's prospects are grim. She can work in a factory and lose her health; she can become a prostitute and lose her self-dignity as well; she can marry a farmer and lose her mind. Or she can be crushed in a sledding accident and lose all three at once. It makes no difference. Poverty, premature old age, and shattered dreams comprise her inevitable reward no matter what she does. The fact that Wharton cripples Mattie, but will not let her die, reflects not the author's but the culture's cruelty. Like

---

8. Anna Garlin Spencer, Woman's Share in Social Culture (Philadelphia: J. B. Lippincott, Co., 1912), pp. 244–46, 247.
9. The Woman's Book, 1: 62.

Lily Bart[1] at the opposite end of the social scale, Mattie Silver has not been prepared for an economically independent life. The system is designed to keep her a parasite or drudge, or both.

Edith Wharton's sympathy goes out to Ethan Frome. Poverty and a succession of insane, dependent women prohibit his ever having the liberty to follow his aspirations. Naturally he longs "for change and freedom," fantasizes Zeena's death, and sees in Mattie the incarnation of his repressed dreams. Any man in his place would. But for Ethan "there was no way out—none. He was a prisoner for life." The prison, Wharton makes clear by setting the story at the simplest and therefore the most obvious level of society, was the American economic system itself, which laid on most men too much work and responsibility and on most women barely enough variety and adult human contact to keep one's spirit alive. (Significantly, Zeena recovers a degree of cheer and vigor when she has Mattie to take care of.) For every well-trained New Woman like Wharton's Justine Brent[2] there were thousands of wasted women shut away from corporate life and bitter about their static existences. At least Ethan meets fellow workers when he carts his timber to sale or goes into town for supplies and mail. Farmers' womenfolk normally went nowhere and did nothing but repeat identical tasks in unvaried monotony. To make that isolation of women stark and to emphasize the sterility of life at the level of *Ethan Frome*, Wharton gives the couple no children; and the woman's name she chooses for bold-faced inscription on the only tombstone described in the Frome family plot is also instructive: ENDURANCE. If Ethan's life is hard, and it is, woman's is harder yet, and it is sad but not surprising that isolated, housebound women make man feel the full burden of their misery. He is their only connection with the outer world, the vast economic and social system that consigns them to solitary, monotonous domestic lives from which their only escape is madness or death.

In Wharton's fairy tale good girls do not grow up into happy wives, and good-hearted, worthy lovers do not ride off into the western sun with the maiden of their dreams. Most important, witches do not get vanquished and disappear. They multiply. First there is Ethan's mother, then Zeena, then Mattie; and they represent only three of the many women gone "queer" in this wintry American landscape. Wharton's moral is as cold and grim as her Starkfield setting. As long as women are kept isolated and dependent, *Ethan Frome* implies, Mattie Silvers will become Zeena Fromes: frigid crippled wrecks of human beings whose pleasure in life derives from depriving others of theirs. Edith Wharton sneered at the New England realism of Sarah Orne Jewett and Mary Wilkins Freeman, claiming that they looked at the problems of

1. Wharton's doomed heroine in *The House of Mirth* [Editor].
2. Nurse-heroine of *The Fruit of the Tree* [Editor].

the region through "rose-colored spectacles."[3] The charge is exaggerated, but not pointless if it is *Ethan Frome* that one uses as the measure.

But why have a young man provide the "vision" of Ethan's story? Why not present *Ethan Frome* directly? A brief look at the tale's evolution is useful here. Edith Wharton began writing Ethan's story in 1906 or 1907 as an exercise in French for her language tutor in Paris. The original sketch, which is really just a fragment, has no narrative frame and suggests that Wharton first conceived her story as nothing more than a piece of realism about rural New England. In the draft, Hart (the Ethan-figure), is torn between love for Mattie, his wife's niece who lives with them, and fear of his carping, sickly wife, Anna. Anna leaves for two days to see a doctor in Worcester, and Hart spends the evening in town to avoid being alone in the farmhouse with Mattie. He does not want to compromise the girl or risk being discovered with her by his jealous wife, who he suspects may be laying a trap for him. When Anna returns from Worcester she announces that her poor health has forced her to engage a new, more robust serving-girl so Mattie must leave. The fragment ends with Hart and Mattie, hopeless, driving through the snow to the depot, the two of them admitting their love and Mattie, tempted to kill herself, forbidding Hart to leave Anna.

Although elements of the finished story exist in the early draft, the differences are critical. In the French fragment there is no intimate supper in the wife's absence, no red glass pickle dish, no cat, no suggestion that Anna can haunt her husband (her weapon would be to lay a trap), no echo of Snow-White in the description of Mattie (she has blue eyes and golden curls), no network of symbolic numbers. There are seeds of the later atmosphere in the romanticized descriptions of nature and the vignette of Anna standing in the doorway late at night—ashen, gaunt, menacing. But most of the fairy-tale imagery and symbolism appears only in the finished version of *Ethan Frome*, which Wharton presents to us through the eyes of her narrator. He serves as a surprising double for Ethan. Young and well educated, he is the engineer that Ethan hoped to become, until a series of women blighted his world. (To impress the parallel, they also have in common their compassion for animals, their interest in pure science, and fond memories of a trip to Florida each of them has taken.)

Wharton's use of this particular narrator encourages us to believe that his "vision" of *Ethan Frome* is close to what Ethan's might be, were he able to articulate it. Other people—Harmon Gow and Mrs. Hale, for two—could give us the plain facts of the story. Ethan, Zeena, and Mattie lived together; Zeena hired a new girl and Mattie was forced to leave; Ethan and Mattie took the tragic sled-ride on the evening he drove her to the depot; the three of them, much changed, ended up living together

3. Edith Wharton, *A Backward Glance* (New York: D. Appleton-Century, 1934), p. 293. [Excerpted in this volume, pp. 78–80—*Editor.*]

again in permanent poverty and misery. What makes of these facts a fairy tale is the sympathetic young outsider's "vision," the way the transient engineer imagines Zeena as a witch, Mattie as a Snow-White, Ethan as a ruined prince—a man whose head must have sat "gallantly" on his strong shoulders before the accident, a man who even in affliction has a profile "like the bronze image of a hero."

The narrator exists to unlock the deepest, the psychosexual, level of *Ethan Frome*. Empathically, he projects himself into young Ethan's situation and sees in it the realization of a specific male fear: the fear that woman will turn into witch. The fear that mother will turn into witch (love into hate, day into night, life into death) we all, man or woman, have known. It is the fear, in fact, that the fairy tale *Snow-White* recognizes and deals with constructively, as Bruno Bettelheim explains in *The Uses of Enchantment*.[4] The fear, however, that woman—a larger category than mother—will simply quit serving and, instead, become self-centered and even demanding of service (the fear that Mattie will become Zeena) is a specifically male fear. Women do not expect other women, as a class, to serve them. But men, historically, have expected that deference; and when the expectation is violated, when woman ceases to meet man's needs, the mythic transformation that we see in *Ethan Frome* takes place. As Simone de Beauvoir explains: "In place of the myth of the laborious honeybee or the mother hen is substituted the myth of the devouring female insect: the praying mantis, the spider. . . . The same dialectic makes the erotic object into a wielder of black magic, the servant into a traitress, Cinderella into an ogress, and changes all women into enemies."[5] Precisely this inversion occurs in *Ethan Frome*, and because the terror is man's it makes emotional and intellectual sense to have a man, and one temperamentally close to Ethan, visualize it for us.

In part Wharton treats fear of maternal rejection in *Ethan Frome*. First Ethan's mother abandons his needs; then Zeena, his mother's replacement, does the same. But airy Mattie Silver is not a mother figure and her transformation moves the pattern beyond fear of maternal betrayal to fear of female betrayal in general. That fear plus perpetuation of the social system that makes it well-founded—Mattie Silvers *do* turn into Zeena Fromes—are the combined focus of Wharton's horror story. The tale looks at man's romantic dream of feminine solace and transport and, with a hideous twist, allows Ethan's fantasy to materialize. Mattie Silver does become "his"; but with, rather than without, Zeena; and the two witchlike women hold him prisoner for life in the severely limited economy and social landscape that traps all three of them.

How well the narrator understands the psychological and social prob-

---

4. Bruno Bettelheim, *The Uses of Enchantment: The Meaning and Importance of Fairy Tales* (New York: Alfred A. Knopf, 1976), pp. 199–215.
5. Beauvoir, *The Second Sex*, p. 179.

lem he dramatizes in *Ethan Frome* is uncertain. Being an ordinary sort of fellow, probably he is a better imaginer of its existence than analyst of its meaning. Edith Wharton, however, stands behind him fully in control of the tale's depth. As indicated in her choice of the Hawthornian names Ethan and Zenobia—neither of which is used in the early French draft—this multileveled book belongs in the continuum of classic American romance.

The name Ethan and Wharton's gloomy Berkshire setting bring to mind Hawthorne's "Ethan Brand," the tale of a man as alienated from woman (though for different reasons) as Wharton's protagonist. The name Zeena—short for Zenobia—similarly calls up *The Blithedale Romance* (1852), a book that specifically deals with male fear of woman in two men, the narrator/participant Coverdale, and the authoritarian perverter of the Blithedale commune, Hollingsworth. Both men (acting out a pattern that anticipates the moral of Wharton's cynical early parable, "The Valley of Childish Things")[6] decide to love childlike Priscilla rather than her mature sister Zenobia. There is no strict equation between Hawthorne's and Wharton's books.[7] Neither Ethan nor Wharton's narrator in *Ethan Frome* is a Hollingsworth, and neither resembles Hawthorne's Coverdale, a pathetic would-be poet. But Ethan's and his narrator's mythicized vision of Mattie Silver—an etherealized virgin-princess for Ethan to husband and protect—does recall Hollingsworth's (and conventional Coverdale's) decision in favor of Priscilla. Furthermore, Wharton's grotesque Zenobia Pierce Frome, who embodies the fate of Mattie, is the perfect antithesis of Hawthorne's hearty yet doomed feminist. His Zenobia is beautiful, healthy, sexual; Wharton's Zeena is ugly, sickly, frigid. She is, in psychological and mythic terms, the male dream of Mattie (or Priscilla) brought to its sterile conclusion: she is the adorable blonde from "The Valley of Childish Things" brought to shriveled middle life. *Ethan Frome* self-consciously places itself in the tradition of American symbolic fiction and envisions the living death— for women, for men—that the dream of Mattie Silver implies: crippled females, "queer" women of the region.

In her French draft Edith Wharton explicitly states that Mattie "exemplified all the dull anguish of the long line of women who, for two hundred years, had been buffeted by life and who had eaten out their hearts in the constricted and gloomy existence of the American countryside." In the finished version of *Ethan Frome* Wharton is more subtle, but no less clear. Witchlike Zenobia Frome, a terrifying and repulsive figure archetypally, is in social terms not at all mysterious: it is

---

6. Early Wharton short story in which a man chooses the perpetually infantile female [*Editor*].

7. * * * In fact, Wharton's story (like Hawthorne's) is about large communal issues, and one of the principal ways in which she emphasizes the pervasiveness of the psychosocial problem involved is by giving the story (unlike Hawthorne) to a narrator who is not even a participant in the action, much less the center of interest. He is just an average young man who shares Ethan's fears of woman so deeply that he can serve as a medium to give them expression.

a commonplace of scholarship about the persecution of witches that many of them were ordinary women bent and twisted by the conditions of their lives as women, their isolation and powerlessness. Stated simply, Zeena Frome is the witch that conservative New England will make of unskilled young Mattie; and Wharton's inverted fairy tale about the multiplication of witches in Ethan's life, a story appropriately told by a horrified young man whose job it is to build the future, finally serves as a lesson in sociology. Witches do exist, Wharton's tale says, and the culture creates them.

JUDITH FRYER

[The Spaces of *Ethan Frome*†]

In Hawthorne's "Ethan Brand," an old Jew appears in a mountain village with a diorama. Looking into the show-box, Ethan Brand, the returned lime-burner, is startled by the "heavy matter" he sees. But what he sees, according to the next viewer, is "nothing."[1] In Hawthorne's heavily symbolic landscapes, Ethan Brand has no place. "Oh, Mother Earth," he cries, just before taking his own life, "who art no more my Mother, . . . Oh, mankind, whose brotherhood I have cast off. . . !" Among the lonely characters of Nathaniel Hawthorne, none, perhaps, so haunts and lingers in the reader's consciousness as Ethan Brand. "The bleak and terrible loneliness in which this man had enveloped himself," as well as that of Hawthorne's Zenobia, the "tragedy-queen" of *The Blithedale Romance*, must have lingered in Edith Wharton's consciousness as she meditated on her own New England tale.[2] Both Ethan Brand and Zenobia are suicides. Wharton's Ethan Frome is a failed suicide, but as one of the village residents tells the narrator of Wharton's tale, "I don't see's there's much difference between the Fromes up at the

† From *Felicitous Space: The Imaginative Structures of Edith Wharton and Willa Cather* (Chapel Hill: University of North Carolina Press, 1986), pp. 180–193. Reprinted by permission.
1. In 1799 Robert Fulton, the American inventor, brought to Paris the first large diorama, a grandiose, circular panorama of New World scenery, accurate in every detail, a landscape without the disturbing presence of a single actor. The diorama was an immediate success. Soon a theater opened, devoted exclusively to dioramas, dedicated "to the reproduction on a theatrical scale of those views which are most worthy of exciting public curiosity from the historical and picturesque point of view," and organized by, among others, a young Frenchman who would soon make a name for himself as a pioneer photographer, Louis Daguerre. This first theater without actors, devoted to a display of landscapes without people, marks a shift from the Renaissance notion that "all the world's a stage" to one that would increasingly set scenes in domestic interiors and present private and psychological problems hidden from the public world. Jackson, "Landscape as Theater," pp. 74–75.
2. Nathaniel Hawthorne, *Tales and Sketches* (New York: Library of America, 1982), pp. 1065, 1063. Wharton uses the name Brand for her characters Sylvester and Ora Brand, a father and ghost of a dead daughter, in her story "Bewitched." As in her *Ethan Frome*, this tale is set in Starkfield, a snowbound and silent winter landscape.

farm and the Fromes down in the graveyard; 'cept that down there they're all quiet, and the women have got to hold their tongues."[3] Hawthorne's characters suffer the dilemma of head and heart—where Ethan Brand became a fiend "from the moment that his moral nature had ceased to keep the pace of improvement with his intellect," Zenobia, envisioning and speaking for a radical restructuring of society in which the relationships between the sexes would fundamentally be altered, suffers an unbearable wound to her heart. In separating himself from "the brotherhood of mankind," Ethan Brand will be reduced, finally, to a marble heart (a residue of which appears in the fragmentary tale told in Wharton's autobiography); "as the bright and gorgeous flower, and rich, delicious fruit of his life's labor—he had produced the Unpardonable Sin!" In defying Destiny by daring to swerve "out of the beaten track," Zenobia, as the exotic flower in her hair indicates, demonstrates a similar "pride and pomp, which had a luxuriant growth in . . . [her] character."[4] Wharton was less interested in the sinfulness than in the loneliness of such separation from humankind, on the one hand, and the masks or veils necessary to social role-playing—the name "Zenobia" was a mask in which Hawthorne's heroine appeared before the public— on the other. Coverdale, the narrator in *The Blithedale Romance*, who as his name suggests veils his own heart, seeks to learn what lies behind the masks; but like Ethan Brand, Coverdale would pry into the hearts of his fellow human beings and truly sympathize with none.

One need not linger too long on the actual correspondence between Hawthorne's and Wharton's characters. As Henry James said about the resemblance of Hawthorne's Zenobia to Margaret Fuller, there are facts of correspondence—Fuller's pride, passion, eloquence, her connection with the Transcendental community—and of "divergence from the plain and strenuous invalid" in "the beautiful and sumptuous Zenobia": it is an idle inquiry "to compare the image at all strictly with the model."[5] In other words, an author takes what she or he needs from a germ of life—or literature—and draws for the rest upon the imagination. Wharton's "germ" for Zenobia seems to have been this "plain and strenuous invalid," one, Hawthorne noted in his journal, whose "strong, heavy, unpliable, and in many respects defective and evil nature" was adorned "with a mosaic of admirable qualities."[6]

We know Zenobia, of course, through the narrator Coverdale, who would turn the whole affair—Zenobia's tragedy—into a ballad, just as we know Hester Prynne through the imagination of the narrator who

3. Edith Wharton, *Ethan Frome* (New York: Scribner's, 1911, with 1922 introduction by Edith Wharton), p. 181.
4. Hawthorne, *Tales*, p. 1064; *The Blithedale Romance* (1852) (New York: Library of America, 1983, p. 645.
5. Henry James, *Hawthorne* (New York: Harper, 1879), pp. 131, 130.
6. Newton Arvin, ed., *The Heart of Hawthorne's Journals* (Boston: Houghton Mifflin, 1929), p. 272.

finds her talisman and the bare record of her case in the attic of the
Custom House. And this is the way we know Ethan Frome. In fact, we
are told, there are several versions of "the Starkfield chronicle," the
"deeper meaning" of which is in the gaps—the parts left to the imagination. And we as readers are invited to make up our own versions.

A female reader, for example, might make up a version different from
the narrator's. He imagines Ethan as a victim of a shrewish, hypochondriac wife seven years his senior. But what was Frome's cousin like when
she first came to the farm to help nurse Ethan's dying mother? For
Ethan who, the narrator imagines, had lived with a deepening silence
year by year and felt, once his mother had fallen ill, the loneliness of
the house to be even more oppressive than that of the fields, Zenobia's
volubility must have been "music in his ears" after the mortal silence of
his long imprisonment:

> His mother had been a talker in her day, but after her "trouble" the
> sound of her voice was seldom heard, though she had not lost the
> power of speech. Sometimes, in the long winter evenings, when in
> desperation her son asked her why she didn't "say something," she
> would lift her finger and answer: "Because I'm listening"; and on
> stormy nights, when the loud wind was about the house, she would
> complain, if he spoke to her: "They're talking so out there that I
> can't hear you."

Then, she, too, fell silent, the narrator imagines. "Perhaps it was the
inevitable effect of life on the farm, or perhaps, as she sometimes said,
it was because Ethan 'never listened.' The charge was not wholly
unfounded."

Whether, given her name, Zenobia has some tragedy of her own
behind her, some suppressed passion buried before she married Ethan,
clearly this marriage is as confining for her as for him. What must it be
like to be Zenobia, a woman imprisoned on an isolated farm with only
the taciturn and inarticulate Ethan for company? No wonder she is turning "queer." Men in such situations at least have contact with farm
hands, other farmers, folks gathered at the post office, the stage driver;
but Zenobia, when the chill and snow seals her off from all human
interaction, must be driven inward in a way conducive to madness. As
she feels herself shriveling up, growing more unattractive, another
cousin arrives: colorful, cheerful, active, bright Mattie Silver. Her husband begins to shave daily and in many little ways to reveal that he is
attracted to the younger and prettier newcomer. Then there is the
"smash-up": no one knows just why Ethan and Mattie were sledding
when he was supposed to be taking her to the train and picking up the
new hired girl, but at any rate, there are the two injured people to care
for now, and Mattie, the intruder, will be permanently paralyzed, Zenobia's burden.

This is not, of course, the story Edith Wharton's narrator makes up, but we as readers are given some license to imagine "other versions," and indeed, when *Ethan Frome* was dramatized by Owen and Donald Davis in 1936, quite a new Zenobia emerged. Leon Edel wrote to Wharton, after seeing *Ethan Frome* performed, that while the play was "beautifully mounted, winter scenes crisp and white against deep blue-night backgrounds, and interiors scrupulously conveying the atmosphere of the New England farmhouse," the principal characters "have been arbitrarily altered. Mattie Silver has turned into a giddy young girl, fluttery and insipid. Contrasted with her, Zeena emerges mature, dignified, and even sympathetic to an audience alienated by Mattie's excessive exuberance. Ethan is weak, indecisive, robbed of much of his stature and nobility." The play was, he felt, "yours and yet not yours."[7]

The given, the "situation" for any version of the tale begins with the landscape. Ethan, Zenobia, Mattie all succumb to the exigencies of the snow-bound village, where in the isolated farm-houses "insanity, incest and slow mental and moral starvation were hidden away." Like the land, Wharton said in her introduction to the tale, her characters were a series of "granite outcroppings"; the story "*contains its own form and dimensions.*"[8] "It was not until I wrote 'Ethan Frome' that I suddenly felt the artisan's full control of his implements," Wharton would recall some twenty-three years after she wrote the tale. "When 'Ethan Frome' first appeared I was severely criticized by the reviewers for what was considered the clumsy structure of the tale. I had pondered long on this structure, had felt its peculiar difficulties, and possible awkwardnesses"—a set of simple and inarticulate characters, a more sophisticated "looker-on" who interprets them. "I am still sure that its structure is not its weak point."[9] If the situation—here the bleakness and privation of the New England landscape—"seizes the characters in its steely grip," she would point out in *The Writing of Fiction*, "the central characters tend to be the least real." They are standard-bearers of the author's convictions "or the expressions of his secret inclinations. They are *his* in the sense of tending to do and say what he would do, or imagines he would do, in given circumstances, . . . mere projections of his own personality."[1]

7. Jan. 31, 1936, Wharton Archives, Beinecke Library, Yale University, New Haven, Conn.
8. Wharton's introduction to *Ethan Frome*. pp. vi–vii, emphasis original. See John Stilgoe's essay, "Winter as Landscape," *Orion Nature Quarterly* 3 (Winter 1984): 5–11, for a description of harsh New England winters in the writings of William Bradford, Cotton Mather, Henry D. Thoreau, John Greenleaf Whittier, Robert Frost and various popular sources. Insulated as we are from the older experience of winter, Stilgoe writes, "blue shadows and white silence, . . . raw winter threatens to congeal the voluptuous warmth of contemporary metropolitan civilization. Old Man Winter now stalks ever more fragile defenses" (p. 5).
9. *A Backward Glance*, p. 209.
1. *The Writing of Fiction*, p. 133, emphasis original. There is, of course, a class distinction to be made between Wharton and her narrator on the one hand and Ethan Frome on the other, and this consciousness of class underlies—in a way I find disturbing—her "principles" of gardening and decor.

In just this way are the lonely and inarticulate people buried alive in the snow-bound landscape bound up with the narrator of *Ethan Frome*, the more sophisticated looker-on, who is *free* to interpret and imagine. This newfound freedom, this ability to make of situations *stories*, must account for the joy and power Edith Wharton herself felt in creating *Ethan Frome*. Underneath the snow that buries the little village of Starkfield, the structure of her tale reveals, lie clues of Edith Wharton's secret garden.

As in *The Blithedale Romance* and *The Scarlet Letter*, then, as well as in ghost stories like Henry James's *The Turn of the Screw* and Edith Wharton's "The Eyes," *Ethan Frome* is two stories, one about the narrator and one that the narrator makes up. To take first the tale made up by the narrator, the one the reader remembers: Ethan Frome, in order to support his ailing, nagging wife and her semiparalyzed cousin who lives with them, is tied to a mill and a farm from which he barely ekes out a living. He and the cousin had years before been much drawn to each other, we learn, and Zenobia, perceiving the growing attraction between Ethan and Mattie, determined to send Mattie away. In the narrator's version, Ethan dreams of fleeing with Mattie, but his financial and imaginative poverty makes freedom impossible. As he drives Mattie to the station, the pleasant thought occurs to him that they might have a farewell sled ride together. Then, at Mattie's urging, they take one more ride, this time aiming for the giant elm at the foot of the steep slope, intending, since they cannot live together, to die together. The plan miscarries: with a horrible irony, the lamed and scarred Ethan is, for the rest of his life, imprisoned with *two* dependent ailing women.

Edith Wharton wrote this part of the story several years before she completed the novella *Ethan Frome*.[2] Wishing to improve her French after moving to Paris, she wrote later in A *Backward Glance*, she engaged a young French tutor for conversations two or three times a week. The tutor, "too amiable ever to correct my spoken mistakes, . . . finally hit on the expedient of asking me to prepare an 'exercise' before each visit. The easiest thing for me was to write a story; and thus the French version of 'Ethan Frome' was begun, and carried on for a few weeks. Then the lessons were given up, and the copy-book containing my 'exercise' vanished forever. But a few years later, during one of our summer sojourns at the Mount, a distant glimpse of Bear Mountain brought Ethan back to my memory, and the following winter in Paris I wrote the tale as it now stands."[3] Several things happened in between. Wharton had a good deal of writing behind her by the time she began

2. Cynthia Griffin Wolff dates the first version as about 1906 or 1907, based on Wharton's meeting her French tutor in 1905 and publishing a story in proficient French in 1908. A *Feast of Words: The Triumph of Edith Wharton* (New York: Oxford University Press, 1977), pp. 161, 426, n. 124.

3. A *Backward Glance*, pp. 295–96. The "black book" is in the Wharton Archives, Beinecke Library, Yale University, New Haven, Conn.

to revise her tale, for one thing: four novels, two novellas, four books of nonfiction, four collections of stories and two books of verse. She had met and fallen in love with Morton Fullerton, for another. By 1911 the affair was over, but this newly experienced passion would give an increased range and depth to her fiction, and her characters, from this point on, would have alternatives to entrapment, even if they did not use them or made bad use of them. Finally, Wharton had begun to read Joseph Conrad, whose narrator and his double in "The Secret Sharer" and "Heart of Darkness" would leave their mark on *Ethan Frome*.[4]

There are significant differences in the two versions of the story. In the first one, there is no narrator, no tragic accident, no "backward glance" or "making up," for the action all takes place in the space of a few days—and thus no lamed Ethan, no paralyzed Mattie; there is little detail given about the Frome house and the land seems, with its hard bright glitter, equally inaccessible and alienating, but less ominously threatening. In the earlier version, Ethan and Mattie have neither the one evening nor the sled ride together. When his wife (named Anna in the earlier version) goes away, Hart (the earlier Ethan) is afraid to be alone with Mattie: he loiters about the town instead of going home, finally warming himself up with a stiff drink. In the final scene Mattie and Hart bid each other a tearful farewell at the train station, she suicidally depressed, but forbidding Hart to do anything that would humiliate Anna or bring infamy upon herself.

In the later construction of *Ethan Frome*, a character with options is superimposed upon a character without options; this narrator comments on and interprets the story of his counterpart as Wharton did in making up the story, literally telling the tale as she wrote it: "I wrote the tale as it now stands, reading my morning's work aloud each evening to Walter Berry. . . . We talked the tale over page by page, so that its accuracy of 'atmosphere' is doubly assured."[5] Wharton's narrator, too, like the narrator of *The Scarlet Letter* in "The Custom House," is concerned with the accuracy of the atmosphere; it is in this way that the dreamworld— the place Hawthorne called "moonlight in a familiar room"—becomes real to the imagination. When the situation is real, the narrator can say: what if *I* were like Ethan Frome? I might have been like Ethan Frome. But the difference between us is that he is inarticulate, while I, in telling this story, free myself from such a trap.

That the narrator *is* Ethan Frome's counterpart is clear from the details about Ethan in the inner story which the narrator cannot have *known* in any objective sense. All that can be verified by direct observation or corroborated by reports of others—as opposed to what is "made up"—is the following: Ethan Frome at fifty-two looks like an old man;

---

4. See R. W. B. Lewis, *Edith Wharton*, and Cynthia Griffin Wolff, *Feast of Words*, for accounts of Wharton's affair with Morton Fullerton and of her reading.
5. *A Backward Glance*, p. 296.

he walks with a limp, the result of a "smash-up" twenty-four years ago that has left his right side so shortened and warped that every step costs him a great effort and his forehead badly scarred with a deep red gash. He drives in every day from his farm to the post office, where the narrator sees him, and where Frome receives no communications from the outside world except the *Bettsbridge Eagle* and letters or packages addressed to his wife from patent-medicine manufacturers. The narrator learns from Harmon Gow, the stage driver, that Ethan Frome has always had to care for those around him—first his father, then his mother, then his wife—and that Ethan's "been in Starkfield too many winters. . . . Most of the smart ones get away," words that will linger in the narrator's mind. From Mrs. Hale, with whom he lodges, the narrator learns only that Mattie, before the accident, had a sweet nature and that the accident itself is, for Mrs. Hale, too terrible to talk about. Mattie Silver was Ruth Varnum's friend, before her marriage to Ned Hale, and it was to Lawyer Varnum's house that Mattie was brought after the smash-up. "If she'd ha' died, Ethan might ha' lived," she tells the narrator. From these hints, from the provocation of Mrs. Hale's silence, from his impressions of winter in Starkfield, when the village "lay under a sheet of snow perpetually renewed from the pale skies, . . . [a] mute melancholy landscape, an incarnation of . . . frozen woe, . . . a depth of moral isolation too remote for casual access," and from daily contact with Ethan Frome, the narrator pieces together his story.

The narrator is an engineer, "sent up by my employers on a job connected with the big power-house at Corbury Junction, and a long-drawn carpenters' strike had so delayed the work that I found myself anchored at Starkfield—the nearest habitable spot—for the best part of the winter." He hires Ethan Frome to drive him daily to the train, and through this regular contact he learns enough to piece together his description of Frome. That Frome is a "ruin of a man" with "something bleak and unapproachable in his face" is due not only to the smash-up, the narrator decides, but to crushed hopes and a defeated sense of self. For example, when the narrator mentions his job in Florida the previous winter, Frome says that he, too, had once been "down there," and when the narrator leaves in Frome's sleigh a book that deals with new research in biochemistry, Frome begins to read it, telling the narrator that such things "used to" interest him. In the narrator's story, Frome "had always wanted to be an engineer, and to live in towns, where there were lectures and big libraries and 'fellows doing things' "; he had studied engineering at Worcester and had gone down to Florida on an engineering job before he was called back to the farm by his father's illness. Since then, "the inexorable facts [had] closed in on him like prison-wardens handcuffing a convict. There was no way out—none."

One day there is a snowstorm so thick and constant that the narrator's train is blocked and Ethan Frome drives him all the way to Corbury

Junction. On the road, they pass the Frome farm, the "exanimate" saw-mill, the cluster of sheds "sagging under their white load," the orchard of "starved" trees, and a field or two, "their boundaries lost under drifts; and above the fields, huddled against the white immensities of land and sky, one of those lonely New England farm-houses that make the landscape lonelier." The narrator sees a house "unusually forlorn and stunted" because it lacks what is known in New England as the "L"— that long, deep-roofed adjunct usually built at right angles to the main house and connecting it, by way of store-rooms and tool-house, with the wood-shed and cow barn. "Whether because of its symbolic sense," the narrator reflects, "the image it presents of a life linked with the soil, and enclosing in itself the chief sources of warmth and nourishment, or whether merely because of the consolatory thought that it enables the dwellers in that harsh climate to get to their morning's work without facing the weather, it is certain that the 'L' rather than the house itself seems to be the centre, the actual hearth-stone of the New England farm." With Frome beside him, he hears the wistfulness in his compan-ion's words and sees "in the diminished dwelling the image of his own [Frome's] shrunken body."

The house now faces an unused road. It once looked out upon an artery of connection to the world, but since the trains began running, "nobody ever comes by here to speak of," and Frome's mother, he sug-gests (like Mrs. Manstey in an earlier story), dies when she is cut off from the outside world. The sense of just how cut off becomes clear that evening, when the continuing snow becomes part of the "thickening darkness, . . . the winter night itself descending on us layer by layer," and even the small ray of Frome's lantern is lost in this "smothering medium." Floundering through the deep drifts in the darkness, the two men at last reach Frome's place and decide to go no further for the night. Lifting his lantern inside the door, Frome reveals "a low unlit passage, at the back of which a ladder-like staircase rose into obscurity"; to the right "a line of light marked the door of the room which had sent its ray across the night," and from behind the door came the sound of a woman's voice "droning querulously." It is at this moment when the interior of Frome's house is revealed to him, the narrator says, that he "found the clue to Ethan Frome, and began to put together this vision of his story."

So clearly is the house presented through the movements and gestures of its inhabitants that we can visualize its plan and understand the pat-terns of movement of the people who live there. The original house plan was an image of classical harmony and balance. A typical New England hall-and-parlor house, it has a central front door that opens onto a passageway dividing the kitchen on the right from the parlor on the left. The stairs lead from the entryway to two bedrooms, one on the right and one on the left. The central floor plan promotes order in that

Ethan can leave his muddy boots and raincoat in the passageway before entering the kitchen. Unlike visitors to an earlier version of a New England house who would have been ushered directly into the "hall"— the multipurpose kitchen, sleeping room, and visiting place—guests at this house must wait in the passageway to be ushered either into the kitchen or into the parlor.[6] Moreover, the front porch announces a tie to "the most considerable mansion in the village," the Hales', with its classical portico, small-paned windows through which can be seen the steeple of the Congregational church, and " 'best parlour,' with its black horse-hair and mahogany weakly illuminated by a gurgling Carcel lamp."

The plan of the Fromes' house has, in fact, been subverted. In New England fashion, a small room, like a minister's study, has been added behind the parlor, and the now nonexistent "L" further contributed to the irregular outline of the house. The removal of the "L," however, means that the kitchen door at the back of the house is directly accessible from the outside, and it is Ethan's habit to go around to the back and enter the house in this way. His farm-hands also enter directly into the kitchen through this back door. Moreover, the kitchen is the only room in the house that is really inhabited. The Fromes are too poor to keep another fire going in the parlor, and the small room at the back, Ethan's room, is rarely used. It was to the parlor that Mattie was carried to begin her invalidism after the smash-up. The narrator must have slept in the small room behind the parlor.

The kitchen ought to be—as it is in the stories of Sarah Orne Jewett[7]—a center of warmth, conversation, hospitality. The Frome kitchen is very cold when Ethan and the narrator enter, and not only because someone has allowed the fire to go out. It is a poor-looking place, even for that part of the country: one chair—Zenobia's—looks like a soiled relic of luxury bought at a country auction, and the rest of the furniture is of the roughest kind, "coarse," "broken," "unpainted," "meagre," like the food—the unappetizing "remains of a cold mince-pie in a battered pie-dish." Ethan is trapped, the narrator imagines, in this house which seems an image of his own shrunken body, but which is really Zenobia's domain: he moves from her bedroom, where he lies beside her without moving, staring at the ceiling, to her kitchen, where he eats her meager portions and listens not to conversation but to querulous droning. In the narrator's version of the story there is a cat, which when Zenobia is not present sleeps in her rocking chair, but even the cat is not an image of warmth. Wharton did not like cats. ("The cat: a snake in fur," she wrote

---

6. For information on New England house plans, see Henry Glassie, *Pattern in the Material Culture of the Eastern United States* (Philadelphia: University of Pennsylvania Press, 1968), pp. 124–31; Abbott Lowell Cummings, *The Framed Houses of Massachusetts Bay 1625–1725* (Cambridge, Mass.: Harvard University Press, 1979), Chapter 3; J. Frederick Kelly, *The Early Domestic Architecture of Connecticut* (New Haven: Yale University Press, 1924), Chapter 5.
7. Well-known writer of New England *[Editor]*.

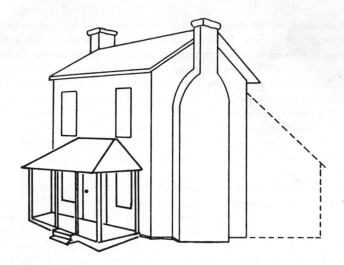

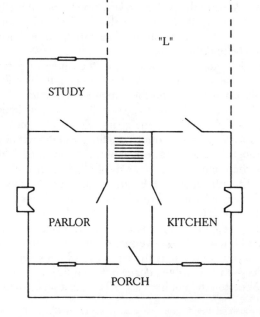

"L"

STUDY

PARLOR

KITCHEN

PORCH

in her diary in 1924.[8]) Bound together in a proximity that does not warm, everyone in this tragic little circle is starved, cold, inarticulate and enslaved by poverty, their bodies, one another, by their inability to imagine for themselves, as the narrator can, other possibilities. Neither is redemption offered by the surrounding land: if Ethan does not go through the farmyard—"bare's a milkpan when the cat's been round"— to get to his house, then he must go through the graveyard, passing the headstone that reads:

SACRED TO THE MEMORY OF

ETHAN FROME AND ENDURANCE HIS WIFE,

WHO DWELLED TOGETHER IN PEACE

FOR FIFTY YEARS.

And in winter, the heavy, unceasing snows threaten to obliterate not only the boundaries and identifying marks of the land, but to extinguish human life itself. The narrator's story begins, "The village lay under two feet of snow."

At the moment that the narrator stands in the passageway of Ethan Frome's house, he begins to imagine the story of the life that goes on in the room with the light; he imagines himself as Ethan, trapped in that house, on that land. So Ethan in the beginning of the story stands in the frosty darkness outside the window of the church where animated young people are dancing. He looks in at a room that seems "to be seething in a mist of heat"; there are platters heaped with food, there is music, and the people inside are engaged in communication and contact—talking, laughing, touching, moving together to the music. Ethan walks Mattie home from the dance—they talk about the stars, about the big elm at the foot of the hill where Ned Hale and Ruth Varnum were almost killed in a sledding accident, about Mattie's plans—and when they reach the back of the house, Ethan stands looking in, this time at his wife:

> Against the dark background of the kitchen she stood up tall and angular, one hand drawing a quilted counterpane to her flat breast, while the other held a lamp. The light, on a level with her chin, drew out of the darkness her puckered throat and the projecting

8. The complete entry reads: "I am secretly afraid of animals— of *all* animals except dogs, & even of some dogs. I think it is because of the *usness* in their eyes, with the underlying *not-usness* which belies it, & is so tragic a reminder of the lost life when we human beings branched off and left them: left them to eternal inarticulateness & slavery. *Why?* their eyes seem to ask us." Wharton Archives, Beinecke Library, Yale University, New Haven, Conn., emphasis original. Cf. this passage from "Kerfol": "It was as if they [the dogs] had lived a long time with people who never spoke to them or looked at them: as though the silence of the place had gradually benumbed their busy inquisitive natures. And this strange passivity, this almost human lassitude, seemed to me sadder than the misery of starved and beaten animals." *The Ghost Stories of Edith Wharton* (New York: Scribner's 1973), p. 84.

wrist of the hand that clutched the quilt, and deepened fantastically
the hollows and prominences of her high-boned face under its ring
of crimping-pins. To Ethan, still in the rosy haze of his hour with
Mattie, the sight came with the intense precision of the last dream
before waking. He felt as if he had never before known what his
wife looked like.

The scene is repeated precisely when Zenobia goes to town to consult a
new doctor and Ethan comes home to Mattie:

. . . he caught a sound on the stairs and saw a line of light about
the door-frame, as he had seen it the night before. So strange was
the precision with which the incidents of the previous evening were
repeating themselves that he half expected, when he heard the key
turn, to see his wife before him on the threshold; but the door
opened, and Mattie faced him.

She stood just as Zeena had stood, a lifted lamp in her hand,
against the black background of the kitchen. She held the light at
the same level, and it drew out with the same distinctness her slim
young throat and the brown wrist no bigger than a child's. Then,
striking upward, it threw a lustrous fleck on her lips, edged her eyes
with velvet shade, and laid a milky whiteness above the black curve
of her brows.[9]

The repetition prepares us for the way, at the end of the story, Mattie
will have become like Zenobia, a whining, dependent invalid, and suggests that all possibilities of escape for Ethan are delusory. His intercourse with Mattie, we learn throughout the story, is "made up of . . .
inarticulate flashes" not really different from his intercourse with his
wife. When he spends the night alone in his cold study, trying to imagine how he might escape with Mattie, the scene out the window that
would give Vance Weston, in *Hudson River Bracketed*,[1] the vision of
his next novel—a "bit of crooked apple-bough against a little square of
sky"—is for Ethan only "beauty of the night . . . poured out to mock
his wretchedness."[2]

In so small a space as the Fromes', patterns of human behavior
become very complex. The only place for Ethan to shave, for example,
is in the bedroom where Zenobia lies watching him, and it is from this
unusual daily ritual that she knows he is attracted to Mattie. If you have
only two dresses, one for good and one for everyday, if you have only

---

9. In the earlier [French] version, although Mattie does open the door for Hart [Ethan], this
repeated vision is imagined before it occurs. As W. D. MacCallan suggests, Hart represses his
feelings here in a way that Ethan does not. "The French Draft of Ethan Frome," *The Yale
University Library Gazette* 27 (July 1952): 40. This article reprints the French draft (the
"black book").
1. Vance Weston is Wharton's artist-hero in the novel mentioned [Editor].
2. Edith Wharton, *Hudson River Bracketed* (New York: Appleton, 1929), p. 511. Cf. this passage
from *The Glimpses of the Moon*: ". . . she saw bits of moon-flooded sky incrusted like silver in
a sharp black patterning of plane-boughs." (New York: Appleton, 1922), p. 5.

one special dish among the common ones, then the putting on of that best dress as Zenobia does when she goes to town, the setting of the table with that special dish as Mattie does when she and Ethan have supper alone, are actions that acquire a great, even an ominous significance. If there is no garden, only barren farmland and a relationship to the land that is everything—including death—and "nothing," then keeping geraniums and hyacinths alive in winter, as Zenobia does, bids us look at her again, invites us to piece out yet another story from the gaps in this one. If there are only two chairs by the hearth to sit on and only one room to sit in, if you sit in the chair that is by custom someone else's, it is a more audacious statement than it would be in a house full of rooms and chairs. If you are "by nature grave and inarticulate," and in the dark vastness of the out-of-doors you are moved by such locutions as Mattie's description of the starry sky—"It looks just as if it was painted!"—believing, as Ethan does, that "the art of definition could go no farther, and that words had at last been found to utter his secret soul," then the lamplit room "with all its ancient implications of conformity and order," the only order you know, bids you out of habit to hold your tongue and not touch that which you have no right to touch. The "order" is, however, of that eerie sort peculiar to dreams, like the fragments of the broken pickle dish laid edge to edge on the shelf, an ominous portent of Mattie's own smash-up.

Ethan Frome affects us as readers so powerfully precisely because of this quality of nightmare.[3] Reading it again and again, knowing that the querulous droning voice we hear at the end of the narrator's introduction is that of the bright and vivacious Mattie Silver at the beginning of the story does not lessen the horror of the dream as we experience it one more time. *Ethan Frome* takes the structures of everyday life, the structures Edith Wharton knew—the carefully balanced house plan, a particular relationship between house and land mediated by some connecting extension of the house, the repeated rituals of daily living—and reduces them to their barest essence, takes from them all warmth and nourishment and possibility of human intercourse. Outside is the obliterating vastness of unbounded space; inside are the clearly marked boundaries of imprisonment.

Ethan Frome dreams, in the narrator's version, of being able to speak: during his hiatus with Mattie he feels constraint vanish, he sees her face change with each turn of their talk "like a wheat-field under a summer breeze," and becoming intoxicated with the sound of his own clumsy

3. The setting of *Ethan Frome* is like a recurring dream in Wharton's fiction: most of the ghost stories are set in large country estates like Wharton's where one "feel[s] all the place had to communicate," especially the quality of silence, as in "Kerfol"; in deserted spaces and wastes of snow, as in "The Lady's Maid's Bell"; in the winter silence and entrapment of Starkfield in "Bewitched"; "day after day, winter after winter, year after year . . . [the] speechless, soundless," loneliness of "Mr. Jones"; the empty, silent winterhouse of "All Souls'." *Ghost Stories*, pp. 81, 193.

words, he longs to try new ways of using this "magic." Words, he senses, can overcome his imprisonment, can turn winter into summer, barrenness into a garden. The narrator, too, dreams the story of Ethan Frome. It does not come to him all at once as he stands in the dark passageway of the Frome house. The house affects him powerfully, as does the land in which he finds himself marooned for the winter. But like Wharton, who had the bones of the story several years before she was able to turn it into a successful work of fiction, the narrator must mull over the pieces, sort out the clues and dream the story for several years before he is able finally to set it down. In the telling, he makes the tale his own; he has control—like Wharton, who experiences the relief of the dreamer awakened, the joy of learning to connect her two worlds.

JEAN FRANTZ BLACKALL

Edith Wharton's Art of Ellipsis†

> I am sorry to have delayed the galleys so long, & if it were possible to gain time by having the page proofs corrected in N.Y., I am willing to have it done. I have revised the galleys thoroughly—it is a second or third revision—so any one who would look after the typographical part carefully could do it. The punctuation must be respected!
>
> Edith Wharton[1]

The use of ellipses is a consistent practice in Edith Wharton's fiction. Of *Fast and Loose*, Wharton's first preserved manuscript, written at the age of fourteen, her editor complains: "A printed text reproducing all her idiosyncracies would be . . . virtually unreadable. . . . I have made conventional substitutions or deletions where the dashes seemed to me clearly unintended. . . . The use of many dots to indicate ellipsis . . . has been modernized." Of Edith Wharton's correspondence with Scribner's in 1907, R. W. B. Lewis writes: "There was also a long and intricate to-do about the spacing of dots at the end of sentences left unfinished in the text—to the point where Edith wondered dourly why the English handled their galleys so much better."[2] And Elizabeth Ammons complains that one modern Scribner's reprint of *Ethan Frome* (The Scribner Library: Contemporary Classics, 1970) obscures the fact

---

† From *The Journal of Narrative Technique* 17 (Spring 1987): 145–62. Reprinted by permission of *The Journal of Narrative Technique*.

1. Unpublished letter dated August 16, 1910, from Edith Wharton to William Crary Brownell, her Scribner's editor. This and other unpublished letters cited in this article are to be found in the Archives of Charles Scribner's Sons, Scribner's Authors File 1, box 167, at the Princeton University Library. I am indebted to Jean F. Preston, Curator of Manuscripts, and her staff for making these materials available to me. Published with permission of Princeton University Library. I am also indebted to Charles Scribner's Sons and to William R. Tyler, owner of the Edith Wharton estate, for permission to quote from these letters.
2. *Edith Wharton: A Biography*, p. 82.

that Wharton originally separated the frame story from the inner narrative by no less than three lines of dots.

Such instances as these call attention to a pervasive characteristic of Edith Wharton's style, which is manifest in all periods and all genres in which she wrote. Wharton used certain devices, among them ellipsis, with which I shall be concerned here, in a highly calculated and contrived way to achieve certain kinds of effects. Though these usages differ greatly in given instances, ellipsis does appear to be associated with specific purposes, among these, to suggest the colloquial quality of speech, to emulate the rhythms of thought, and to mark a point of mental realignment. They may represent the inexpressible, or that which a character is unwilling to express, or that which the author chooses to withhold. Most important, Wharton uses ellipses to entice the reader to enter into imaginative collaboration with the writer.[3]

Wharton's understanding of what she was about is at times integrated into her texts in remarks made by the characters or by the authorial persona that intimate her awareness of the value of an absence, a pause, a silence, a gap. There are many such passages as these.

From "The Pretext" (1908):

> "Ghosts vanish when one names them!"

From *Summer* (1917):

> He spoke slowly, with pauses that seemed to invite his hearers to silent participation in his thought; and Charity perceived a light of response in their faces.

From *The Age of Innocence* (1920):

> "Anyhow, he—eventually—married her." There were volumes of innuendo in the way the "eventually" was spaced, and each syllable given its due stress.

From "The Debt" (1910):

> He was as inexpressive as he is today, and yet oddly obtrusive: one of those uncomfortable presences whose silence is an interruption.

3. The present overview of Wharton's strategic use of ellipsis is based on an examination of the 86 short stories brought together by R. W. B. Lewis in *The Collected Short Stories of Edith Wharton*, though I have included illustrations from several other works when these were particularly apposite. To facilitate the reader's access to the stories, I quote from Lewis' reprint edition—parenthetic citations in the text refer to Lewis—and from other accessible modern reprints. I have, however, checked quotations against English first editions, since Wharton apparently regarded these as being most reliable typographically. There are some variations among editions in the placing of three or four dots at the end of a sentence, but these do not appear to affect the function of terminal ellipses. Wharton's own preference was for three spaced dots but, above all, for consistency. (Regarding these matters see ms. letter to W. C. Brownell, August 6, 1907.) More significant departures from first editions will be noted individually. The dates appearing in parentheses in the text are those of the first publication in book form or, for uncollected stories, the periodical date, and are included to reveal how consistent over years Wharton's practices were. All ellipses appearing in quotations from Wharton's fiction are Wharton's own.

From "The Recovery" (1901):

> They moved about from room to room without exchanging a word.
> The vast noiseless spaces seemed full of sound, like the roar of a
> distant multitude heard only by the inner ear. Had their speech
> been articulate their language would have been incomprehensible.

Nora Frenway, in "Atrophy" (1930), looking out the train window,
sees

> miles and miles of alluring tarred roads slipping away into mystery.
> How often she had dreamed of dashing off down an unknown road
> with Christopher!

This image of roads leading to unrevealed conclusions, into mystery or,
as modified, leading into unknown circumstances, seems to correspond
to Wharton's use of ellipses at certain points—the end of a section, the
end of a story—to invite the reader to follow up the line of thought, the
consequences, the possibilities of a relationship, unassisted.

*   *   *

The emphatic use of ellipses in *Ethan Frome* is unusual in Wharton's
fiction, and has drawn attention. Departure from and return to the
frame of that narrative are marked by almost three lines of dots at the
beginning and by a conventional ellipsis plus three additional lines of
dots at the end of the inner narrative. Such emphasis invites response,
and both Elizabeth Ammons and Cynthia Wolff have integrated mention of the ellipses into an interpretation of the *nouvelle*.[4] For Ammons
the ellipses signify a change of genre, from the realistic outer narrative
to the fairy tale within. The inner story subtly evokes *Snow-White*, only
to violate the reader's expectations by its ironic inversion of the traditional fairy-tale ending. "As a fairy story, *Ethan Frome* terrifies because
it ends askew. Incredibly, the witch [Zeena] triumphs. Mattie Silver
becomes Zeena's double rather than Ethan's complement." I would suggest, rather, that the ellipses function as an instrument of intensification. If a change of genre is implied, the ellipses mark the
transformation of drama into narrative. *Ethan Frome*, the inner story, is
a tragic drama, observing almost classical unities, focusing upon the
moment of crisis in the relationship of the three principals, the three-
day sequence when the jealous wife raises her hand against the lovers
and thereby forces them to counteract her move. Out of this cataclysmic
confrontation comes the tragic denouement that stretches on endlessly
into the future, metamorphosing the drama into a narrative fiction. It is
Wharton's strategic manipulation of time, her sustaining the anguish of
the moment over years and years, that renders the peculiar intensity
and horror of Ethan Frome's story. The augmented ellipses mark this

4. Ammons's and Wolff's essays appear in this volume, pp. 145–157 and pp. 130–145 *[Editor]*.

transition into the critical moment and out of it into enduring time.[5] There is a comparable effect of indefinite extension in time in several other tales which end with an ellipsis, among these "The Moving Finger" (1901), "The Daunt Diana" (1910), and "The Long Run" (1916).[6]

In an iconoclastic reading Cynthia Wolff argues that *Ethan Frome* is the narrator's story. The engineer is an obsessed narrator and his "vision" (Wharton's own word), apart from factual details given in the frame, is a sinister fabrication rather than an objective rendering of Ethan's story. Wharton is subjectively implicated in her own fiction, and fears the entrapment and lack of initiative that the narrator's vision of Ethan's story records. Her containment of the narrator's "private nightmare" within a controlled fiction distances her from these fears and from the narrator's own temptation to yield to "a seductive and enveloping void." In defending her reading Wolff argues that "Everything that the reader can accept as reliably true can be found in the narrative frame; every-

5. Cf. Wharton's letters to A. H. Scribner concerning the page proofs for the first edition of *Ethan Frome*. On August 19, 1911, she writes: "On p. 186 there is a sharp break in the narrative, shown by a double line of dots. On seeing the page proofs I have decided that this is not a sufficient indication of the pause, & interval in time, which must be shown here; & I should like the lower part of p. 186 (after the two rows of dots) to be left blank, and the next paragraph to begin on p. 187." Acknowledging the corrected proofs, she adds, on August 23, 1911, "If some kind of sign—a sort of brief colophon—could be put in the lower part of p. 186, to give a still more complete impression of a break, it might be better. German prints [printers/?] use these signs very effectively in such cases, but I am not clear what would be used in English books. At any rate, I think another line of dots would help." After the "colophon" alternative is discussed at length, Wharton leaves it to the editor to decide, in a letter dated August 27, 1911.

6. Two other stories employ augmented ellipses such as we find in *Ethan Frome* (1911), "The Duchess at Prayer" (1901) and "Kerfol" (1916). In the American first edition of *Crucial Instances* but not in the English first edition a complete line of dots begins Part IV of "The Duchess at Prayer"; in both these editions a line of dots occurs after the first paragraph of Part V. The first row (found in the American text) clearly marks a transition from the frame, in which a first-person narrator describes the garden setting in which he will presently hear an old man's tale, to his aged *cicerone*'s tale of the Duchess. The story of the Duchess comprises the inner narrative and the whole of Part IV of the story. The beginning of Part V returns to the first-person narrator's descriptive frame—gray sky, a wind, purple hills across the valley— and in both editions a complete line of dots separates this brief descriptive paragraph from the first-person narrator's first question to the *cicerone* after hearing his tale. Hence we see that here as in *Ethan Frome* the augmented ellipses seal off the inner tale from the frame, and that the inner tale involves a transition into remote time past. Presumably the augmented ellipses are deleted at the beginning of the inner tale (the beginning of Part IV of the story) in the English first edition because the ellipses coincide with a parts division and are therefore in effect redundant. A row of dots following on a Roman numeral looks silly. (Like the English first edition, *The Collected Short Stories of Edith Wharton* deletes the line of dots that separates the frame from the beginning of the inner tale [I:233]. It differs from both first editions in deleting the row of dots that separates the end of the inner tale from the frame [I:244]).

There are two other complete lines of dots to be noted. Both Anne de Cornault in "Kerfol" and the Duchess in "The Duchess at Prayer" pass into unconsciousness upon confronting what is to them a horrible reality (though not a reality substantiated by either text). Anne de Cornault believes that her husband was murdered by ghostly dogs ("Kerfol," *Xingu*, Macmillan, p. 181); the Duchess believes that her husband has immured her lover, alive, in the chapel crypt ("The Duchess at Prayer," *Crucial Instances*, John Murray, p. 41). Augmented ellipses occur at this point. In either tale the succeeding paragraph returns to the world apart from the character's subjective vision, to a detached, fabricated, official version of "truth." Hence the augmented ellipses in these instances emphatically mark transitions. Cf. ns. p. 11 above. (*The Collected Short Stories of Edith Wharton* reduces the augmented ellipses in "Kerfol" to a conventional ellipsis [II:299] and omits the augmented ellipses in "The Duchess at Prayer" [I:243–244])

thing else bears the imprint of the narrator's own interpretation. . . . Even at the end of the narrator's vision, in the concluding scene with Mrs. Hale, Wharton is scrupulously careful not to credit the vision by giving it independent confirmation."

That such a reading is possible illustrates the skill with which Wharton has applied her art of ellipsis. The ellipses in the final scene in Ruth Hale's remarks to the narrator illustrate Wharton's understanding of the value of a blank. The author causes the reader to "think the evil" for himself, to fill in the blank according to his own imaginative resources. Wolff fills in the blank as being the author's personal absorption in the narrator's fearful vision. I fill in the blank by saying that Ruth Hale heard Mattie say something upon awakening after the sledding accident that revealed to her the love affair between Mattie and Ethan and, consequently, that they had attempted suicide.

> (Ruth Hale speaking)
> "then all of a sudden she woke up just like herself, and looked straight at me out of her big eyes, and said . . . Oh, I don't know why I'm telling you all this," Mrs. Hale broke off, crying.
> "they all thought Mattie couldn't live. Well, I say it's a pity she *did*. I said it right out to our minister once, and he was shocked at me. Only he wasn't with me that morning when she first came to . . ."

Hence I see Mrs. Hale as corroborating the narrator's intuited discovery of the adulterous triangle. The ellipses reflect her reticence, her unwillingness to name the evil of which she alone has firsthand knowledge. For the narrator, therefore, that knowledge of illicit love and willed self-destruction remains an inference, an imaginative invention, which becomes his story. His stance would seem to be comparable to that assumed by the narrator of "All Souls'" at the beginning and end of her narrative:

> I'll efface myself, and tell the tale, not in my cousin's words, for they were too confused and fragmentary, but as I built it up gradually out of her half-avowals and nervous reticences. If the thing happened at all—and I must leave you to judge of that—I think it must have happened in this way. . . .

At the end she remarks: "Such is my—conjectural—explanation of the strange happenings at Whitegates." So, too, the *Ethan Frome* narrator offers the reader a conjectural account. It was "the provocation of Mrs. Hale's silence" and "the accident of personal contact with the man" that instigated him to probe into Ethan's story.

In their subtler aspects, then, ellipses in Wharton's fiction demand of the reader a mental initiative. The reader must fill in the blank: complete the thought, fathom the joke, enter into the emotional vibrations of the characters, imagine their past, invent their next move or the thoughts that will produce it. These processes are of course simultaneously performed by characters within the fictions, whose agency stimulates the reader's own initiatives. A Whartonian silence is, therefore, like Bartleby, an obtrusive presence, because it tacitly demands an imaginative response.[7]

LEV RAPHAEL

From *Edith Wharton's Prisoners of Shame*†

* * *

The narrator of *Ethan Frome*, on first observing Frome at Starkfield, is struck by Frome's 'lameness checking each step like the jerk of a chain.' Ethan Frome is chained to an even darker fate than Lily's,[1] because he doesn't escape into death, yet his story too is one of disappointment, failure, powerlessness and shame—for him and in lesser ways for Mattie Silver and even his wife Zeena. The physical burden is matched by an emotional chain that constantly pulls Ethan short, that silences him, that constricts his life: shame over a lifetime of disappointments, culminating in being trapped ('most of the smart ones get away' from Starkfield), and over his deep inadequacies as a man. In *Ethan Frome*, shame becomes more and more potent a force as the novella progresses and its conflicts intensify.

Kaufman notes that 'the affective source of silence is shame, which is the affect that causes the self to hide. Shame itself is an impediment to speech.'[2] In the narrator's first extended contact with Frome, he reflects that Frome 'seemed a part of the mute melancholy landscape, an incarnation of its frozen woe, with all that was warm and sentient in him fast bound below the surface. . . .' Living in Starkfield, 'silence had deepened about him year by year.' We gain our first glimpses below that surface of silence watching Frome interact with the narrator, who is visiting Starkfield on an engineering job. Frome finds 'a volume of pop-

---

7. Gary H. Lindberg makes a similar point about Wharton's narrative technique in his observing that lapses in time between narrative blocks in *The House of Mirth*, *The Custom of the Country*, and *The Age of Innocence* cause the reader to "reconstruct" the intervening segment. "The gaps between a novelist's scenes have a curious power to implicate us, for somehow we must tacitly account for the lapsed time, and to this degree we participate in constructing the narrative movement itself." (*Edith Wharton and the Novel of Manners* [Charlottesville: University Press of Virginia, 1975], pp. 47–49).

† From *Edith Wharton's Prisoners of Shame: A New Perspective on her Neglected Fiction* (New York: St. Martin's, 1991), pp. 284–89. Copyright © Lev Raphael. Reprinted with permission of St. Martin's Press, Incorporated.

1. Lily Bart is in Wharton's *The House of Mirth* [Editor].

2. Gershen Kaufman, *The Psychology of Shame: Theory and Treatment of Shame-Based Syndromes* (New York: Springer, 1989), p. 200.

ular science' that the narrator left behind, and with 'a queer note of resentment in his voice' says the book is full of things he knows nothing about: 'He was evidently surprised and slightly aggrieved at his own ignorance.' For the narrator, these comments point up 'the contrast . . . between his outer situation and his inner needs.' Frome's 'old veil of reticence' is a mask for the bitter life of disappointment. And even in a town where people have suffered enough to feel 'indifferent' to other's troubles, Frome is seen as having 'had his plate full up with [sickness and trouble] ever since the very first helping.'

In the narrative built up about Frome, we learn of the early roots of his shame in disappointment. Though he had gone to a technical college for a year and been interested in physics, the death of his father 'and the misfortunes following it' ended the possibility of study, and through that, escape from the constricting life of Starkfield. Unlike Lily Bart, Ethan Frome has no personal gifts or talents that can offer even the fantasy of a better life. His life of isolation changes, however, when Mattie Silver comes to stay with him and his wife.

Mattie's circumstances recall Lily's in some ways (she too can 'trim a hat'). She is the daughter of a cousin of Zeena's, whose misfortune has 'indentured her' to the Fromes. Mattie's father 'had inflamed his clan with mingled sentiments of envy and admiration' by a successful move to Connecticut, marriage and business ventures. But he mishandled money that relatives had given him, all of which was revealed after his death. The shameful disclosure killed his wife, and left Mattie a victim. 'Her nearest relations . . . ungrudgingly acquitted themselves of the Christian duty of returning good for evil by giving [her] all the advice at their disposal.' Zeena only took Mattie in because her doctor said she needed help around the house: 'The clan instantly saw the chance of exacting a compensation from Mattie.' Like Lily, Mattie is proof of someone else's beneficence, and her 'liberation' is a kind of imprisonment, since she has to 'pay' for her father's success *and* his failure.

For Frome, Mattie's youth and enthusiasm offer him a pathway out of isolation. She is someone he can share his observations and thoughts with: 'He could show her things and tell her things . . . .' He also enjoys her 'admiration for his learning'—she can make him feel happy and proud. Yet because of her new importance in his life, she is also a source of shame. Waiting to take her home from a squaredance in town, he is struck by not feeling special. Through a window he sees 'two or three gestures, which, in his fatuity, he had thought she kept for him . . . the sight made him unhappy.' Even more painfully, he wonders 'how he could ever have thought his dull talk interested her. To him, who was never gay but in her presence, her gaiety seemed plain proof of *indifference*' [my emphasis]. When she is leaving the dance,

[a] wave of *shyness* pulled him back into the dark angle of the wall, and he stood there *in silence* instead of making his presence known to her. It had been one of the wonders of their intercourse that from the first, she, the quicker, finer, more expressive, *instead of crushing him by the contrast, had given him something of her own ease and freedom*; but now he felt as *heavy* and *loutish* as in his student days, when he had tried to 'jolly' the Worcester girls at a picnic [my emphases].

Frome is 'by nature grave and inarticulate [and] admired recklessness and gaiety in others'; one of Mattie's great gifts is to ease Frome's shame. Mattie's impact on Frome recalls Lily's skillful easing of Percy Gryce's profound embarrassment on the train to Bellomont. But Mattie is naturally capable of doing what in Lily is planned and reasoned. Wharton's intuitive understanding of shame is clear here; of course someone stiff and shy like Ethan would be struck by the contrast between himself and someone natural and free, and that invidious comparison would potentially be the source of shame. So much depends on her—and Frome attaches 'a fantastic importance to every change in her look and tone.' Doesn't this terrible dependence on others for one's own self-esteem remind us of characters throughout Wharton's fiction?

The night Ethan picks Mattie up at the dance, he is jealous of young, well-off Denis Eady, who had danced with Mattie. Later, thinking about Mattie and Denis, he will feel 'ashamed of the storm of jealousy in his breast. It seemed unworthy of the girl that his thoughts of her should be so violent.' Now, he is relieved when Mattie resists riding with Denis, but then Mattie's 'indifference was the more chilling after the flush of joy into which she had plunged him by dismissing Denis Eady.' Their idyllic walk home, 'as if they were floating on a summer stream,' ends with a grim reality: withered, censorious Zeena is waiting for him, and he goes up to their bedroom 'with *lowered head*' [my emphasis]. Shame is certainly a key element of his relationship with Zeena, the cousin who came to nurse his mother, and who stayed after Mrs Frome died. Unlike Mattie, she arouses little that is positive in Ethan. Zeena's 'efficiency shamed and dazzled him' and he keenly felt a 'magnified . . . sense of what he owed her.' Zeena's own shame helps trap him in Starkfield, which they had originally agreed to leave:

she had let her husband see from the first that life on an isolated farm was not what she had expected when she married . . . She chose to look down on Starkfield, but she could not have lived in a place which looked down on her. Even Bettsbridge or Shadd's Falls would not have been sufficiently aware of her, and in the greater cities which attracted Ethan she would have suffered a complete loss of identity.

Her feelings are thus clearly much more than what Richard Lawson describes as a 'disinclination to accept any change.'[3] Her power over Ethan manifests itself in a critical silence, hinting at 'suspicions and resentments impossible to guess.' Still, though vaguely threatened by Zeena, he is not reduced to *complete* powerlessness: 'There had never been anything in her that one could appeal to; but as long as he could ignore and command he had remained indifferent.'

The balance between them changes when Zeena goes off for more doctor's advice and Ethan and Mattie spend some time together alone—their first such occasion, which is both festive and furtive. Ethan is 'suffocated with the sense of well-being' coming in from his hard day's work for dinner, but when Zeena comes up in their conversation, Mattie feels 'the contagion of his embarrassment' and she flushes. The next day he feels intoxicated 'to find . . . magic in his clumsy words,' but he makes Mattie blush when he mentions having seen engaged friends of hers kissing: 'now he felt as if her blush had set a flaming guard about her. He supposed it was his natural awkwardness that made him feel so.'

Zeena's return with the diagnosis of 'complications'—which confers morbid 'distinction . . . in the neighbourhood'—precipitates the first fight between Ethan and herself 'in their seven sad years together.' Zeena claims that she will need full-time help around the house that Mattie cannot supply, and bursts out that she would have been ashamed to admit to the doctor that her husband begrudged her the help, that she lost her health nursing his mother, and her family said he 'couldn't do no less than marry' Zeena in the circumstances. Ethan explodes, and is 'seized with horror at the scene and shame at his own share in it.' Zeena taunts him with the possibility she might end up in a poorhouse, as other Fromes have done, and then Ethan's big lie is exposed. He had clumsily said he couldn't drive her to her train because he was going to get a payment for lumber from Andrew Hale. When he tried to get that unprecedented advance from Hale, Hale flushed, leaving Ethan 'embarrassed.' Shame kept him from pleading an emergency: since he had struggled to become solvent after his father's death, 'he did not want Andrew Hale, or any one else in Starkfield, to think he was going under again.' Frome naturally responds with anger when Hale asks if he is in financial trouble, because he of course feels further exposed.

Now, facing Zeena, Ethan blushes and stammers, trying to explain that there was no money coming in, and he is devastated when his wife announces she has hired a girl and that Mattie *must* go: he is 'seized with the despairing sense of his helplessness.' Ethan tries to shame Zeena into keeping Mattie, pointing out that people will frown on her kicking out a poor, friendless girl, but Zeena is adamant, leaving Ethan 'suddenly weak and powerless'—and enraged:

3. *Edith Wharton* (New York: Ungar, 1977), p. 68.

All the long misery of his baffled past, of his youth of failure, hardship and vain effort, rose up in his soul in bitterness and seemed to
take shape before him in the woman who at every turn had barred
his way. She had taken everything else from him; and now she
meant to take the one thing that made up for all the others.

Ethan is so distraught that he blurts out to Mattie that she has to leave,
and then feels 'overcome with shame at his lack of self-control in flinging the news at her so brutally.' The grim evening ends with Zeena's
discovery that her prized pickle dish, a never-used wedding present, was
broken during her absence when Mattie and Ethan were having dinner,
and that Ethan had tried to hide the breakage. Glad that Mattie—with
whom she compares so poorly—is leaving, Zeena's joy turns to profound sorrow at the destruction of the one treasure in her miserable
life.

Ethan longs for escape with Mattie to the West—but he hasn't
enough money: 'The inexorable facts closed in on him like prisonward-
ers handcuffing a convict. There was no way out—none. He was a prisoner for life, and now his one ray of light was to be extinguished.' In a
way like Lily, 'the passion of rebellion' breaks out in him and he plans
to ask Andrew Hale for money to pay for Zeena's new hired girl (though
the money would really be for his 'escape'). After all, Hale knows
Ethan's money troubles well enough for Ethan 'to renew his appeal
without too much loss of pride' [my emphasis]. On the brink of making
this request, however, unexpected sympathy from Mrs Hale turns Ethan
away, with 'the blood in his face.' Having been accustomed to think
people 'were either indifferent to his troubles, or disposed to think
[them] natural,' he is warmed by her compassionate 'You've had an
awful mean time, Ethan Frome.' Like Lily, unable to use Selden's letters despite Rosedale's seductive offer, he is 'pulled up sharply.' How
can he dishonestly take money from the Hales when they sympathize
with the way life has cheated him?

Still, Ethan's 'manhood was humbled by the part he was compelled
to play . . . as a helpless spectator at Mattie's banishment.' When she
later weepingly wishes she were dead, Ethan will feel ashamed too. Taking Mattie away, they stop at the pond where they first realized at a
picnic that they loved each other; it is a 'shy secret spot, full of the same
dumb melancholy that Ethan felt in his heart' [my emphasis]. Their
blissful reprieve of sledding turns into an attempted mutual suicide, but
as in so many other things, Ethan fails to pull it off, and he and Mattie
are left crippled and even more dependent on Zeena. Ethan is so
ashamed of what his life has come to that no stranger sets 'foot in [his]
house for over twenty years.'

All this, of course, is the *vision* of the narrator, and Frome is 'the
man he might become if the reassuring appurtenances of busy, active,

professional, adult mobility were taken from him.'[4] The life of silence
and constriction Ethan Frome leads is indeed a nightmare, as Cynthia
Griffin Wolff has eloquently shown, but I see this as a nightmare in
which shame has reduced human possibilities and even human speech
to an almost unbearable minimum. Ethan's fantasies of being buried
next to Mattie, his 'warm sense of continuance and stability' at the sight
of the family graveyard, is a longing not for passivity but for *release* from
the crushing weight of a lifetime of humiliating failure and disappointment. Wolff makes a compelling case for echoes in *Ethan Frome* of
Wharton's complex involvement with the aging Henry James, querulous and unpredictable Teddy Wharton. Certainly a marriage like hers,
especially as it blundered towards dissolution, was a source of intense
shame.[5]

CANDACE WAID

["A Vision of Unrelenting Infertility"]†

* * *

* * *In becoming a mutilated and crippled man, he also seems to
become the barren and infertile woman. Ethan Frome himself represents the failure of fertility and the insistent barrenness described
throughout the novel.[1]

The vision of *Ethan Frome* is finally a vision of unrelenting infertility.
The suicide attempt that cripples Mattie and Ethan is prefigured in the
smashed pickle dish, "the bits of broken glass" that Zeena discovers and
holds "as if she carried a dead body . . ." (Wharton's ellipses). The shattered pickle dish that is Zeena's most treasured wedding gift and the
dead cucumber vine that makes Frome imagine Zeena's death are
emblems of a lost or past fertility. The smashed glass under the foot of

---

4. See Wolff's essay in this volume, p. 130–145 [Editor].
5. See [Cynthia Griffin Wolff's] "Cold Ethan and Hot Ethan," *College Literature* (1987) vol. xiv,
   no. 3.
† From Candace Waid, *Edith Wharton's Letters from the Underworld: Fictions of Women and
   Writing* (Chapel Hill: The University of North Carolina Press, 1991), pp. 75–78. Copyright
   © 1991 by the University of North Carolina Press. Used by permission of the author and publisher.
1. * * *Kenneth Bernard emphasizes the imagery of castration in the novel, but he also suggests
   that the chilled atmosphere is related to Zeena's frigidity. Her sexual coldness is related to the
   barrenness suggested in the name Starkfield. Bernard comments that "barrenness, infertility is
   at the heart of Frome's frozen woe." See "Imagery and Symbolism in *Ethan Frome*," *College
   English* 23 (1961): 182. For the most complete discussion of the imagery of a void that Wharton uses to describe the New England of *Ethan Frome* and *Summer*, see Henry Alan Rose,
   "Such Depths of Sad Initiation': Edith Wharton and New England," *New England Quarterly*
   50 (1977): 423–39. Rose writes, "In this cultural emptiness, Wharton's imagination was free
   to range in a manner not duplicated in her cluttered urban world." He argues that in the
   "barren settings" of New England, Wharton felt "the full extent of the negation, the sense of
   void" (423–24).

the bridegroom should symbolize the loss of virginity and the beginning of fertility; but the pickle dish, used or unused, can symbolize infertility only. The dead cucumber vine that "dangled from the porch like a crape streamer tied to the door for a death" suggests the past fertility of an umbilical cord that now marks the barren interior of a house deprived of its "actual hearth-stone". One critic[2] has remarked that a "cucumber is no more than a pickle," yet without entering the ongoing critical debate about the vegetable symbols in the novel, it is essential to acknowledge that a pickle is a preserve that cannot reproduce itself. In the magical supper that Frome and Mattie have during their evening alone, the pickle dish and pickles form a display, a kind of rehearsal, for the eroticized scene of the accident that finally breaks the vessel of the young woman's body and preserves her in infertility. Both the broken pickle dish and the breaking of the body of the young woman suggest the horror of fertility rituals gone awry.

In the narrator's vision, the fragments of the dish and Mattie Silver's body cannot be put back together again. Only the narrator's story projected onto the shards of the past (which he claims to have gathered "bit by bit") can form the mocking semblance of a whole and seamless narrative. The narrative also has an ominous inevitability and circularity. *Ethan Frome* has its beginning in its ending: at the beginning of the story the narrator describes the crippled Frome, whose face "looks as if he was dead and in hell now!" The vision of the narrator must end in this hell because the future of the story he tells will always be in the past. In the introduction Wharton remarks that her "tale was not one on which many variations could be played." The narrator's vision may contain variations, but the story must end in the same place, around the same barren hearth.

Frome's "bleak and unapproachable" face and the unspeaking presence that makes him seem "a part of the mute melancholy landscape" also suggest the impenetrable structures of the novel itself, structures that are repeatedly figured in the image of the closed door. The closed door, like the unspeaking Frome and the "provocation of Mrs. Hale's silence," compels the narrator to piece together his fiction. However, the end of the vision suggests an impenetrable exteriority that extends to the narrative structure of the book itself. Intent on suicide, the characters of the narrator's vision encounter the existence of an impenetrable boundary; they drive "down on the black projecting mass." We have seen that key points of the narrative are marked by the opening of the door. At one crucial moment the narrator says, "Then the door opened and he saw his wife." The description of the sled ride down the hill ends with the broken phrase: "and then the elm . . ." (Wharton's ellipses). The elm that Frome and Mattie smash into is the door that does not

---

2. Bernard in above note [*Editor*].

open. Like the narrative structure of the novel, it frames and estranges the characters, sealing them in their heartless life: the living death that the narrator knows is behind the door of the Frome kitchen. The narrator projects his vision at the moment we are to see behind the closed door, and his fiction fills the elliptical center of the book, but what we see is an image of brooding silence.

In his desire to penetrate the mysteries of Ethan Frome, the narrator wants to act like "Life" in the "reed-bed," who (in the words of the reed) "rapt me from my silent tribe,/Pierced, fashioned, lipped me, sounding for a voice."[3] Yet even in his vision, even in the identification which might lead Wharton's authorial stand-in to feel that (in Vesalius's[4] words) "that other" "on the hearth" "is his actual self," he finally imagines Ethan Frome not merely as taciturn but as a writer who cannot write. On the night before he decides to commit suicide with the woman who "seemed the embodied instrument of fate," Frome reads a message from Mattie Silver and tries to write a letter.

The narrator, who has imagined that Frome took "a year's course at a technological college at Worcester, and dabbled in the laboratory with a friendly professor of physics," pictures him in his "cold dark 'study' " with his books and "an engraving of Abraham Lincoln and a calendar with 'Thoughts from the Poets.' " Earlier in the empty kitchen Frome has found "a scrap of paper torn from the back of a seedsman's catalogue, on which three words were written: 'Don't trouble, Ethan.' " He reads "the message again and again." Although at first "the possession of the paper gave him a strange new sense of her nearness," he realizes that "henceforth they would have no other way of communicating with each other" besides "cold paper and dead words!" (Later when Mattie says, "You must write to me sometimes," he responds, "Oh, what good'll writing do?") He starts to write a letter to his wife telling her that he has run off with Mattie, but after reading "the seductive words" of an advertisement for trips to the West, he has second thoughts: "The paper fell from his hand and he pushed aside his unfinished letter."

Like Lily Bart, Frome tries to imagine an alternate plot for his unbearable story, but leaving his letter unfinished, he resigns himself to being a prisoner for life. Moments before Ethan and Mattie decide to attempt suicide, Mattie produces the unfinished letter: "She tore the letter in shreds and sent them fluttering off into the snow." Soon her "words" of desperation are "like fragments torn from his heart," and the failed sui-

---

3. "Life" is Wharton's poem which the reed narrates [Editor].
4. Historically, Vesalius was a Belgian anatomist (1514–1564), condemned for dissecting a woman's body. Wharton's imaginative reconstruction in her poem, "Vesalius in Zante," concerns his return after death to his successor and competitor, Fallopius (discoverer of the female fallopian tubes, after whom they are named), and their dispute over each's contributions and discoveries. Hence, here, Vesalius imagining himself in Fallopius would be the engineer imagining himself as Ethan. The importance to the discussion here lies in the complexity of the engineer's vision and the underlying exploration of the failure of fertility through words [Editor].

cide attempt leaves both of them torn and shattered. Mattie's elliptical message written on "the seeds-man's catalogue" emphasizes Ethan's failure as a seedman. Later he strokes her hair so that the feeling of it "would sleep there like a seed in winter," but these winter seeds bear no fruit. Like the woman whose "page" is torn by Vesalius,[5] her life will be "ripened" only to a "bud of death"—in the words of Wharton's Margaret of Cortona,[6] a "lifeless blossom in the Book of Life." Writing under the calendar with 'Thoughts from the Poets,' Frome sees only "cold paper and dead words." Here the seeds of writing, despite the possibility of "seductive words," are not the seeds of the pomegranate—either the maternal fertility of Demeter or the transgressive eroticism of Persephone.[7] The words on the seed catalogue cannot even lead to an alternate underworld of death. The cost of vision in this story is a failure of mortality as well as immortality as the characters are left imprisoned in a living death. The "symbol of a man,/The sign-board creaking o'er an empty inn,"[8] that pictures the barrenness of both women and rockbound New England in the novel is also a sign for the failure of words to generate life.

5. Another return to Vesalius, who desired to know the secret of woman through dissection; hence, "read" the "secret" of woman through mutilation *[Editor]*.
6. "Margaret of Cortona" is another poem of Wharton's in which the historical fourteenth-century saint expresses her conflict between earthly and divine love, arguing that love of Christ leads to a barren existence in a convent *[Editor]*.
7. Demeter, Greek goddess of corn, whose daughter, Persephone, was abducted to Hades. The grieving mother caused a drought on earth. Zeus intervened, and Persephone was allowed to return for two-thirds of the year, but not forever, because she had eaten pomegranate seeds in Hades (Hell). The imagery again explores the relationship of writing and fertility *[Editor]*.
8. Quote is from "Vesalius in Zante," expressing his frustration and sense of sterility *[Editor]*.

Edith Wharton: A Chronology[†]

1862   Edith Newbold Jones born, January 24, in New York City.

1878   Makes her debut in society; her collection of poetry, *Verses*, is privately published; a poem appears in the *Atlantic Monthly*.

1882   Her father, George Frederic Jones, dies.

1885   Marries Edward ("Teddy") Wharton on April 29.

1890   Short story, "Mrs. Manstey's View," published in *Scribner's*.

1897   *The Decoration of Houses*, written with Ogden Codman, is published.

1899   First collection of short stories, *The Greater Inclination*, published.

1900   *The Touchstone*, a short novel, published.

1901   Her mother, Lucretia Rhinelander Jones, dies; second collection of short stories, *Crucial Instances*, issued.

1902   *The Valley of Decision*, Wharton's first long novel, published; Wharton and her husband move into the house she designed in western Massachusetts, The Mount.

1903   *Sanctuary*, a short novel, published.

1904   Third volume of short stories, *The Descent of Man*, published.

1905   *The House of Mirth*, a novel, published.

1907   *The Fruit of the Tree*, a novel, published.

1908   Love affair with Morton Fullerton, which will last about two years, begins; *A Motor-Flight through France*, a book of travel writing, published.

1909   *Artemis to Actaeon*, a collection of poems, published.

1911   *Ethan Frome*, a short novel, published.

1912   *The Reef*, a novel, published.

1913   Divorce from Teddy Wharton; *The Custom of the Country*, a novel, published.

1914   Permanently residing in France, Wharton becomes actively involved in war-relief work.

1915   *Fighting France*, pro-French propaganda essays, published.

1916   *The Book of the Homeless*, edited by Wharton and designed to

† From Edith Wharton, *The House of Mirth*: A Norton Critical Edition, edited by Elizabeth Ammons (New York: Norton, 1990). Reprinted by permission of Elizabeth Ammons and W. W. Norton & Company, Inc.

raise money for war-relief work, published; *Xingu and Other Stories* appears.

1917 *Summer*, short novel, published.

1918 *The Marne* published.

1919 *French Ways and Their Meanings*, essays, published.

1920 *The Age of Innocence*, novel, appears; *In Morocco*, travel essays, published.

1921 Awarded the Pulitzer Prize for *The Age of Innocence*.

1922 *The Glimpses of the Moon*, novel, published.

1923 Receives honorary degree from Yale University; last visit to the United States; *A Son at the Front*, a war novel, appears.

1924 *Old New York*, a collection of four novellas, published.

1925 *The Mother's Recompense*, a novel, published; *The Writing of Fiction*, a collection of theoretical pieces, issued.

1927 *Twilight Sleep*, a novel, published.

1928 Teddy Wharton dies; *The Children*, a novel, published.

1929 The novel *Hudson River Bracketed* appears.

1930 *Certain People*, short stories, brought out.

1932 Sequel to *Hudson River Bracketed*, *The Gods Arrive*, published.

1934 *A Backward Glance*, memoirs, published; at work on *The Buccaneers*, novel left unfinished at her death.

1937 Dies on August 11; buried in the Cimetiere des Gonards in Versailles, France.

Selected Bibliography

This bibliography does not include works excerpted in this volume.

The most complete bibliography of biographical and critical sources through 1987 is *Edith Wharton: An Annotated Secondary Bibliography*, edited by Kristin O. Lauer and Margaret P. Murray (New York: Garland, 1990). Editions of *Ethan Frome* and important material on the text itself can be found in *Edith Wharton: A Descriptive Bibliography*, edited by Stephen Garrison (Pittsburgh: University of Pittsburgh Press, 1990). The definitive biography is *Edith Wharton: A Biography* by R. W. B. Lewis (New York: Harper and Row, 1975). For biographical material with extensive critical commentary, see Cynthia Griffin Wolff, *A Feast of Words: The Triumph of Edith Wharton* (New York: Oxford University Press, 1977).

Other material of particular importance to students of Wharton's work, particularly *Ethan Frome*, other than sources excerpted in this edition, follows.

Auchincloss, Louis. *Edith Wharton: A Woman in Her Time*. New York: Viking, 1971.

Bendixen, Alfred and Zilversmit, Annette, eds. *Edith Wharton: New Critical Essays*. New York: Garland, 1992.

Benstock, Shari. *No Gifts from Chance: A Biography of Edith Wharton*. New York: Scribners, 1994.

Bernard, Kenneth. "Imagery and Symbolism in *Ethan Frome*." *College English* 22 (December 1961): 178–84.

Bjorkman, Edwin A. "The Greater Edith Wharton." *Voices of Tomorrow: Critical Studies of the New Spirit in Literature*. New York: Mitchell Kennerley, 1913.

Blackall, Jean Frantz. "The Sledding Accident in Ethan Frome." *Studies in Short Fiction* 21 (Spring 1984): 145–46.

Bloom, Harold. *Edith Wharton*. New York: Chelsea House, 1986.

Deegan, Dorothy Y. *The Stereotype of the Single Woman in American Novels*. New York: Octagon, 1951.

Donovan, Josephine. *After the Fall: The Demeter-Persephone Myth in Wharton, Cather and Glasgow*. University Park: Pennsylvania State University Press, 1989.

Dwight, Eleanor. *Edith Wharton, An Extraordinary Life*. New York: Harry N. Abrams, 1994.

Eggenschwiler, David. "The Ordered Disorder of Ethan Frome." *Studies in the Novel* 9 (1977): 237–46.

Erlich, Gloria. *The Sexual Education of Edith Wharton*. Berkeley: University of California Press, 1992.

Gimbel, Wendy. *Orphancy and Survival*. Landmark Dissertations in Women's Studies. Edited by Annette Baxter. New York: Praeger, 1984.

Goodman, Susan. *Edith Wharton's Women: Friends and Rivals*. Hanover and London: University Press of New England, 1990.

Goodwyn, Janet. *Traveller in the Land of Letters*. New York: St. Martin's, 1990.

Hafley, James. "The Case Against *Ethan Frome*." *Fresco* 1 (1961): 194–201.

Happel, Richard V. "Notes and Footnotes." *The Berkshire Eagle*, 25 February 1976, p. 20.

Hays, Peter S. "First and Last in *Ethan Frome*." *NMAL: Notes on Modern American Literature* 1 (1977): Item #15.

———. "Wharton's Splintered Realism." *Edith Wharton Newsletter* 2.1 (Spring 1985): 6.

Herron, Ima Honaker. *The Small Town in American Drama*. Dallas: Southern Methodist University Press, 1969.

Holzer, Harold. "Edith Wharton's First Real Home: Remembering Life and Work at the Mount." *American History Illustrated* 17 (September 1982): 10–15.

Hovey, R. B. "*Ethan Frome*: A Controversy about Modernizing It." *American Literary Realism* 19 (Fall 1986): 4–20.

Howe, Irving. *Edith Wharton: A Collection of Critical Essays*. Twentieth Century Views. Englewood Cliffs, New Jersey: Prentice-Hall, 1962.

Iyengoor, K. R. Srinivasa. "A Note on *Ethan Frome*." *Literary Criterion* 5 (Winter 1962): 168–78.

Joslin, Katherine. *Women Writers: Edith Wharton*. London: Macmillan, 1991.
———, and Alan Price, eds. *Wretched Exotic: Essays on Edith Wharton in Europe*. New York: Peter Lang, 1993.
Kazin, Alfred. "Afterword." *Ethan Frome*. New York: Collier, 1987.
Lawson, Richard H. *Edith Wharton*. New York: Ungar, 1977.
McDowell, Margaret B. *Edith Wharton*. Rev. Ed. Twayne Series. Boston: G. K. Hall, 1991.
Murad, Orlene. "Edith Wharton and *Ethan Frome*." *Modern Language Studies* 13 (Summer 1983): 90–103.
Nevius, Blake. *Edith Wharton's* Ethan Frome: *The Story, with Sources and Commentary*. New York: Scribner's, 1968.
Puknat, E. M., and S. B. Puknat. "Edith Wharton and Gottfried Keller." *Comparative Literature* 21 (Summer 1969): 245–54.
Ransom, John Crowe. "Characters and Character: A Note on Fiction." *American Review* 6 (January 1936): 271–88.
Rose, Alan Henry. "Such Depths of Sad Initiation: Edith Wharton and New England." *New England Quarterly* 50 (1977): 423–39.
Rusch, Frederick S. "Reality and the Puritan Mind: Jonathan Edwards and Ethan Frome." *Journal of Evolutionary Psychology* 4.3–4 (1983): 238–47.
Sagarin, Edward. "Ethan Frome: Atonement Endures Until Darkness Descends." *Raskolnikov and Others: Literary Images of Crime, Punishment, Redemption and Atonement*. New York: St. Martin's, 1981.
Thomas, J. D. "Marginalia on *Ethan Frome*." *American Literature* 27 (Nov. 1955): 405–09.
———. "Three American Tragedies: Notes on the Responsibilities of Fiction." *The South Central Bulletin* 20 (Winter 1960): 11–15.
Tuttleton, James, and Kristin O. Lauer and Margaret P. Murray. *Edith Wharton: The Contemporary Reviews*. New York: Cambridge, 1992.
———. "Mocking Fate: Romantic Idealism in Edith Wharton's *The Reef*." *Studies in the Novel* 19.4 (Winter 1987): 459–74.
Vita-Finzi, Penelope. *Edith Wharton and the Art of Fiction*. New York: St. Martin's, 1990.
Wershoven, Carol. *The Female Intruder in the Novels of Edith Wharton*. Rutherford: Fairleigh Dickinson University Press, 1982.